1974

Yale Russian and East European Studies 1

DOSTOEVSKY'S QUEST FOR FORM

A Study of His Philosophy of Art

by ROBERT LOUIS JACKSON

New Haven and London, Yale University Press, 1966

Sagen Sie
Ihm, dass er für die Träume seiner Jugend
Soll Achtung tragen, wenn er Mann sein wird,
Nicht öffnen soll dem tötenden Insekte
Gerühmter besserer Vernunft das Herz
Der zarten Götterblume—dass er nicht
Soll irre werden, wenn des Staubes Weisheit
Begeisterung, die Himmelstochter, lästert.

FRIEDRICH SCHILLER: *Don Carlos,* ACT IV

Or discendiam quaggiù nel cieco mondo
(Incominciò 'l poeta tutto smorto).
Io sarò primo, e tu sarai secondo.

DANTE ALIGHIERI: *Inferno,* CANTO IV

To my daughters Robin and Kathy

Preface

THE PURPOSE of this book is to bring before the reader, as vividly and succinctly as possible, the central body of Dostoevsky's aesthetic thought and to reveal its centrality to his world outlook.

The subject of Dostoevsky's aesthetics is not new. Dostoevsky scholars for the past fifty years have been concerned in one way or another with his implicit and explicit aesthetics. It is enough to recall the scholarly studies of L. P. Grossman, A. S. Dolinin, M. Bakhtin, A. Bem, G. Chulkov, I. I. Lapshin, or, more recently, V. Kirpotin, G. M. Fridlender, and J. van der Eng. Yet with the exception of Lapshin's short study, *Estetika Dostoevskogo,* which appeared in 1923, no single work has appeared which attempts to gather together and interpret in its own terms Dostoevsky's aesthetic thought—his pronouncements on beauty, the nature of artistic representation of reality, the function of literature, and similar matters—in order to determine and then demonstrate the coherence of this thought.

The limits of this study are determined by its strict focus: the aesthetic thought of Dostoevsky as it may be ascertained from an examination of his critical writings, letters, notebooks, and the testimony of those who were close to him. Reference is made to Dostoevsky's novels insofar as they contain direct commentary on his aesthetics. The philosophical context of his novelistic universe is always kept in mind. But, with the exception of a brief discussion of *Poor Folk,* analysis of his stories and novels in themselves plays almost no role in this study. The main effort throughout has been to keep the aesthetic ideas of Dostoevsky clearly in the foreground.

"Well, now, I've just conceived of an idea in the form of a novel," Dostoevsky writes S. A. Ivanova, March 8, 1869. This remark points to a central truth about Dostoevsky: he was in no sense a professional philosopher or aesthetician; more important, and crucial to his reality as an artist, he was unable to express outside of his belles lettres, outside of imagery, the full complexity of his thought. He did not write in the logical, structured form of an expository writer. "Through an attribute of my nature," he observed in the January 1881 number of his *Diary of a Writer,* "I begin from the end, and not from the beginning, present my whole thought at once. I have never been able to write gradually, make measured approaches and present my idea only after having preliminarily chewed it over and proved it as far as possible." To present a whole thought at once, of course, is to present an image. One might add that the peculiarly elliptical, dialectical, and permanently unresolved character of his thought made it difficult for him to express himself fully in the expository style. He felt the complexity of life too deeply to be able to capture it in anything but the living image.

It is necessary to turn to his belles lettres, then, for the whole Dostoevsky. A careful study of his art of the novel, such as one finds in the writings of L. P. Grossman, leads directly to the intricate realm of Dostoevsky's voiced and, equally important, unvoiced assumptions about the nature and function of art. Nonetheless, the deliberate pronouncements of a writer—and particularly one as articulate as Dostoevsky—remain of great importance. Dostoevsky's aesthetic thought is of interest in itself and may be apprehended quite apart from the context of a study of his novels. But its particular interest is in the fact that, resting, as it were, on the surface of his creative endeavor, it constitutes a vast system of directional signals controlled by, or responding to, the hidden dynamism of his creative thought. We say "system," yet, in fact, Dostoevsky's views on the nature and function of art, especially as we find them scattered through his works, do not constitute a closed system. His aesthetic thought is the thought of a poet: it is alive precisely through its fractured character, yet it has a center, in the language of Yeats, that holds.

It is the thesis of this work that Dostoevsky's aesthetic ideas, in all their unsystematic and often quite contradictory character, reveal a figure in the carpet. It is not possible to speak of him as a philosopher of art, but it is possible to speak of his philosophy of art, or, putting it another way, of his view of human and transcendental reality; in this view the aesthetic element, the element of beauty as exemplified in the great works of art of classical and early Christian and Renaissance culture, constitutes a central unifying focus. Dostoevsky's vision of reality is basically religious; the focal point of his vision is ultimately the image of Christ. But it is an aesthetically conceived image. Faith in Christ is faith in embodied form, in an image of beauty, perfection, and transfiguration. Dostoevsky died a Christian, but he found his salvation in art. Like the great German poet and humanist, Friedrich Schiller, whom he revered in his youth, Dostoevsky's principal appeal to his countrymen and to humanity was for "more beauty, more fine impressions, more enveloping love, more education. But now," he wrote, October 27, 1867, in his notebook, "there is a thirst for *beauty and the ideal and at the same time a lack of faith in it,* or faith but no love for it." The notion of beauty and the ideal—as it has migrated from Plato through medieval Christian aesthetics down to the romantic aesthetics of Schiller and Chateaubriand, Schelling and Hegel—structures and dominates Dostoevsky's entire world outlook; it is the controlling center of his views about art. It is impossible to understand the creative tension in Dostoevsky's belles lettres apart from this passionate commitment to a notion of beauty and the ideal.

The organization of this study is mainly thematic. The first four chapters, however, examine Dostoevsky's aesthetic thought in a chronological framework: they cover the period from his early youth through his return from exile in 1859. Dostoevsky's letters in this period—those that have been preserved—offer relatively little material for any detailed discussion of his aesthetic ideas; he left no critical writings, apart from some feuilletons written in the middle of the 1840s. Our knowledge of Dostoevsky's aesthetic thought—apart from what may be deduced from a study of his belles lettres—comes from his abundant critical writings, letters, and notebooks in the period 1861–81. It is largely on the basis of this material that the main part of this study—Chapters 5 through 10—has been organized.

Do the ideas expressed in the period 1861–81 reflect Dostoevsky's aesthetic thought in this period and this period alone? Dostoevsky's thinking on art certainly was greatly enriched in the literary polemics of the 1850s and 1860s, in which he participated on his return from exile; it was enormously stimulated through contact with the literary life of St. Petersburg, through association with major critics like N. N. Strakhov and A. Grigoriev, and, of course, through reading; it was activated, above all, by his own creative work, his search for a novel-form and novelistic techniques which would enable him to convey his own imaginative concept of Russian social and spiritual reality in a period of upheaval and chaos in post-reform Russian society. But the basic structure of Dostoevky's aesthetic thought—his higher aesthetic and his concept of reality, his notion of the aesthetic mission of art in culture—was deeply rooted in the romantic idealistic philosophy of the Russian 1840s. Finally, Dostoevsky's aesthetic thought in its initial stages of development was influenced by the major radical critic of the 1840s —Vissarion Belinsky.

But whatever the roots of Dostoevsky's aesthetic ideas, the period of their most mature expression was certainly in the 1860s and 1870s. His essay, "Mr. —bov and the Question of Art," which appeared in 1861, is pivotal. It unquestionably reflects his intensive thinking in the 1850s about the nature and mission of art, and it anticipates, though sometimes lightly and obliquely, the content of his aesthetic ideas as they will be clarified and developed in the subsequent two decades. The essay is not examined independently (though it deserves careful study as a unique example of Dostoevsky's expository style), but the material in the essay enters almost every chapter of this study.

The final chapter, "Correspondences," attempts to focus some of Dostoevsky's aesthetic thought against the background of philosophical thought in the late eighteenth and early nineteenth centuries. It would have been possible, of course, to treat Dostoevsky's aesthetics throughout the study with a constant eye to its resemblances with European aesthetic thought. This approach was rejected for two reasons: first, such a method tends to break up the integral picture of Dostoevsky's aesthetic outlook; second, it tends to place excessive emphasis on the problem of derivation. What is important about Dostoevsky's aesthetic ideas is the original synthesis they constitute and the manifestation of this synthesis in his art —not the fact that these ideas came to him from Schiller or Hegel. "L'écrivain original n'est pas celui qui n'imite personne," wrote Chateaubriand, "mais celui que personne ne peut imiter." Nevertheless, Dostoevsky's aesthetic thought is certainly illuminated against the background of other thinkers. It is essential to recognize, moreover, not only Dostoevsky's indebtedness to these thinkers but his community with them. He was, when all is said and done, a peer among peers. But in his art and thinking, the problems of aesthetics leave the lecture room to live intensely, freely.

I want to thank Professor René Wellek who encouraged me to write this book; Yale College for a Morse Fellowship which allowed me to devote a whole year to writing; Wayland W. Schmitt, editor, John O. C. McCrillis, designer, Kathy Roberts, editorial assistant, all of Yale University Press, for their help in preparing the manuscript for publication; Elizabeth Berliner for reading the proofs; and my wife, Leslie Jackson, whose design for the jacket is to me a fulfillment of the quest for form.

R. L. J.

Truro, Mass.
August 1965

Contents

Introduction

ONE OF THE recurrent and fundamental thoughts in Dostoevsky's writing is that life itself is a whole art and that to live means to make an artistic work out of oneself. An early hero of Dostoevsky announces that he is the artist of his own life, while Dostoevsky observes in his notebook many years later that "man does not live his whole life, but composes himself."[1] The model, or desired shape, of that self-composition is suggested by Versilov in *The Raw Youth*. "Life is also an artistic work of the Creator, a perfect and irreproachable form like a Pushkin poem." "Form, form!" Dostoevsky exclaims in his notebook as he struggled with the material of *The Raw Youth*. "Write in an ordered manner, briefly à la Pushkin . . . (*Imitate Pushkin*)."[2] Pushkin was Dostoevsky's ideal from the very beginning of his creative career. "I want every work of mine to be fine to precision," Dostoevsky wrote in a letter in 1845. "Look at Pushkin and Gogol."[3]

A quest for form—and precisely a classical ideal of form—dominates Dostoevsky's creative thought and strivings. This quest is experienced as a subjective need by a number of Dostoevsky's heroes (e.g. Makar Devushkin, Prince Myshkin, Dmitry Karamazov); it is projected by Dostoevsky, as it was much earlier by Friedrich Schiller, as man's path to freedom. It is, however, one of the most significant paradoxes of Dostoevsky as man, thinker, and artist that his experience of this quest for form was marked by intense struggle, anxiety, and doubt. The artist, Schiller wrote in his philosophical letters *On the Aesthetic Education of Man,* "will take his content from the present, but his form he will borrow from a nobler time, indeed, from beyond all time, from the absolute, unchangeable unity of his being."[4] All his life Dostoevsky worshipped ideal form as the symbol and embodiment of moral and spiritual transfiguration. But he did not find this form, this unchangeable unity of being, either in himself, in Russian man, or in human nature at large.

"How well you write letters," Dostoevsky wrote to his wife in 1867. "How am I going to write like that and express my heart, my feelings in that manner. . . . I do not have any form, gesture. My late brother Misha often woefully reproached me for this."[5] Dostoevsky gave exaggerated expression to the curious notion of aesthetic inadequacy in his characterization of Prince Myshkin in *The Idiot*. Radomsky directly reproaches Myshkin for his "phenomenal lack of measure (to which you yourself already have confessed several times)." And Myshkin, referring to the occasion when he and Rogozhin read and discussed Pushkin together, remarks: "I am always afraid that my absurd manner will compromise the thought and *main idea*. I do not have a sense of gesture. I'm always making the opposite gesture, and this evokes laughter and debases the idea. I've also got no sense of measure, and this is the main thing; it's perhaps the most important thing." Myshkin's whole struggle to emerge from the chaos into which his disease has plunged him—a chaos which is also Russian life as Myshkin experiences it—takes shape as a craving for the values of classical form: measure, proportion, harmony. These values Dostoevsky found perfectly embodied in Pushkin. It is not without significance that Myshkin is particularly conscious of his lack of form when reading Pushkin. The "main idea" of Pushkin is not merely the central point or issue of a poem or story; the main idea of Pushkin which Myshkin fears that he will compromise is *form*.

Myshkin, of course, is not Dostoevsky. But problematical features or aspects of Dostoevsky's personality and thinking are posed in Myshkin. We note throughout Dostoevsky's creative life a persistent, nagging tendency to underrate himself as an artist-craftsman, a creator of form. "I know very well that I write worse than Turgenev," Dostoevsky writes his brother Mikhail in 1859, "but, after all, not so much more poorly and, finally, I hope to write not quite so poorly."[6] Turgenev for Dostoevsky was the "most artistic of all modern writers,"[7] and he brackets him (in *Crime and Punishment*) with Pushkin as a pure artist. His constant complaint, until all but the last years of his life, is that he lacked time to polish and finish his works. He envied Tolstoy, Turgenev, and Goncharov for their leisure. Even late in his life he speaks of himself as "more of a poet than an artist."[8]

Dostoevsky's admiration for the artistry of Turgenev and Tolstoy was fully justified, but his underevaluation of himself as an artist-craftsman was entirely without foundation. Whatever the personal roots of this underevaluation of self, on the plane of aesthetic consciousness and ideas it seems related to his lifelong identification of the notion of form with classical aesthetic values and of art with the function of moral-aesthetic edification. The Venus of Milo, Raphael's Sistine Madonna, the entire works of Pushkin are for Dostoevsky embodiments of perfect forms, of edifying beauty. The greatest tribute Dostoevsky could pay to Turgenev in his Pushkin Address in 1880 was to say that the character of Liza (in *A Nest of Gentry Folk*) came close to equalling Pushkin's Tatyana as a type of real, positive beauty. And despite his jealous refusal to see in Tolstoy a bearer of a "New Word" in Russian literature (in contrast to Lomonosov and Pushkin), Dostoevsky acknowledged in him a "god of art," a writer loved by all shades of the Russian public because he was a creator of "positive beauty."[9] Turgenev, Tolstoy, and Goncharov, Dostoevsky acknowledged, all "came directly from Pushkin."[10]

We may note, finally, apropos of Dostoevsky's awareness of and love for pure "artistry" and "positive beauty," that in his own creative work he tirelessly dreamed about and sought to create positive types of moral and spiritual beauty. But the stubborn paradox of his creative work and thought remains: while he adhered as a critic and thinker to a classical higher aesthetic, to a vision of ideal beauty, as a writer he turned himself over to the embodiment of what Schiller called the shapeless matter of the moral world. The ideal, sculptured forms and images he admired in Pushkin are hardly typical in the landscape of the Dostoevsky novel.[11] Nor did he ever owe his popularity with the public—even to this very day —to his depiction of positive beauty, ideal types. Toward the end of his life he privately confided to his notebook that his great achievement as a writer lay in being "the first to depict the real man of the Russian majority and the first to disclose his disfigured and tragic side." Did Dostoevsky realize the great distance that separated his realistic art from that of Turgenev, Goncharov, and Tolstoy? His own comments on the special character of his realism in his letters, notebooks, and critical writings in the 1860s and 1870s indicate such an awareness. He very clearly establishes the lines of demarcation between his realism and that of Tolstoy and Goncharov. But he was unable, or unwilling, in critical terms to come to grips with the contradiction between his philosophical adherence to a classical higher aesthetic (with its imperative to form "à la Pushkin") and his practical, working aesthetic (with its interest in the "real man" of the Russian majority). In his art, however, Dostoevsky succeeded in embodying the contradiction in his aesthetic thought in a creative dialectic. Here his lofty aesthetic idealism, his ideal of higher beauty, is projected as the eternal and luminous goal of human striving. Man's transitory, earthly life is marked by suffering, by the disfiguration of his earthly nature. But throughout all man's moral and spiritual confusion Dostoevsky perceives a norm, a point of striving: it is to be found, symbolically, in the iconographic representation of the Madonna, in the paintings of the Italian masters (Raphael, Carracci, and others), in the sculpture of classical antiquity, in *The Iliad,* in the "lofty harmony of sounds" of Mozart and Beethoven, in all the "ideals of beauty created by the past"; it is to be found, finally, in the image of beauty of Christ and in the preservation of that ideal—and the idea of the possibility of realizing that ideal—within man himself.

The quest for form is a tragic quest as far as man's earthly transitional life is concerned. All that can be hoped for is a creative tension within man between the opposite strivings of his nature. Dostoevsky's novels, in their moral and spiritual content, are essentially a representation of that tension in man, in moments of the highest strivings, but more often in the long moments of slackening, disintegration, and despair.

1   A Strange Contradiction

"IT WAS the month of May; it was hot. We drove with hired horses almost at a footpace and would halt at stations for two and three hours. I remember how wearied we became, finally, of this trip which had lasted almost a week." Dostoevsky is recalling in his *Diary of a Writer* (January, 1876) his trip to St. Petersburg in 1837 to matriculate in the Engineering School. The remarkable decade of the 1840s comes into focus.

> My brother and I were making our way then into a new life, we were dreaming about something with terrible intensity, about all the "beautiful and sublime"—at that time this phrase was still fresh and was uttered without irony. And how many such beautiful phrases were current at that time! We believed in something passionately, and although we both knew quite well all the demands that the mathematics examination would make upon us, we dreamed nevertheless only about poetry and about poets. My brother was writing verse, every day three poems, even on the road, and I was ceaselessly composing in my head a novel about Venetian life.[1]

Dostoevsky's account does not stop here; at one of the way stations, he continues, he watched a departing courier strike blow upon blow on the back of the neck of his coachman; the latter, in turn, lashed his horses mercilessly until, at length, they flew off. "This repulsive little scene has remained in my memory all my life," Dostoevsky remarks. "I was never able to forget that courier, and many an infamous and cruel thing in the Russian people I was inclined to explain, willy-nilly and for a long time afterwards, in an obviously too one-sided sense." He adds that in the late 1840s, in the period of his "most sacred and passionate dreams," it once occurred to him to found a philanthropic society with the courier's troika on the seal of the society.[2]

Dostoevsky recalls this incident from his youth in the course of an article stressing the educational role of the "Russian Society for the Protection of Animals." Not only little dogs and horses are precious to the Society, he writes, "but man, Russian man, whom it is necessary to *re-form* and to humanize." And Dostoevsky remarks at this point in a footnote that the word *obrazit'* (re-form) "is a folk word meaning to give an image to, to restore in man a human image. One has always said to the drunkard, with reproach: 'Now you ought to go and *re-form* yourself.' I heard the convicts say this."[3]

In the reminiscences we have cited Dostoevsky limns the features of the decade of the 1840s: an ecstatic philosophic mood, a lofty aesthetic humanism, an intense preoccupation with creation, and, finally, a sharp disjunction between the ideal, the dream, and disfigured social reality.[4] This decade must be the point of departure and point of return in any discussion of Dostoevsky's aesthetic thought. His primary aesthetic education was effected in the heightened romantic and philosophic atmosphere of this decade. His aesthetic humanism, his lifelong preoccupation with the restoration of the human image, his fervent belief in ideal form and beauty are nourished in this period. What begins as a naïve and sentimental idealism, however, rapidly evolves into a tragic humanism.

Turgenev in his novel *Rudin* described the "enchanted" philosophical circles of the 1840s, in which philosophy, art, science, and life were discussed, illumined, explained. "Nothing remained senseless, accidental; in everything was manifested reasonable necessity and beauty, everything acquired a clear and at the same time mysterious meaning . . . and we ourselves, with a kind of sacred reverential awe, with a sweet heartfelt tremor, felt as though we were living vessels of eternal truth, its instruments, called upon for something great."

The problem of cultural identity—a problem of national self-consciousness—is the dynamic core of Russian intellectual consciousness in the several decades that open into the 1840s. Peter Chaadaev in his almost emblematic "Philosophical Letter" (1836) posed negatively the problem of Russian culture, stressing its backwardness, inferiority, and formlessness, compared with European culture; this problem of Russian culture—poetically resolved by the genius of Alexander Pushkin in his immense sifting and synthesis of European and Russian traditions, in his creation of perfect literary forms—remains the theme of the 1840s. *"We have no literature,"* the central critic of the period, Vissarion Belinsky, complains in 1834. And he calls for a literature which will be a "symbol of the inner life of the people," an authentic national literature which will express some part of the *"great idea of the universe in its endlessly diverse manifestations!"*[5]

The quest for cultural self-identity is a quest for the creative principle—for Belinsky, as for Herder, the folk principle—and for its embodiment in art. "Only in art and literature, and consequently in aesthetic and literary criticism," Belinsky declared in 1842, "does the intellectual consciousness of our society find expression."[6] The aesthetic emphasis here is not accidental; art and literature gave expression to Russian intellectual consciousness, but they were also what the national intellectual consciousness sought: embodiment, unity, identity—aesthetically, *form.*

Here German culture-philosophy and romantic idealism, fermented in the national upheaval of the German principalities, played an enormous role in shaping Russia's philosophic and literary consciousness and in determining the special aesthetic emphasis of Russian self-speculation. Herder's teaching that great poetry is the product of a national spirit; Schelling's exaltation of art as the means through which philosophy expresses itself in the external world, as the link between nature and history, between the real and the ideal; Schiller's idea (expressed in both his poetry and critical writings) of the moral regeneration of man through the awakening of his aesthetic sensibility; Hegel's identification of art's highest destiny with religion and philosophy, and of philosophy as the means of comprehending the process of world development, of revealing the eternal in the present, temporary, and transitory— all these contributed heavily to the form and character of Russian intellectual consciousness.

The great wave of German romantic philosophic idealism, which moved through the early decades of the Russian nineteenth century, lifted Russian consciousness into vast, transcendental realms; but the same idealism provoked and evoked a tormenting consciousness of the wide gap between the ideal and the real, between the felicitous German Absolute and the unhappy Russian present. A deep social consciousness, supported again by powerful currents of Western European social and philanthropic thought (in particular, the social teachings of the French utopian socialists), gave a radical content to the romantic ideal. The critical, philosophizing spirit struck at the foundations of all individual and social existence. "The spirit of analysis and investigation," wrote Belinsky, "is the spirit of our time. Now everything is subject to *criticism, even criticism* itself. Our time accepts nothing unconditionally, does not believe authorities, rejects tradition."[7] "The *question—* here is the alpha and omega of our time."[8]

Thus, starting from the innermost core of ego, of the relation of self and nonself, the transitory and the Absolute, the quest for self-identity in Russia reached out toward the most lofty idealism, the outermost reaches of transcendental self-renunciation. Truth, justice, beauty, however, did not remain abstract philosophical concepts but became real ideals, real goals to be lived by. The ideal-become-reality released an ecstasy of emotion, a moral passion and energy that galvanized a new social humanism and gave a new thrust to literature. Something of this passion can be felt in Dostoevsky's recollection of how he felt about Belinsky's reception of his first novel, *Poor Folk* (1846). Belinsky had enthusiastically praised him for his lofty embodiment of "truth in art." When Dostoevsky left Belinsky's home he was ecstatic: "I will prove worthy," he thought to himself. "I will try to become just as beautiful as they, I will be 'faithful'! . . . they are alone, but only they have verity, and verity, goodness, truth always will conquer and triumph over vice and evil; we will triumph; oh, to be with them, to be one with them!"[9]

Poor Folk itself was one of the early fruits of the new social realism in literature in the 1840s. Native tendencies toward realism, already powerfully stimulated by the prose of Pushkin and Lermontov, took new form in the so-called "natural school" of Gogol—a literary movement of which Belinsky was spokesman and ideologist. The new social realism, with its democratic and philanthropic emphasis, was strongly influenced by literary trends and social thought in the West: the writings, for example, of Balzac with their depiction of social groups and classes and their interest in typology, and especially the novels of George Sand with their deep concern with social questions and their fervent idealism.

In his remarkable tribute to George Sand at the time of her death in 1876, Dostoevsky wrote that, simply reading the newspapers about her, "I understood what this name meant to me in my life, what an ecstatic response, what accolades this poet had drawn from me at the time, and how many joys, how much happiness she once gave me! I put down each of these words boldly, because all this was literally true." The name of George Sand evokes for Dostoevsky an entire era. She was "one of our (i.e. *our*) contemporaries, quite entirely, an idealist of the Thirties and Forties. Hers is one of those names of our mighty, self-confident, and, at the same time, sick century, full of the most unclarified ideals and the most unresolved desires—one of those names which, arising over there in the 'land of sacred miracles,' enticed from us, from our eternally creating Russia, too many thoughts, too much love, an overabundance of sacred and generous bursts of energy, of living life and precious convictions." Yet Dostoevsky stresses he is not complaining; in worshipping and exalting such names, he affirms, "Russians were serving and serve their direct destiny." Schiller, another one of the great names of the Russian 1840s mentioned by Dostoevsky, was "much more national and much more akin to the barbaric Russians" than to the French or to anyone else in the nineteenth century.[10] Schiller, Dostoevsky wrote elsewhere, was part of the "flesh and blood of Russian society. . . . We were educated on him, he is native to us and in many ways is reflected in our development."[11]

Dostoevsky's warm, almost loving tribute to George Sand, Schiller, and the ethos of the 1840s, is deeply felt; in its peculiarly poignant, nostalgic quality it resembles Nina Zarechny's backward glance in the last act of Chekhov's *The Sea Gull:* "How nice it was then. . . . What a bright, warm, joyful, pure life, what feelings— feelings like tender, delicate flowers." Yet Dostoevsky's tribute to George Sand inadequately reflects the crash of illusions he experienced between the 1840s and the 1860s—a crash or "fall" involving fundamental assumptions of the idealistic ethos of the 1840s on the nature of man and on his readiness for the good life.

Belinsky noted at the very beginning of his career a tendency of Schiller to present "only the beautiful in life," his sacred ideals and dreams, while making improbable, or distorting through exaggeration, the "evil in life."[12] Later he called attention to a distinct duality in Schiller: on the one hand, the pathos of his poetry is in his passionate love, based on reason and consciousness, for man and mankind; on the other, he is "a romantic in the sense of the Middle Ages! A strange contradiction!" Belinsky goes on to note that "Schiller is lofty in his contemplation of love; but this love is dreamy, fantastic: it fears the earth so as not to be soiled by its filth, and it holds itself up near the heavens, precisely in an atmospheric zone where the air is rare and not good for breathing, and the rays of the sun shine without warming."[13] The strange contradiction that Belinsky observed in Schiller was characteristic of the idealist ethos of the 1840s. The attempt to resolve that contradiction—to bring the ideal down to earth—constitutes the dynamic impetus in Belinsky's criticism and in much of the literature of the "natural school" in the 1840s.

In his early writings Dostoevsky is preoccupied with the tragedy of the "dreamer," with the fatal consequences for the individual of psychological withdrawal or isolation from actuality. But the theme of the dreamer in Dostoevsky's writings reaches its fullest development only when the psychological and social tragedy of the dreamer telescopes with the theme of the tragedy of the idealist ethos of the 1840s. Dostoevsky himself experienced the fate of the dreamer in the brutal awakening of his arrest and exile to Siberia in 1849. His political idealism collapsed. No more eloquent testimony to Dostoevsky's profound reevaluation of the radical idealist ethos of the 1840s is to be found than in his novel *The Insulted and Injured* (1861). The theme of this work is the tragedy of naïve, abstract, "Schilleresque" idealism and the impotence of "natural good" before evil in life. The narrator, Ivan Petrovich, remarks, apropos of the inability of one character to recognize evil, that she had that "attribute which most good-natured people have . . . of praising people too highly, of stubbornly considering them better than they are in actuality, fervently exaggerating the good in them." "And what a disillusionment always is in store for [good-natured] people like that. It would be far better if they were to sit tranquilly in their corners and not go out into the world" (Pt. II, Ch. 6).[14] The narrator of the story—a writer who has written a story identical in content, it would seem, to *Poor Folk*—emerges as a disillusioned lover of humanity, a man with his "golden age" in the past. Ivan Petrovich, of course, is not Dostoevsky, but his tragic story reflects Dostoevsky's new critical appraisal of the 1840s.

Ivan Petrovich may perish in his disillusionment; the narrator, Alexander Petrovich Goryanchikov, in *Notes from the House of the Dead* will not survive his confrontation with raw Russian reality. But Dostoevsky's passionate idealism of the 1840s is reborn on a new religious-aesthetic plane. Schiller's purely moral-aesthetic ideal of beauty coalesces, as it were, with the ideal beauty of Christ. The "strange contradiction" that Belinsky observed in Schiller— the terrible disjunction between the ideal and real—reemerges in Dostoevsky's philosophy as the central contradiction of human existence. Man strives for an ideal unrealizable in earthly existence, continually sullied by earthly being and striving, but continually purified in the form of a dream in man's suffering consciousness. This dream has many shapes and manifestations in Dostoevsky's novelistic universe: it is the lost paradise, the Sistine Madonna, or the image of Christ; but everywhere this dream is beauty, the embodied idea of a transfigured humanity. "Beauty must be exhibited as the necessary condition of humanity," Schiller wrote in his philosophical letters *On the Aesthetic Education of Man.* This idea is at the center of Dostoevsky's aesthetic philosophy; in his lifelong dedication to it he remains a child of the 1840s.

2   The Romantic Image of the Poet

AT THE CONCLUSION of a letter to his brother Mikhail, August 16, 1839—a letter in which he comments with peculiar reserve upon the death of his father—Dostoevsky writes: "What can I say about myself?" More and more frequently, he continues, he views his surroundings with complete indifference. Yet there is a strong awakening within him. He yearns for freedom, will sacrifice everything for it, but wonders what freedom will bring. "What will I be, alone, in the unknown crowd?" Dostoevsky writes of his uncertainties but also of those moments when he is sure that he will realize his "sacred hopes." His faith in life is acquiring a purer and more lofty source, he observes, and his spirit is no longer subject to stormy outbursts.

> Everything in it is tranquil, as in the heart of a man who has hidden a deep mystery; to learn "what man and life mean"— in this I am succeeding fairly well; I can study characters from writers with whom the best part of my life flows freely and joyfully; I will not say anything more about myself. Man is a mystery. It is necessary to divine it, and if you are to be divining it all your life, then you can't say that you have been wasting your time; I am occupied with this mystery, because I want to be a man.[1]

Dostoevsky's awakening to art is an awakening to life. His observations are remarkable in the way they disclose the permanent bent of his artistic and philosophical consciousness: a central concern with man, the view of him as an enigma, and the thought that to be a man one must have an active interest in the human condition. This is almost a credo defining Dostoevsky's quest as an artist. Toward the end of his life he describes Shakespeare as the "prophet sent by God to announce to us a mystery—of man, of the human soul."[2] "With a total realism to seek man in man," he writes in his notebook in the last year of his life, "I am only a realist in the higher sense, that is, I depict all the depths of the human soul."[3]

It is no surprise, against the background of an age dominated by German romantic aesthetics, to find Dostoevsky positing art as a form of philosophical inquiry. Philosophy, he writes his brother in 1838, cannot be taken as a simple mathematical problem in which the unknown is nature. "Note that the poet in a burst of inspiration divines God, hence fulfills the task of philosophy. Hence poetic ecstasy is the ecstasy of philosophy. Hence philosophy is the same as poetry, only a higher degree of it."[4] The object of philosophical inquiry, then, is simultaneously the object of poetic creation: the poetic process here might be defined as cognition through divination (inspiration, revelation). Dostoevsky takes his brother to task for underrating the role of feeling in the soul's cognition of the universe. Nature, the soul, love "are known by the heart and not the mind." Humans must divine but cannot embrace thought suddenly. "*Mind* is the conductor of thought through a perishable envelope into the structure of the soul. Mind is a material capacity, but the soul or spirit lives by thought which the heart whispers to it. Thought is born in the soul. Mind is a tool, a machine, driven by spiritual fire."[5] However, in the "realm of knowledge," according to Dostoevsky, mind functions independently of feeling and heart.

The later, mature Dostoevsky frees himself from the ornate, transcendental phraseology of German idealist philosophy. He centers his artistic quest on man in his concrete environment; but Dostoevsky does not, like Zola, ground it there. The basic concept of poet as philosopher and seer, of art as revelation; the conception of ultimate reality as spiritual; the view of mind (reason) as ancillary to feeling, and of the creative process as fundamentally irrational, or intuitional—all this remains as a permanent understructure in Dostoevsky's thinking on art and literature.

The poet divines the soul, nature, God, but his inspired creation, like the realm of the transcendental which he would divine, partakes of the ineffable. "How is it possible to share one's ecstasy on paper? The spirit always hides more than can be expressed in words, colors, or sounds," Dostoevsky writes in 1839. "For this reason it is difficult to execute the idea of a creative work." In this connection Dostoevsky remarks that "there is no more holy a martyr than the poet."[6]

Inspiration sparks creation, the work of art; at the same time it enters into creation as its permanent, inspirational essence. Fame,

Dostoevsky writes his brother in 1838, also facilitates the inspiration of the poet, but not Byron's petty and vain idea of fame. "But the thought alone that someday long after your past ecstasy there will burst from the ashes a pure, sublimely beautiful spirit, the thought that inspiration like a heavenly mystery will illuminate the pages over which you wept and over which posterity will weep—I don't think that this thought couldn't creep into the soul of the poet even at the very moment of creation." But as though contemplating rejection the young Dostoevsky immediately banishes his thought about a responsive public and observes in a gesture of wounded self-pride: "The devil with the insignificant shout of the crowd. Ah! I have just remembered the second verse of Pushkin where he describes the crowd and the poet: 'And let (the crowd) spit on the altar where your flame burns / And with childlike playfulness rock your sacrificial stand.' Now isn't that charming!"[7] One perceives in this abrupt shift in mood the nervous sensibility and vanity that marks Dostoevsky's reaction to the critical reception of his first works in the 1840s.

The image of the poet that emerges in Dostoevsky's few early extant letters (1838–40) is a thoroughly romantic one. The poet is a lofty spiritual being; he is the sensitive man aloof from the mundane, everyday world, yet suffering from a basic dichotomy. He is a Hamlet-like figure. The atmosphere of man's soul, Dostoevsky writes his brother in 1838, consists of a "union of heaven with earth" in which the "law of spiritual nature is violated." Dostoevsky writes with romantic, melancholy emphasis that the world has

> taken on negative meaning and out of a lofty, refined spirituality has come satire. Let a person turn up in this picture who does not share either effect or thought with the whole, in a word, a quite alien person—and what will happen? The picture is spoiled and cannot exist. But just to see the coarse envelope under which anguishes the universe, to know that one burst of will is enough to smash it and join with eternity, to know this and to be the last of creations—this is frightful! How weak in spirit is man! Hamlet! Hamlet!

Those "stormy wild speeches in which sound the groans of a frozen world" crush the young Dostoevsky's soul with misery. "Once Pascal made a *bon mot:* he who protests against philosophy is himself a philosopher. A pitiful philosophy!"[8] Dostoevsky's own empathy with Hamlet, his own Hamlet-like protest, brings to mind Belinsky's interpretation of Hamlet's discord with reality (in an essay in the spring of 1838 on a production of *Hamlet* in St. Petersburg). The stage of youthfulness, of unconscious harmony of man's spirit with nature, according to Belinsky, is followed by a transition to maturity. "This transition is always a stage of disintegration, disharmony, hence, sin. Man is no longer satisfied with natural consciousness and simple feeling: he wants to know." The crisis occurs, according to Belinsky, at that moment when reality diverges from man's dreams, man's ideals. Hamlet, "our *beautiful soul,* our thoughtful dreamer," is plunged into a crisis of discord. "Passage from this disharmony of disintegration to a harmony of spirit by means of inner struggle and consciousness is the lot only of the *best* people."[9]

Dostoevsky—also a beautiful soul and thoughtful dreamer of the 1830s—quite clearly made an early transition (in Belinsky's sense) to maturity. The problem of discord between man and his world, between mundane and ideal reality as it is embodied in man —a central philosophical problem of his art—was a critical focus of Dostoevsky's nascent creative consciousness. The crisis of discord, experienced by Dostoevsky in all its romantic overtones, early took the form of a quest for knowledge of man, a search for the passage from disharmony to harmony of spirit.

The young Dostoevsky's image of the poet clearly found embodiment in the figure of his young poet friend, I. D. Shidlovsky. Dostoevsky writes of him in a letter to his brother in 1840. "He lived for a whole year in Petersburg without doing anything or working in the service. . . . Just look at him: this is a martyr! He has wasted away; his cheeks are sunken; his rheumy eyes are dry and burning; the spiritual beauty of his face has been ennobled by his physical breakdown. He suffered! suffered greatly! My God, how he loves some girl (Marie, it seems). . . . He has married somebody. Without this love he would not be the pure, exalted selfless priest of poetry." Shidlovsky not unexpectedly strikes Dostoevsky as "a beautiful, exalted creation, the correct sketch of a man as both Shakespeare and Schiller represented him to us; but he was already prepared at that time to fall into the gloomy mania of Byronic characters."[10]

The affinity between Dostoevsky and Shidlovsky, however, appears to have been deeper than Dostoevsky's ecstatic remarks would suggest at first glance. "Ah, soon, soon I will re-read the new poems of Ivan Nikolaevich [Shidlovsky]," Dostoevsky wrote his brother in a letter in 1838. "How much poetry! How many ideas inspired by genius!"[11] The few poems of Shidlovsky that have been preserved reveal a deeply romantic philosophical consciousness. Shidlovsky's personality, his poetry, his tragic self-division—as M. P. Alekseev has pointed out—between the two poles of romantic self-assertion and religious self-renunciation, his striving to harmonize the rebelliousness of personal will with a longing for another world—all evoked a sympathetic response in the young Dostoevsky and undoubtedly helped to shape his own religious-philosophical consciousness.[12]

"In the life of man there are many, many sorrows, misery, and —joys," Dostoevsky wrote his brother Mikhail in 1840. "In the life of the poet these are thorns and roses. Lyricism is the eternal fellow traveler of the poet, because he is a verbal creature."[13] But the poet for Dostoevsky is more than an ecstatic, lyrical, suffering creature. He is a creature with ideals. It is not accidental that Dostoevsky idolized Schiller. "I have learned Schiller by heart," he wrote his brother in 1840, "talked him, raved him. And I think fate never did anything more fortunate in my life than in making known to me a great poet in this epoch of my life."[14] The "generous" and "passionate" Don Carlos, the Marquis de Posa, and Mortimer— here is the substance of the poet's ecstasy. In amazement Dostoevsky asks his brother in 1840 if it is possible that he finds no poetry in Racine and Corneille. "No poetry in Racine? The flaming, passionate Racine, the Racine in love with his ideals, is there no poetry here?" "Have you read *Le Cid?*" Dostoevsky asks in the course of a dithyramb on Corneille. "Read it, pitiful man, read it and fall in the dust before Corneille. . . . What does romanticism demand if its lofty ideas are not developed in the *Cid?*" Corneille with his "giant characters," with his ideals of love and honor, is the very "spirit of romanticism." In the same letter Dostoevsky lauds Victor Hugo as a "lyricist with a pure angelic character, with a Christian, childlike tendency in poetry, and in this nobody compares with him. . . . Only Homer with that same unshakeable confidence in his calling, with that youthful faith in the god of poetry."[15]

Literature for the young Dostoevsky clearly was the broadest avenue for the study of mankind, its ideals, meaning, and destiny. *Hamlet,* as we have seen, posed the most fundamental questions about man's situation in the universe. "Balzac is great!" Dostoevsky exclaims in 1838. "His characters are the works of a universal mind! Not the spirit of the time, but whole thousand-year periods have prepared through their struggle such a dénouement in the soul of man."[16] Homer, Dostoevsky wrote, was in significance "parallel only to Christ . . . in the *Iliad* [he] gave to the ancient world organization both of earthly and religious life, just as powerfully as Christ did for the new [world]."[17] We may perhaps surmise from Dostoevsky's remarks on Hugo's Christian tendency in poetry, his conception of Schiller as a Christian poet, his interest in Chateaubriand's *Le Génie du Christianisme,* as well as his infatuation with Shidlovsky that a strong religious interest already was shaping his literary and aesthetic consciousness. "Yes! Write me about the chief idea of Chateaubriand's *Génie du Christianisme,*" Dostoevsky wrote to his brother in 1838.[18] It is a noteworthy fact that the conception of Christianity not only as truth, but as beauty—the chief idea of *Le Génie du Christianisme*—is the core of Dostoevsky's Christian aesthetic outlook as it takes shape in his writings of the post-exile period.

3   Into the Vortex

THE YEARS between 1840, when Dostoevsky wrote of his infatuation with Schiller, and 1846, when he published *Poor Folk,* were marked by rapid evolution in his literary development. "Brother, in respect to literature I am *not the same person* I was two years ago," he wrote his brother Mikhail, February 24, 1845. "That was childishness, rubbish. Two years of study have brought much and taken much away."[1] The intensity and breadth of Dostoevsky's interest in literature is suggested by his letter to his brother in January, 1840.[2] It is in this period that Dostoevsky began to write. In February, 1841, he read excerpts from his dramas *Maria Stuart* and *Boris Godunov* (the dramas, however, were not preserved).[3] The desire to give himself over more completely to literature grew more intense. "Oh brother, dear brother! More quickly to the pier, more quickly to freedom!" he wrote in the same year. "Freedom and one's vocation—this is a great thing. I dream of it, imagine it, again, as never before. The soul somehow broadens out to conceive the greatness of life."[4] Even before Dostoevsky retired from the government service in 1844 he collaborated with his brother in the translation of foreign literature into Russian—Schiller's works, on a large scale, but also those of Eugène Sue, George Sand, and Balzac. Dostoevsky mentions a "finished drama," entitled *The Jew Jankel,* in January, 1844 and notes that he has just translated Balzac's *Eugénie Grandet*—"a miraculous work! a miraculous work!"[5] "You say that drama is my salvation," he wrote in September, 1844. "Yes, but producing a play requires time. Money also." But he had a hope. "I am finishing a *novel* the size of *Eugénie Grandet.* The novel is rather original." The work Dostoevsky had in mind was *Poor Folk.*[6]

Dostoevsky's literary evolution in the years leading up to *Poor Folk* is imaginatively recreated in his feuilleton "Petersburg Visions in Verse and Prose" in 1861.[7] The narrator-feuilletonist describes the fantasies he indulged in as a youth. "What did I not dream through in my youth, what did I not experience with my heart, with my whole soul in golden and passionate dreams, as though from opium. There were no moments in my life more complete, more holy, and more pure. I dreamed to such a degree that I let my youth slip by." The narrator relates how he would come home from work, sit reading Schiller and Hoffmann, dream in his attic room, imagine himself in various roles, go into ecstasies, suffer, love, imagine himself before Elizabeth, Louisa, Amalia.[8] "But the real Amalia I also let slip by." "I became the artist of my own life," remarks a similar dreamer in Dostoevsky's story "White Nights" (1848).

The transition in the artist-dreamer from narcissistic self-examination and self-exaltation to a sober examination of the life around him is dramatized in the narrator's "vision" at the Neva River. Hurrying home from the Vyborg side one wintry January evening, the narrator stopped at the river and glanced into the smoky, frosty distance. Night lay over the city "under the last gleam of sun." Columns of smoke rose like giants from the roofs on both embankments

and rushed upward through the cold sky, twining and untwining on the way, so that it seemed as if new buildings were rising over the old ones, as if a new city was forming in the air. It seemed, finally, that this whole world with all its inhabitants, strong and weak, with all their domiciles, shelters of the poor or golden palaces, in this twilight hour resembled a fantastic, magical vision, a dream which in its turn would vanish immediately and evaporate in steam in the dark blue sky. Some strange thought suddenly stirred in me. I shuddered, and my heart was as though flooded at this moment with a hot rush of blood that boiled up suddenly from the surge of a powerful but hitherto unknown sensation. I seemed to have understood something in that moment which till then had only been stirring in me but was still uninterpreted; it was as if I had peered into something new, into a completely new world, unfamiliar to me and known only by certain dark rumors, by certain mysterious signs. I suppose that from precisely that moment my existence began.[9]

This vision at the Neva also appears at the conclusion of "A Weak Heart" (1848); looking at this same scene, a "strange thought" came to Arkady, and his heart was filled with a new sensation. "It was as though he only now understood all this anguish and had learned why his poor Vasya, unable to bear his happiness, had gone mad. . . . He peered into something new in that minute." The vision of Arkady and of the narrator-feuilletonist is an awakening to the tragic reality of St. Petersburg.

The narrator reveals what it was that he saw when he peered into the "completely new world." In his romantic Amalia days, he writes, he had lived with a clerk, Amalia's suitor, "who wore an overcoat with a cat skin collar which could be taken for marten." He had not wanted even to think about that marten fur. But then suddenly, living by himself, he began to think about it.

> And I began to look into the matter and suddenly I saw some other strange persons. All of them were strange, miraculous figures, quite prosaic, not at all Don Carlos and Posas, but quite entirely titulary councillors, and at the same time, as it were, quite fantastic titulary councillors. Somebody grimaced before me, somebody who had hidden behind this whole fantastic crowd and who was pulling some strings, springs, and these dolls moved, while he roared with laughter and just went on roaring! And I dreamed at that time of another story, of a certain titulary heart that lived in obscurity, honest and pure, moral and devoted to the hierarchy of officialdom; and along with him [I dreamed of] a certain girl, abused and unhappy, and their whole story profoundly lacerated my heart. And if I were to gather up that whole crowd which I dreamed of at that time, a splendid masquerade would emerge.[10]

The grimacing puppeteer is unquestionably Gogol. Gogol, Dostoevsky wrote in 1861 in another article, "constantly was laughing; he laughed his whole life both at himself and at us, and we laughed with him, laughed to such an extent that, finally, we began to weep from our laughter. He grasped the purpose of Lt. Pirogov; out of an official who lost an overcoat he created for us a fearful tragedy. . . . Oh, this was a colossal demon the like of which you never had in Europe."[11] Gogol's writing profoundly influenced Dostoevsky in the crucial period of the formation of his literary consciousness. "We have all come from out of Gogol's overcoat,"

Dostoevsky reportedly remarked.[12] But Dostoevsky's literary awakening involved both a step toward and a step away from Gogol; it was—as Dostoevsky's account in "Petersburg Visions" strongly suggests—an act of self-definition, an establishment of lines of demarcation between his own vision of reality and Gogol's. This double movement is manifest in his first work, *Poor Folk*.

Dostoevsky's literary evolution in the early 1840s took place under the aegis of the new school of realism—the Gogol "natural school"—championed by Belinsky. "Out of nothing to do we founded the natural school," Dostoevsky wrote with irony in 1861. "In those days everything was done according to principle; we lived by principle and were fearfully afraid of doing anything that was not in accordance with the new ideas."[13] Dostoevsky first met Belinsky in 1845, but, as he wrote later in his *Diary of a Writer*, he already had been reading Belinsky "passionately" for several years.[14] Belinsky saw in *Poor Folk* an embodiment of the principles of the natural school. He hailed the work for its "simplicity and truth," its "humane thought," its unmelodramatic depiction of the "workaday, everyday life" of the poor and oppressed. Here was a poet gifted with a profound sense of justice and humanity, capable of revealing the interior spiritual beauty of these poor folk, of depicting their tragedy and arousing in the reader a sense of democratic protest. "Honor and glory to the young poet whose muse loves people in attics and cellars and says of them to the inhabitants of the gilded palaces: 'But these are also people, your brothers!' "[15]

"I spend a great deal of time at Belinsky's," Dostoevsky wrote at the time of the publication of *Poor Folk*. "He is extraordinarily well-disposed toward me and seriously sees in me *proof before the public* and justification of his views."[16] "Belinsky," he wrote again, "said that he has complete confidence in me, because I can take up entirely different elements."[17] A few months later Dostoevsky wrote again in a letter: "Just think, all *our people* and even Belinsky, have found that I have moved far even from Gogol. . . . People find in me a new original current (Belinsky and the rest) consisting in the fact that I function by analysis and not by synthesis, i.e. I go into the depths and, analyzing atom by atom, I seek out the whole, whereas Gogol on the other hand goes straight at the whole and therefore is not as profound as I."[18] Dostoevsky is carried away here by the success of *Poor Folk*. What is of particular interest in his sketchy comments, however, is the notion that *Poor Folk*, in other than purely artistic respects, represents some kind of advance over Gogol.

What was Dostoevsky's own view of the relation of art and reality in the period of *Poor Folk?* To what extent did he regard his art as a deepening of Gogol's representation of man and social reality? His extant letters contain hardly any observations on these questions. *Poor Folk* itself, on the other hand, provides much material for an understanding of Dostoevsky's literary poetics at the threshold of his career; in some respects this work can be viewed as a manifesto in imagery of the author's literary principles and positions.

Makar Devushkin, the naïve and uneducated clerk in *Poor Folk,* fancies himself a budding writer; he takes an interest in literature and even sits in on a group of third-rate literary amateurs where pseudohistorical tales and potboilers in romantic style are read and discussed. In one of Devushkin's letters (June 26) to Varvara he sets down some of the notions on art that he has garnered from conversation and reading:

> Literature is a fine thing, Varenka, very fine; this I learned from them the other day. A profound thing! Strengthening the heart of people, providing instruction. . . . Literature is a picture, that is, in a certain sense a picture and a mirror; the expression of the passions, really subtle criticism, instructions for edification, and a document.

This simplistic view of art as a mirror and of art as edification forms an ironic prelude, for the reader, to Devushkin's confrontation later on (letters of July 1, July 8) with Pushkin's "The Station Master" (1830) and Gogol's "The Overcoat" (1842). Dostoevsky's own views on the artistic representation of reality may be discerned in his handling of this confrontation.

Devushkin reports his impressions of Pushkin's "The Station Master" almost in a state of melting ecstasy. In this story he finds his innermost heart, his circumstances, his identity, his "whole life" in detail. "Really, I feel the same thing, absolutely the same thing as in the book. . . . And how many Samson Vyrins there are who go about among us!" Devushkin exclaims. But he reacts with rigid hostility to Gogol's "The Overcoat." On the one hand, the story plainly troubles him because it appears to sanction, if not arouse, attitudes of social insubordination and protest—unacknowledged and strongly repressed attitudes present in Devushkin himself. On the other hand, Devushkin recoils from Gogol's story because he sees it as a comic lampoon on the life of the little man, a sketch with a particularly rude and humiliating emphasis upon the everyday details of the poor man's private existence. Devushkin fails entirely to perceive Gogol's own humanistic, even sentimental attitude toward his hero. He finds "The Station Master" thoroughly "natural," true to life; "The Overcoat," however, is "simply lacking in truthfulness because it couldn't happen that there could be such a clerk."

Here one may note that Devushkin's reaction to Gogol's story is almost a fictional realization of one of Belinsky's ideas. Gogol, the Russian critic observed in 1843, despite his supreme artistry is not high in the esteem of the Russian public.

> The comic, the humorous, the ironic, is not accessible to everybody, and everything that evokes laughter is usually considered by the majority to be below that which evokes lofty ecstasy. . . . Comedy is the fruit of civilization . . . to understand the comic one must stand on a high level of education. . . . The crowd only understands external comedy; it does not understand that there are points at which the comic merges with the tragic and evokes no longer a light and joyful, but a painful and bitter laugh. . . . Thus the poet who arouses in the reader a contemplation of the lofty and beautiful and an anguish for the ideal through the depiction of the low and vulgar life, in the eyes of the crowd, can never appear the priest of that very same refined taste which the poets serve who have depicted the lofty in life. [The crowd] will always see the *lowly comic* in his profound humor, and, looking at the truthfully reproduced phenomena of a vulgar day-to-day existence, it does not see because of them the bright images present precisely here.[19]

Devushkin's reaction to "The Overcoat," one might say, is "proof and justification" of Belinsky's view of the crowd's reaction to Gogol. We must not, in any sense, confuse Devushkin's reaction to "The Overcoat" with Dostoevsky's own reaction to it. "There is instinct in our public, as in every crowd, but there is no education," Dostoevsky wrote his brother early in 1846. "They do not understand how one can write in such a style. They are accustomed to see the mug of the author in everything; but I didn't show mine. They don't seem to guess that it is Devushkin who is speaking and not I, and that Devushkin cannot speak in any other way."[20] The same observation applies, of course, to Devushkin's literary judgments. But we may find in Dostoevsky's way of mirroring Devushkin through a reading of Pushkin and Gogol the author's preference, not for one masterpiece as opposed to another, but for a realistic method which renders a more complete account of man's reality.

Devushkin finds no truth in "The Overcoat." The deeper truth, of course, is that Devushkin recognizes himself in Gogol's story, but his reaction is essentially the same as when he sees himself reflected in a real mirror outside a bureaucrat's office: "I looked into the mirror on the right and could simply have gone crazy over what I saw." The scarecrow image that he perceives in the real mirror conveys, in all its surface realism, the appalling truth of his tragic condition. Devushkin is here, and yet Devushkin is not here: the bizarre mirror image conveys nothing of the depth or inner tenderness of his being. In the mirror everything is degraded, everything limited to the external "description" that Devushkin loathes; yet in his consciousness there is a profound sensitivity which gives dignity to that degradation. The real mirror, in short, conveys nothing of Devushkin's own subjective conception—a humanized one—of his image, nothing of his self-image.

Akaky Akakievich, like Devushkin's mirror image, is essentially a passive object—both of his fellowman's ridicule and of his creator's humanistic solicitude. Devushkin, on the other hand, is the active bearer of his own humanity. Dostoevsky spares Devushkin none of the humiliating burden and detail of everyday "low" existence, but he endows him with self-consciousness, spiritual receptivity, an idealism, and a nascent aesthetic sense. Devushkin may be simple, uneducated, unformed, but he is recognizably *man.*

Gogol passionately believed that reality in art must be illumined from within by a lofty ideal. But he did not succeed in transfiguring any of his characters with this ideal, though he succeeded in making a few of them (including Akaky Akakievich) pathetic symbols of a disfigured humanity. The "bright images" that Belinsky found hidden in the tedium and vulgarity of the Gogolian landscape are outside of man. The Gogolian character is transfixed by his own grimace; what Belinsky said of the characters in Gogol's play *Inspector General* (*Revizor*, 1836)—"strictly speaking they have neither vices nor virtues in them"—is essentially true of all of Gogol's characters.[21] In his characterization of Devushkin, Dostoevsky humanizes the little man, restores to man his human image, figuratively speaking, "re-forms" him.[22] It is of signal importance, one may note in this connection, that Dostoevsky endows his delicate hero with a powerful, though primitive, aesthetic sense. Devushkin's consuming interest in literature, his practical and theoretical preoccupation (however naïve and ridiculous) with his writing and "style," all bear witness to a deep striving for form. His rejection of "The Overcoat," of the portrayal of Akaky Akakievich, is essentially a rejection of the mask of disfiguration; conversely, his responsiveness to "The Station Master" is a responsiveness to form—form in the broad moral-aesthetic sense that Pushkin's art came to represent for Dostoevsky. In Dostoevsky's novelistic universe Devushkin is the first figure—as Dmitry Karamazov is the last—in whom the striving for human dignity and shape, the problem of moral form itself, is perceived and examined in its aesthetic aspect. In this sense Devushkin, as a creation, gives perfect expression to Dostoevsky's aesthetic humanism and to the ethos of the 1840s.

Art for the young Dostoevsky, then, is not a "picture or a mirror," as Devushkin conceives it; art does not passively reflect reality; rather—like Dostoevsky's vision at the Neva—it "peers into" reality, seeks out the inner man, and presents him in the dynamic of his full reality, his full truth. In *Poor Folk*—as later in the drafts to his Pushkin speech in 1880—Dostoevsky as a writer expresses a preference for the "full truth" of Pushkin's characters, as opposed to the half-truth of Gogol's satirical types.[23]

Dostoevsky's method of characterizing Devushkin is, finally, a clear parody of the "mirror" concept of art. The reader sees Devushkin as Devushkin sees himself in the contrasting mirrors of Gogol and Pushkin (in the mirror of "The Station Master" the

knowledgeable reader will even see Samson Vyrin reflected in another mirror—the pictures of the prodigal son story which line the
walls of his station). The complete Devushkin, of course, is mirrored neither in "The Overcoat" nor "The Station Master" nor the
real mirror into which our hero peers; nor is he fully reflected in
Varvara's letters or even in his own reflections on himself. In *Poor
Folk* Dostoevsky shatters the proverbial mirror of reality, and man
is revealed anew in the multiple and complex perspective of its
fragments.

"*Reality*—here is the device and last word of the contemporary
world!" Belinsky wrote in 1842. "Reality in facts, in knowledge,
in the convictions of feeling and the conclusions of intellect—
everywhere and in everything reality is the first and last word of our
age."[24] We feel the same intoxication with reality, with the contemporary world and all its manifestations, in Dostoevsky's early feuilletons. Dostoevsky emerges as a propagandist of reality in a feuilleton of June 1, 1847.[25] The inhabitant of St. Petersburg, stupified
by its winter, he writes, has little time "to examine Petersburg more
attentively, to study its physiognomy, and to read the history of the
city and of our whole epoch in this mass of stones, in these splendid
buildings, palaces, monuments." However it is not the history of
St. Petersburg that arouses Dostoevsky. One may respect the past,
the ancient history of Moscow and Russia, but the Russian national element is not to be found in the dead letter of antiquity and
tradition. It is to be found in the present. The quality of Petersburg that enthralls Dostoevsky is the "element of the contemporary,
the idea of the present moment." Petersburg is the modern "head
and heart of Russia." Here, "all is chaos, all is confusion, there is,
perhaps, much food for caricature; but on the other hand all is life
and movement." Petersburg is "still being created, made; its future
is still in the idea; but this idea belongs to Peter the Great, it is being embodied, it is growing, taking root every day not alone in the
Petersburg bog but throughout Russia, all of which lives through
Petersburg alone." Precisely in this striving for the contemporary
Dostoevsky finds the triumph of the national element. The mark of
a people's health he finds in its love for contemporary reality. Dostoevsky's feuilleton is full of the vigorous excitement of the 1840s.

Never was so much spoken about the contemporary direction of things, about the contemporary idea, etc., as now, as of late. Never before has literature and every manifestation of social life evoked such curiosity. . . . Almost everybody is beginning to examine, analyze the world, and each other, and themselves. Everybody is examining and measuring each other with curious glances. . . . Thousands of new points of view are being opened up even among people one never suspected of having a point of view.

All this ferment and activity appeals to Dostoevsky precisely as an artist. Clearly he measures the health of the artist and of literature with the same yardstick with which he measures the health of the people: the striving for the contemporary and the preoccupation with the national element. Apropos of the work of a caricaturist, G. Nevakhovich, Dostoevsky remarks that it would be

difficult to imagine a time more suitable than now for the appearance of a caricaturist-*artist*. There are many ideas that have been worked out and experienced by society; one does not have to wrack one's brains for topics, although we often hear: "now just what can we speak and write about?" But the greater the talent of the artist, the richer his means to put across his idea to society. For him there exist neither barriers nor ordinary obstacles; for him there is a host of topics, always and everywhere, and in this very century the artist can find food wherever he wishes and speak about everything.

The authentic artist, then, does not stand outside of society and its ferment but is at the very center of its activity and interests. He does not create for himself alone but strives to "put across his idea to society." And his canvas is his city, his epoch, his century—and not merely in its external manifestations or "physiology" but in its "history" and "idea." Dostoevsky was preeminently such an artist —both in his initial years and in the later period of his greatest creations.

While Dostoevsky calls upon the artist and citizen to face reality, to live in it, he is preoccupied in his belles lettres with the individual (both artist and nonartist) who has lost contact with reality.

"Terrible is the dissonance, terrible the imbalance which society presents to us," he writes in a letter to Mikhail in 1847. "The *external* should be in equilibrium with the *internal*. Otherwise, lacking external phenomena, the inner dangerously gets the upper hand. The nerves and fantasy then take up a lot of room in the being. Every external phenomenon from lack of habit seems colossal and somehow frightens. You begin to fear life."[26] The most natural need of man, Dostoevsky insists elsewhere, is to "become conscious of, to realize, to give shape to, his I in real life."[27] The tragedy of the "dreamer" who has lost contact with real life is at the center of a number of Dostoevsky's stories written in the preexile period: "White Nights," "The Landlady," *Netochka Nezvanova*. Artists or characters with a distinct artistic sensibility figure prominently in all three works. In "The Landlady" in particular, Dostoevsky explores the catastrophe to creative consciousness of the dreamer's failure to make contact with reality.

At this time Dostoevsky had entered into close personal and intellectual relations with Belinsky and the group around him. Later he became associated with the Petrashevsky reading circle and became involved in several conspiratorial inner circles. In 1873 Dostoevsky wrote that he had parted ways with Belinsky in 1848 "for a variety of reasons, quite unimportant ones, however, in all respects."[28] He maintains, however, that although he had ceased to visit Belinsky in the last year of his life, he "passionately had accepted at that time all his teachings."[29] There is reason to believe that this is something of an exaggeration. In the same reminiscences Dostoevsky observed that he and Belinsky were at opposite poles on the question of religion; in this sphere Belinsky regarded Dostoevsky as a "naïve man."[30] The problems of religion, of course, pose the fundamental questions of philosophy. Dostoevsky's pronounced divergence from Belinsky on questions of religion and faith imply fundamental differences in other areas. It seems quite probable that at this time—as, indeed, in later life—Dostoevsky succeeded in harmonizing quite contradictory philosophical, literary, and political views.

What, precisely, were Dostoevsky's views on the question of the role of the artist in society, the function of literature in the social cause, in the preexile period? Belinsky expressed many opinions on this question. Art serves society, he wrote in 1840, "not as something existing for it, but as something existing in itself and for itself, containing in itself its purpose and cause." To demand that literature serve social goals, he felt, at that time, could only lead to "rhymed dissertations," or "dry allegories" concealing "dead preachment," or the fulminations of parties. The content of true poetry is "not the questions of the day, but the questions of centuries, not the interests of the country, but the interests of the world, not the fate of parties, but the fate of mankind."[31] Art and society must "each go its own road without interfering with each other."[32] In 1842 Belinsky no longer stressed the lofty autonomy of art; he insisted, however, that "freedom of creation easily harmonizes with service to contemporary society: for this it is not necessary to compel oneself to write on themes, to coerce one's imagination; for this it is necessary only to be a citizen, a son of one's society and one's epoch, to appropriate to oneself its interests, to merge one's strivings with its strivings."[33]

There is nothing in these remarks of Belinsky with which Dostoevsky would quarrel. There is no reason to assume that Dostoevsky and Belinsky differed on the question of the nature of the interests and strivings of society (as Dostoevsky differed on these questions with the radical democrats after his exile).

But along with continued emphasis upon the dangers of dry didacticism in art, there is an increasing emphasis in Belinsky's writing upon the importance of "artistic service," upon the writer's concrete contribution to social development. Here and there utilitarian criteria are evident. "All that does not meet the measure of practical application," he wrote in 1845, "is false and empty."[34] Privately, in a letter to V. O. Botkin in December, 1847, Belinsky wrote:

> I no longer require any more poetry and artistry than is necessary to keep a story true, that is, to keep it from turning into allegory or taking on the character of a dissertation. . . . The chief thing is that it should call forth questions, have a moral effect upon society. If it achieves that goal even entirely without poetry and artistry, it is *nonetheless* interesting for me, and I do not read it but devour it. . . . Of course, if a story arouses questions and has a moral effect on society along with a high level of artistry, I like it all the better; but the main

thing for me still is in the substance and not in the fancy trap-
pings. Let a story be ever so artistic, but if it has no substance,
brother, no substance: *je m'en fous.* I know that I take a one-
sided position, but I do not wish to come out of it, and I feel
sorrow and pity for those who do not share my one-sided-
ness.[35]

Dostoevsky vigorously criticized the radical literary critic N. A.
Dobrolyubov in 1861 for a readiness to divorce aesthetic and
moral criteria. The extant evidence of Dostoevsky's views in the
late 1840s on the question of the function of literature in the social
cause suggests that he did not share Belinsky's increasingly militant and utilitarian outlook. Dostoevsky was arrested with other
members of the Petrashevsky circle in 1849 and brought to trial. In
his "Affidavit," filed before the trial commission, he asserted that
he had quarreled with the literary critic Belinsky in 1848 over the
questions of the "ideas of literature and [the problem] of tendency
in literature." Dostoevsky insisted that his view had been "radically opposed" to Belinsky's and that he had reproached Belinsky
for trying to give literature a "local meaning unworthy of it" by
reducing it to description of newspaper facts or scandalous events.
He told Belinsky (according to the "Affidavit") that nothing would
be gained by "spleen," by buttonholing the passerby and "forcibly
preaching to him and teaching him with mind and reason."[36]
Dostoevsky likewise affirmed that he once spoke at Petrashevsky's in connection with a literary quarrel with Petrashevsky; at
that time Dostoevsky had insisted that

> art needs no tendency, that art was a goal in itself, that the
> author should busy himself with artistry, and the idea will
> come of itself, because it is a necessary condition of artistry.
> In a word, *it is known that this tendency is diametrically op-
> posed to the journalistic* [approach] *and . . .* [to the view that
> literature must serve as a] *fire brigade.* Many also knew that
> this had been my tendency for several years. Finally, every-
> body heard our quarrel at Petrashevsky's; everybody can at-
> test to what I have said.[37]

In additional testimony at the trial, Dostoevsky observed that
Durov, a member of the Petrashevsky circle, had supported him in

the view that literature needs no tendency except the "purely artistic" and in the view that "tendency binds the writer, cramping his freedom, and in the bargain, a splenetic, abusive tendency which ruins artistry."[38] In a note to his testimony at this point Dostoevsky adds: "With which Petrashevsky completely agreed. It turned out that the quarrel resulted from a misunderstanding. All the guests of Petrashevsky were witnesses."[39] The secret government agent and informer, P. D. Antonelli, who spied on the Petrashevsky gatherings, corroborates in part Dostoevsky's testimony. He notes that Petrashevsky used to quarrel with the Dostoevsky brothers, "reproaching them for their manner of writing which, it seemed, would not lead to any development of ideas in society."[40]

Undoubtedly Dostoevsky, in an effort to cover up his conspiratorial activities, exaggerates the importance of his literary differences with Belinsky, Petrashevsky, and others. Dostoevsky, after all, shared substantially the same social and political goals as these men. But his testimony is convincing on the question of his point of view. It is a striking fact, moreover, that in his "Affidavit" in 1849 are to be found in embryo form the central points of his later critique of Dobrolyubov in 1861, namely: the concept of art as a goal in itself, the notion that in free creation the "idea will come of itself," and the belief that tendency may cramp the freedom of the writer. It goes without saying, of course, that when Dostoevsky found himself in basic political disagreement with the radicals of the 1860s, his critique of utilitarian tendency acquired more than theoretical significance.

Dostoevsky's remarks about Belinsky and about tendency appear in the context of a discussion about censorship and the role of literature in society. His words obviously are carefully chosen for a police audience; both strain and studied simplification are noticeable; he appears, nonetheless, to make a particular effort to give as true an expression of his opinions as possible in those realms where the danger was minimal. Literature would appear to have been a realm for relative freedom of expression. Dostoevsky's literary thoughts in his "Affidavit," therefore, deserve attentive, even if cautious, evaluation.

Severe censorship, Dostoevsky insisted in his "Affidavit," had created a "tense, most difficult" state of affairs for literature. "I was unhappy that the vocation of the writer was degraded in our time by some kind of dark suspicion, and that even before the writer wrote anything he was looked upon by the censor as though he were some natural enemy of the government." Works were forbidden sometimes simply because "they ended in a too sad way, because a too gloomy picture was presented, although this picture did not accuse, or throw suspicion on, anybody in society, and although the tragedy itself took place in a completely accidental and external manner." Dostoevsky asserted that he was subjected to censorship for presenting a picture "in too gloomy colors." All this creates a most burdensome situation for the writer who must earn his living. Dostoevsky admits that he complained about this censorship but declares that such complaints cannot be considered "freethinking."[41]

In such an atmosphere of misunderstanding and suspicion, literature, "one of the most important matters in the state," finds it difficult to exist. "Entire genres of art must disappear; satire, tragedy, no longer can exist. Such writers as Griboedov, Fonvizin, and even Pushkin could not exist with the severity of present-day censorship. Satire pokes fun at vice, and most often—vice under the mask of virtue. But how could there be any kind of satire now?" The censor tries to conceal vice and the gloomy side of life.

> But can one write with bright colors alone? How can the bright side of the picture be visible without the gloomy? Can there be a picture without light and shade together? We have a notion of light only because there is shade. They say: describe only valorous deeds, virtues. But we do not know virtue without vice; the very concepts of *good* and *evil* have come from the fact that good and evil constantly have been living together, one right next to the other. . . . I do not stand for the depiction of vice and the gloomy side of life! Both one and the other are in no way congenial to me. But I speak solely and exclusively in the interests of art.[42]

Dostoevsky's remarks do not reveal, of course, the depth either of his political attitudes or of his literary interest: they are carefully tailored; they are interesting, however, precisely as an attempt to defend art in terms of the demands of art. The observation on tragedy which is "accidental" suggests, of course, Dostoevsky's understanding of the nature of real tragedy. The remarks on light and shade and on the coexistence in life of good and evil certainly are commonplaces; nonetheless they anticipate a major problem-emphasis in Dostoevsky's art.

Dostoevsky fervently expresses the wish—in a manner of understatement characteristic of the whole "Affidavit"—that the "sad misunderstanding" between literature and the censor will quickly pass. "Because I love literature and cannot but be interested in it; because I . . . know that literature is one of the expressions of the life of the people, is a mirror of society." Here, however, Dostoevsky outlines the function of literature as one of actively transmitting to the people, defining, naming the new concepts which come with education and civilization, "because the people cannot name them in the present case, because civilization does not come from it, but from above; only that society which accepted civilization before the people can name [the concepts], that is, the upper stratum of society, the class already educated to the acceptance of these ideas. Now who has formulated the new ideas in a form that the people can understand them—now who, if not literature!"[43]

There is much in this statement of the function of literature that could flatter the upper classes; the condescending attitude toward the people is hardly characteristic of the author of *Poor Folk,* let alone the fervent populist of later years. Dostoevsky's remarks before the investigating committee could be interpreted differently by different audiences. In later years he never ceased to emphasize the great importance of literature and culture in Russian life; he emphasized that the educated upper class, or at least the outstanding representatives of this class, certainly could partake of the attribute of the national element (*narodnost'*). "Is it possible that the national element disappears with the development of a people?" Dostoevsky asks in 1861. "Is it possible that we 'educated ones' are no longer the Russian people?"[44]

The appearance of Lomonosov—an establisher of norms in the Russian language—after Peter the Great was not accidental, Dostoevsky observes. Lomonosov's language reforms facilitated Peter's reform. "Without literature society cannot exist," he goes on, "and I saw that it was perishing, and for the tenth time I repeat that the misunderstanding which arose between literature and the censors agitated me, tormented me."[45] The great issues and political passions that lay behind the Petrashevsky trial are veiled and subdued here by laborious understatement. There is real pathos, none-theless, in Dostoevsky's words on a perishing literature. His view on the living interdependence between literature and society reflects not only the great role played by Russian literature in the moral formation of Russian society—a role understood by so many Russian men of culture; his view reflects his own aesthetic humanism and the deep social commitment of his literary interest.

More than a slight misunderstanding, of course, lay between literature and the censors: it sent Dostoevsky to Siberian prison and into exile for ten years.

4   Rebirth of Conviction

"OF COURSE, reality and events . . . in life facilitate the development of the human spirit (of any man) and have a powerful influence even on such a great and independent spiritual power as that of Pushkin," Dostoevsky wrote in the draft to his Pushkin speech in 1880. Dostoevsky objects to the notion that Pushkin's education and youth in St. Petersburg had one meaning, while travel through Russia, his stay in Mikhailovskoye, and the influence of his nurse, Irina Rodiovna, were the cause of another direction in his life. Pushkin's genius was not really dependent on external influences, Dostoevsky wrote, "and without doubt would have developed rightly under any influences."[1] The same must be said, substantially, of Dostoevsky's own life. Siberia powerfully shaped his development. But it brought to fruition only that which had been seeded in his genius in the preexile period. We cannot speak of two independent Dostoevskys, two unconnected periods in Dostoevsky's life; we can only speak of his continuous development in the 1840s and, later, under different and changed circumstances, in the St. Petersburg of the 1860s and 1870s. Siberia is the pivotal center in his development.

Dostoevsky returned to St. Petersburg in 1859 after ten years in prison and exile in Siberia. He had been unable to write in prison at Omsk, he said in a letter to A. N. Maikov in 1856, "yet there was turbulent inner work."[2] "You say that you experienced much, thought over much, lived through much anew," he wrote to his friend. "I too thought and experienced, and there were such circumstances, such influences, that one was obliged to experience, re-think, and meditate too much—beyond one's endurance." Yet, as Dostoevsky continued in the same letter: "ideas change, but the heart remains the same."[3] He later spoke of his period of exile as one of the "rebirth of my convictions."[4] The concept of rebirth, as opposed to change, is particularly relevant to any consideration of the evolution of Dostoevsky's religious consciousness and his aesthetic-philosophical outlook.

We can speak of a radical change in Dostoevsky's political orientation toward both the radical intelligentsia and the government. The writer who returned to St. Petersburg in 1859 did not identify himself with the revolutionary strivings and rigorous utilitarian and materialist outlook of the radical democrats led by N. G. Chernyshevsky (1828–89) and N. A. Dobrolyubov (1836–61). His notebooks in the early 1860s reflect his hostility toward the outlook of the new generation of radicals even more than his pieces of journalism and literary criticism; in the latter, at least in the beginning of his publishing venture with the journals *Vremya* and *Epokha,* Dostoevsky attempted to hold to a centrist position in the hope of winning adherents to his camp. Dostoevsky's first and perhaps major piece of literary criticism in his journal, "Mr. —bov and the Question of Art" (1861), is particular evidence of this attempt at compromise.

One cannot speak of an about-face in Dostoevsky's basic aesthetic-philosophical outlook as one can about his political positions. Belinsky had facilitated Dostoevsky's movement from a transcendental romanticism to a humanistic and socially oriented realism. But there is no evidence that Dostoevsky ever abandoned the fundamental idealist assumptions of German romantic aesthetic; nor is there evidence that he ever succumbed to atheism. The testimony of the Petrashevsky trial already indicates clear differences between Dostoevsky and Belinsky on fundamental questions of the function of literature and the artist in society. It would seem closer to the truth to speak of a vital reactivation in Dostoevsky in the 1850s, a reactivation of a residual philosophically idealist outlook and—in the context of his deepening religious consciousness—a Christianization of that humanist aesthetic which was his legacy from the 1840s.

Of interest in this connection is one of Dostoevsky's letters to A. E. Vrangel in 1856; in it, he remarked that he was preparing an article, "Letters about Art," which was the "fruit of a decade of careful thought. I conceived it all to the last word back in Omsk." He wrote that his article was "essentially on the significance of Christianity in art."[5] Dostoevsky, as we noted earlier, certainly knew about, and possibly read, Chateaubriand's *Le Génie du Christianisme*—the outstanding effort in the nineteenth century to elaborate a distinctly Christian aesthetic. Chateaubriand, like Schiller, gives a central place to the aesthetic element in the moral development of man; but with Chateaubriand, as with Dostoevsky in his major creative period after exile, the aesthetic and moral elements are directly dependent upon the Christian religion. Did Dostoevsky's higher aesthetic have such a Christian focus in the 1840s? An identification of the aesthetic, moral, and religious categories is, perhaps, implicit in certain features of "The Landlady" (1848). Here the heroine Katerina's craving for moral purity and religious expiation is symbolized by her prostration before the iconographic image; in the pattern of Dostoevsky's aesthetic-religious symbolism in his major novels, the icon (in Russian, *obraz*—image, or *ikon*) emerges as the aesthetic embodiment of divine, ideal form, of ineffable beauty.

The identification of the aesthetic ideal with the religious ideal, of ideal form or beauty with the image of Christ, is manifest in Dostoevsky's letter to N. D. Fon-Vizina in 1854. In this letter he speaks of himself (in the matter of religion) as a "child of the century, a child of disbelief and doubt." He writes all the same of his terrible "thirst to believe which is all the more powerful in my soul the more the opposite proofs accumulate in me." Yet there are moments of absolute tranquility in which he formed in himself a symbol of faith. "This symbol is very simple, here it is: to believe there is nothing more beautiful, profound, sympathetic, intelligent, manly, and perfect than Christ, and not only is there nothing, but with jealous love I say there can be nothing." And Dostoevsky adds —and these are the lines we wish to emphasize—"even if somebody proved to me that Christ was outside the truth, and it *really* were true that the truth was outside Christ, then I would rather remain with Christ than with the truth."[6] Some passages in the notebooks to *The Devils* (1871–72) illuminate the problem-content of Dostoevsky's remarks to Mme. Fon-Vizina:

"princess or Sh.
'—. . . Eliminating Christ you eliminate the unattainable ideal of beauty and of good from mankind. But in place of him what do you propose of equal measure?'
Gr—. . . but who prevents you, disbelieving in Christ as God, from yet honoring him as an ideal of perfection and of moral beauty?' "[7]

The solution proposed by Gr— is precisely the one that Dostoevsky proposes as a last resort in 1854; it is also the solution that Stavrogin (in a period preceding the action of the novel) advances. Shatov says to Stavrogin: "But didn't you tell me that if it were mathematically proven to you that the truth was outside of Christ, then you would prefer rather to remain with Christ than with the truth?" (Pt. II, Ch. 7).

The aesthetic element is as central to Dostoevsky's conception of Christ in 1854 as it is in 1870. He will remain with Christ even if it is proven to him that He is not divine. Yet the act of remaining with Christ (beauty) is itself precisely a leap of faith which places Christ back in the circle of revealed truth, which renders false the "opposite proofs." The perception of beauty is inseparable for Dostoevsky from the leap of faith.

In the same letter to Vrangel in which he announces his "Letters about Art," Dostoevsky raises the question as to where he will publish his article. He observes that the journal *Russkij Vestnik* has printed an introduction by Katkov to a collection of Pushkin's works "in which the ideas are completely opposite to mine."[8] This introduction was published in two installments.[9] At the time of his letter, Dostoevsky, then still in Siberia, may have read only the first part of Katkov's introduction, because in the second part Katkov deals with the "question of the practical significance of art," the "question of utility," in a manner little different from Dostoevsky's treatment of these questions in "Mr. —bov and the Question of Art."[10] "The lines of Raphael never decided any practical question of life contemporary to him," Katkov wrote. "But they brought a great benefit and great use for life in the course of time; they powerfully contributed to its humanization."[11] Katkov's views on the moral-aesthetic usefulness of art, like Dostoevsky's views on the same subject, strongly reflect Schiller's philosophical letters *On the Aesthetic Education of Man*.

It is, however, in the first part of his introduction that Katkov advances a point of view on art that differs from Dostoevsky's. He acknowledges that the beautiful is the essential feature in the characterization of art, but at its foundation is that which is the foundation of cognitive thought—truth. "Truth is the first and necessary basis of all poetry; truth is also its inner goal, as also the goal of knowledge." "Poetry in essence is the same as cognitive thinking, the same as knowledge, the same as philosophy." "Poetry is . . . cognitive thought directed at everything that is not subject to abstract thinking."[12] Dostoevsky, as we shall note again, does not deny the cognitive character of art. But it is beauty as embodied in the image (*obraz*) that is the specificum of art to Dostoevsky, that is the foundation of truth, that is the inner goal of all art.

The article centering on the relation of Christianity and art, which Dostoevsky proposed in 1856, did not materialize; or, if it did, it has not been preserved. In the same year Dostoevsky wrote his brother that he believed he could "say something remarkable about art: the entire article is in my head and on paper in the form of notes."[13] Almost two years later he wrote his brother that he had plans and notes for several literary articles, "for example, on *modern poets,* on the *statistical* tendency of *literature,* on the uselessness of *tendencies* in art—articles which are written passionately and even with a sharp edge."[14]

In the subscription prospectus for his new journal *Vremya* in 1861, Dostoevsky announced that the second issue of the journal would deal with the "question of the *significance of art and of its actual relation to real life.* This is the most crucial of the contemporary literary questions which insistently demands resolution."[15] The question of the relation of art and Christianity is not mentioned here, nor is it raised in Dostoevsky's article, "Mr. —bov and the Question of Art," which appeared in the second issue of *Vremya.* The absence of any specific Christian emphasis in Dostoevsky's article is all the more conspicuous in view of the fact that here he projects art and beauty as the embodiment of man's most lofty ideal, of his craving for harmony, tranquility, and beatitude. The omission may have been motivated by Dostoevsky's awareness of the atheistic sentiments of sections of his radical audience. As for his private sentiments, they are clear: "Christ [is] the eternal, centuries-old ideal toward which man strives and must strive by the law of nature," he wrote in his notebook in the early 1860s. "Christ is the *ideal of man in the flesh.*"[16] There is no mention of Christ in "Mr. —bov and the Question of Art," but the deeply idealist content of Dostoevsky's aesthetic and its fundamentally religious spirit suggest a rebirth of convictions long overdue.

5 Two Kinds of Beauty

"BEAUTY will save the world—two kinds of beauty," Dostoevsky observes without further explanation in one of his notebooks to *The Idiot*.[1] This extremely condensed set of idea-signals points not only to the problem center of *The Idiot,* but to the complex dialectic of Dostoevsky's aesthetic thought. The first phrase—"Beauty will save the world"—is a model of syntactic precision and order; it promises direct, unimpeded action. But the second phrase is ominously disruptive; it shatters the integrity of the beauty-savior and bogs down the action in ambiguity and enigma. "Is it true, Prince, that you once said that 'beauty will save the world'?" Ippolit Terentiev asks Myshkin in *The Idiot* and then mockingly adds: "What kind of beauty will save the world?" "The world will become the beauty of Christ," Dostoevsky answers in one of his notes to *The Devils*.[2] But Myshkin gives no answer to Terentiev; elsewhere in the novel he remarks: "It is difficult to judge beauty; I am still not ready. Beauty is an enigma." Dmitry Karamazov also posits the enigma of beauty.

Where is Dostoevsky in this aesthetic confusion? Is he the one who believes in a single omnipotent beauty? Or does he acknowledge more than one kind of beauty? It is to be noted at the outset that when Dostoevsky, as critic or journalist, and speaking for himself, uses the word "beauty," it is invariably in the antique or neo-Platonist and Christian sense of ideal beauty. It is this kind of beauty which will save the world; it is, to Dostoevsky, a beauty which finds an objective correlative in concrete form—form subject to definite formal aesthetic principles. Philosophically, Dostoevsky gives de jure recognition only to this classical beauty. At the same time, in his belles lettres, Dostoevsky quite consciously explores, or one might say poses the problem of, two kinds of beauty. Here he recognizes de facto a category of the beautiful, or of the experience of the beautiful, which is the very antithesis in both formal attributes and moral content to classical beauty; he recognizes, in short, a judgment of beauty of which the determining principle is wholly subjective. What is the relationship between these two areas or structures of aesthetic thought in Dostoevsky's thinking?

We cannot arrive at a proper understanding of Dostoevsky's aesthetic position without recognizing one paradoxical notion: *it is not beauty which is ambivalent, but man who experiences two kinds of beauty.* "But really to them (and indeed to many) this madness seems not a monstrosity but, on the contrary, *beauty*," Dostoevsky wrote N. N. Strakhov in 1871 apropos of the destructiveness of the Paris Commune. He continued: "And thus the aesthetic idea in the new humanity is beclouded. A moral foundation of society (taken from positivism) not only gives no results, but cannot even define itself, is confused in desires and in ideals."[3] Dostoevsky's position is clear. Man in his moral obloquy finds pleasure in ugliness, violence, bloodshed, and falsely calls it beauty. But the "aesthetic idea" alone (the idea of beauty which for Dostoevsky in the post-exile period, if not earlier as well, is always the religious idea), though beclouded in man's consciousness, is universal and absolute.

We must distinguish, then, between Dostoevsky's point of view and the point of view of his characters. This is not to deny that Dostoevsky enjoys a certain complicity with his heroes, even the most morally or ideologically questionable ones, but it is always within, and in relation to, a clearly defined structure of ideas and beliefs. It is especially important to distinguish this basic structure where Dostoevsky's aesthetic thought is concerned.

Dostoevsky sets forth his view of the role of beauty in the life of man in his critique of utilitarian aesthetics, "Mr. —bov and the Question of Art." Here we find Dostoevsky's major formulation of his aesthetic outlook.

The need for beauty and the creation which embodies it is inseparable from man, and without it man, perhaps, would not want to live in the world. Man thirsts for it, finds and accepts beauty *unconditionally* and just because it is beauty; and he bows before it with reverence, without asking what it is useful for and what one can buy for it. And, perhaps, precisely in this consists the greatest secret of art, that the image of beauty created by it immediately becomes an idol, *unconditionally*. And why does it become an idol? Because the need for beauty develops most at the moment man is in discord with reality, in disharmony, in struggle, that is, when *he is living most of all,* because man lives most of all when he is seeking something and striving; at such a time he feels within himself a most natural desire for everything harmonious, for tranquility, and in beauty there is both harmony and tranquility. But when man finds what he has been striving for, then for a time life as it were slows up for him, and we have seen examples in which man, having achieved the ideal of his desires, not knowing what further to strive for, being satiated, would fall into a kind of anguish, would even foment in himself this anguish, seek out another ideal in his life and, out of extreme surfeit of pleasure, not only would not value what he had enjoyed, but consciously would even turn from the direct path, exciting in himself alien tastes, unhealthy, sharp, inharmonic, sometimes monstrous ones, losing measure and aesthetic feeling for healthy beauty and demanding instead of it exceptions. And therefore beauty is immanent in everything healthy, that is, to that which is most alive, and is a necessary need of the human organism. It is harmony; in it lies the guarantee of tranquility; it embodies the ideals of man and of mankind.[4]

This is a philosophical credo—at once a view of beauty and a definition of the human condition. The striking aspect of this whole exposition, of course, is the central place given to the aesthetic element in the life of man; with it, in its "healthy" form, are associated all man's noblest ideals and aspirations; but in its unhealthy form the aesthetic element enters man's being as a destructive force.

Dostoevsky's point of departure is the same as Plato's in *The Symposium:* the concept of love of beauty as necessarily love of something that is wanting to man, the concept of beauty as absolute. The conception of an absolute ideal beauty emerges from the postulation of man as incomplete, at variance with himself, and therefore ever seeking completion, unity, wholeness, and harmony. "Man strives on earth for an ideal which is *contrary* to his nature," Dostoevsky observes in his notebook in the early 1860s.[5] At the core of Dostoevsky's aesthetic philosophy, then, is the tragic view of man's relation to himself and to reality as one of permanent discord, and the view of this discord as constituting a creative dialectic in human existence, the inner force of man's aesthetic strivings.[6] Man's spirit is envisaged in a continual tension toward the ideal, the Absolute. "Peoples form and move," observes Shatov in *The Devils,* "through the inexhaustible desire to come to an end. . . . The spirit of life, as the Scriptures say, 'rivers of living water'. . . . The aesthetic principle, as the philosophers say, the moral principle, with which they identify it. 'The seeking of God,' as I call it much more simply" (Pt. II, Ch. 7).

But when the ideal, or tension toward the ideal, vanishes from man's life, Dostoevsky notes, man loses his moral equilibrium. "Another ideal" replaces his higher ideal, and the striving for the abnormal replaces the vanished craving for the norm. Man in these moments excites in himself "alien tastes, unhealthy, sharp, inharmonic, sometimes monstrous ones, losing measure and aesthetic feeling for healthy beauty and demanding instead of it exceptions." Dostoevsky writes of such moral-aesthetic disintegration in his interpretation of the poetic improvisation, "Cleopatra e i suoi amanti," in Pushkin's story "Egyptian Nights." All hope and faith have disappeared, Dostoevsky explains, from Cleopatra's decadent society; it is at the edge of an abyss.

> Life is choked because of the absence of a goal. There is nothing in the future; one must demand everything from the present; one must fill life with the immediate alone. Everything passes into the body, everything plunges into physical debauchery, and, in order to fill in for the higher spiritual impressions which are lacking, people excite their nerves, their body with everything that can possibly arouse sensations. The most monstrous aberrations, the most abnormal phenomena little by little become customary. Even the feeling of self-preservation disappears. Cleopatra is the representative of this society.[7]

Dostoevsky carefully avoids the use of the word "beauty" in his discussion of man's taste for "another ideal"; he does not explicitly state that man conceives and experiences this other ideal as beauty. Yet the idea of unhealthy beauty is suggested by the very notion of healthy beauty. What is involved here is the notion of a counterideal in the life of man, one that contrasts with the ideal of absolute beauty in that it is both temporal and accessible, fundamentally unhealthy, and full of the force of violence, disharmony, and unrest. There is no question of any good embodied in this other ideal. The phenomenon evoked here is aesthetically attractive evil—in its most basic form, sensuality. This is the "ideal of Sodom"—as opposed to the "ideal of the Madonna"—about which Dmitry speaks in *The Brothers Karamazov;* it is the phenomenon of beauty in Sodom. These two ideals, taken in their dialectical relationship to one another in man, constitute the enigma that is beauty to Dmitry Karamazov. On the aesthetic plane love of beauty in Sodom is posed in *The Brothers Karamazov* as the discordant element in man's inner being. But man does not renounce the ideal of absolute beauty—the ideal of the Madonna. It is precisely in the context of his inner discord, in struggle, as Dostoevsky noted, that the need for harmony, order, and form is felt.

The problem of beauty in Sodom—aesthetically, the problem of ugliness, disfiguration, deformation of the norm—is Dmitry's point of departure in his dramatic peroration on the enigma of beauty in *The Brothers Karamazov:* here is man's condition, his dilemma, his struggle viewed in its earthly aspect. Dostoevsky's point of departure in his disquisition on beauty in "Mr. —bov and the Question of Art" is absolute beauty toward which man strives: here is man's struggle seen in the aspect of his highest destiny, of eternity. The concept of absolute beauty as the highest good and the eternal truth and the corresponding notion of an ideal form which symbolizes harmony and, therefore, beauty constitute the unalterable foundation of Dostoevsky's higher aesthetic.

The concept of the unity of moral and aesthetic categories, of the good and the beautiful, is posited by Dostoevsky in all periods of his creative life. The dreamer in his confusion loses that "moral sense with which man is capable of evaluating all real beauty," Dostoevsky writes at the beginning of his literary career;[8] and at the end: "Only that is moral which coincides with your feeling of beauty and with the ideal in which you embody it."[9] Beauty is immanent in everything healthy. Art, embodying beauty, is an embodiment of moral health. Artistic creation forms an "image of beauty" before which man bows; he bows before this image precisely in its incarnation of his ideal—of the purity and good that he strives for. Dostoevsky writes of the moral purity (*tselomudrennost'*) of the sculpture images of the Venus of Medici and Venus of Milo. "These images produce a lofty, divine impression of art precisely because they are works of art. Here reality is transfigured, *passing through art,* passing through the fire of a pure, chaste inspiration and through the artistic thought of the poet. This is the secret of art and every artist knows about it."[10] Art is a transfiguration. The very act of creation—the creation of form—is a creation of moral value. The need for beauty, therefore, is a need for moral transfiguration. But even art, Dostoevsky cautions, will not have its "whole influence" on an "unprepared or undeveloped nature, or on a coarse and debauched soul. The more developed, the better the soul of man, the more complete and authentic will be the impression of art upon it."[11]

Beauty in its incarnation of the moral ideal is also truth. George Sand, Dostoevsky noted at the end of his life, was entranced in her works by the beauty of the moral truths she preached.[12] The visionary hero of "The Dream of a Ridiculous Man," recalling his vision of earthly paradise (which was imbued with the harmony and tranquility of pure beauty), repeatedly speaks of his discovery of the truth. "I saw the truth, I saw and know that people can be beautiful and happy without losing the capacity to live on earth." The truth here is ideal moral reality; it is moral truth embodied in real visual forms. "The real images and forms of my dream, that is, those which I in fact saw at the very moment of my dream, were filled with such harmony, were so entrancing and beautiful, and were so truthful, that on awakening I wasn't able to embody them in our weak words."

The dream of the Ridiculous Man is a vision of formal beauty itself; he has seen a "living image," he stresses, and he wishes to go forth and preach the truth of his revelation. It is the actuality of an aesthetic experience, the experience of ideal form, of pure beauty, that he wishes to preach. Art acts on man "plastically and through the image," Dostoevsky wrote in one of his articles.[13] The Ridiculous Man's dream acted upon him as would a work of art, and it is as a work of art (the plastic and representational arts) that he would act upon men. Hence his frustration with "our weak words." But the Ridiculous Man, it cannot be forgotten, is not a writer; he lacks the ability to embody his vision in verbal imagery. The writer also creates in images. The author of *Poor Folk*—Dostoevsky recalled Belinsky's excited praise of his first work—had conveyed in one stroke, "in an image," the very essence of what the publicists and critics try to explain "in words." "This is the secret of artistry," Belinsky told Dostoevsky, "here is truth in art!"[14]

Truth exists in the language of the critic or philosopher; but in art, whether plastic or verbal, truth exists only in the image, in the form that embodies it.[15] The problem of conveying truth in art, therefore, is a problem in the creation of form, one that only genuine artistry can solve. There can be no truth in a work that scorns artistry, Dostoevsky insists in "Mr. —bov and the Question of Art." The truth of a work—its living truth and therefore its "usefulness"—is destroyed by poor craftsmanship. "There is no idea, no fact which could not be vulgarized and presented in a ridiculous way."[16] On the other hand, "the artistic finish of a work gives clarity, relief, palpability, and truth to a thought, and artistic power consists just *in truth and in its vivid representation*."[17] Truth here is not just something lifted from nature or social reality and placed within the framework of a work of art; here truth is an attribute of the work of art itself, the end result of an artistic transfiguration of reality.

Beauty to Dostoevsky is the beauty of what may be called ideal form—form that is the incarnation of harmony, measure, and repose. Dostoevsky's formal conception of beauty is the same as that found in Greek aesthetics. Beauty for him is figural, and it is in the plastic and representational arts of the antique and Renaissance periods that he seeks the form or "shape," the model, of his ideal beauty. Dostoevsky writes in 1861 of the "ideals of beauty created by the past,"[18] and in 1871, through Stepan Verkhovensky (in *The Devils*), of the "form of beauty already achieved." He calls attention to the "sublime beauty" of the Apollo of Belvedere;[19] he is infatuated with the beauty of the Venus of Milo and the Venus of Medici.[20] "The Exhibition in the Academy of Arts: 1860–1861" —attributed to Dostoevsky—expresses a preference for the Greek norm and ideal of beauty. The ancient Greeks greatly honored the human body; one reason for this is the Greek "reverence for the beautiful," a reverence which "we" share with the Greeks, "and, of course, nothing in the world is more beautiful than a beautiful body."[21]

But Dostoevsky finds no reverence for the beautiful body in the paintings on exhibit. He is disgusted with the manner in which women are depicted. Here there is no feeling for the ideal. "Where can one get a model so that one could draw a really beautiful body, the kind of model that would not leave a great deal to idealize?" There are no tolerable models, he complains; instead, "Feet are disfigured by shoes, the stomach spoiled like a potato, and by a foolish bind of the skirt, so that the poor artist even has to invent a woman." Dostoevsky is offended by one painting in which the goddess Bacchante is shown with an "excessively large breast," and by another painting—Manet's "Nymph with Satyr" ["La nymphe surprise"]—in which the body of the nymph has the "color of a five-day-old corpse." The latter painting, he suggests, had been exhibited with the intention of showing "to what limits of ugliness [*bezobrazie*] the imagination of the artist can go."[22]

Disfiguration, lack of proportion, deviation from the antique notion of the "beautiful body," is objectionable to Dostoevsky; he frankly insists on idealization in painting, as he does in his article "Apropos of the Exhibition" in 1873.[23] Disfigured bodies in no way evoke that religious reverence which is called forth by the "beautiful body." It is no accident that Dostoevsky, in "Mr. —bov and the Question of Art," assimilates the notion of the "image of beauty" to an idol (*kumir*), to a pagan statue of divinity, that he finds in the sculptured image of the goddess Diana an embodiment of ideal beauty. "Note that human nature unfailingly demands [something] to worship," Dostoevsky writes in his notebook.[24] In bowing before the image of beauty man gives expression to one of his deepest needs—the religious need to worship something.

Here it is important to note the centrality of *obraz* as an aesthetic as well as religious symbol in Dostoevsky's thinking on art. *Obraz* is the axis of beauty in the Russian language;[25] it is "form," "shape," "image"; it is also the iconographic image, or icon—the visible symbol of the beauty of God. In a letter to Apollon Maikov in 1868, Dostoevsky admires the poet's poem, "At the Chapel" ("U chasovni"), at the center of which is an icon. He is troubled only by Maikov's tone: "You seem to *apologize* for the icon, *justify*," and Dostoevsky goes on to indicate in a few words his great regard (in the past as well as present) for the popular cult of the icon.[26] The icon, particularly the iconographic representation of the Madonna, appears in Dostoevsky's artistic universe as a religious-aesthetic symbol of great importance—a literal image of beauty toward which man turns in reverence and longing. "Her eyes were dimmed by a mute, tormenting anguish," Dostoevsky writes of the heroine Katerina in "The Landlady." "She slowly rose, took two steps forward, and with a piercing wail fell down before the image [of the Madonna]." Dostoevsky's whole conception of the role of beauty in the life of man is conveyed in his conception of Katerina: a woman torn between her voluntary enslavement to a corrupt passion and an anguished yearning for purity and unity. Man is created in the image and likeness of God, Dostoevsky repeats in his writings; his highest striving is to "imitate the perfection of that image."

The Platonic and Christian ideals of beauty—the ideal of pure beauty and the image of the Madonna—merge for Dostoevsky in the " 'image of pure beauty' " (Aglaya's expression in *The Idiot*) of Pushkin's "poor knight" ("Zhil na svete rytsar' bednyj"). "The poet wanted to combine in one extraordinary image the whole huge concept of medieval chivalric Platonic love of some pure and highminded knight," Aglaya says. "Naturally, all this is the ideal" (Pt. II, Ch. 6). The knight's image of pure beauty, in Pushkin's poem, finds embodiment in the mystic sign "A[ve] M[ater] D[ei]."[27]

"The Greeks," Shatov remarks in *The Devils*, "deified nature and bequeathed to the world their religion, that is, philosophy and art." The feelings aroused by beauty are basically religious to Dostoevsky. Man "bows" before beauty.[28] The notion of an organic union of the religious and aesthetic elements, of beauty and prayer, in art is at the root of Dostoevsky's analysis, in "Mr. —bov and the Question of Art," of a poem by the lyric poet A. A. Fet, entitled "Diana":

I saw between the trees over clear waters,
In all the magnificence of splendid nakedness

The rounded features of the virgin goddess.
With colorless, oval eyes,
The wide brow was upraised—
Its undistracted glance all lapped in peace;
And the stone virgin, sensitive, gave heed
To prayers of maidens suffering pangs of birth.
But the wind swept among the leaves—
A bright image of the goddess danced on the waters;
I waited—she will come forth with bow and arrows,
Flickering through the trees with a milky whiteness,
To glance at somnolent Rome, the eternal city of glory,
The Tiber of the yellow floods, the clustered colonnades,
The long broad avenues—But the still marble
Paled before me with its inaccessible beauty.[29]

The statue of Diana—the structural and thematic center of the poem—is literally an image of beauty for the poet. The classical ideal of figural beauty is expressed in the poised motionlessness, rounded features, and lofty demeanor of the goddess; all this is focused against the background of the classical landscape of Rome. The poet's conception of this goddess as unattainable beauty, veiled in the mystery of birth, of dawn, echoes Plato's view of divine, harmonious beauty as "destiny or goddess of parturition who presides at birth, and therefore, when approaching beauty, the conceiving power is propitious."[30] The poet Fet has done what the painter Manet failed to do: he has started with an ideal model and he has sung a hymn to harmonious creation, to divine beauty.

"In this enthusiasm (Byronic as we call it) before the ideals of beauty created by the past and left us in eternal inheritance," Dostoevsky writes, "we pour out often the whole anguish for the present, and not from impotence before our own life, but, on the contrary, from a flaming thirst for life and from anguish for the ideal which we reach out toward in pain." Fet's poem "Diana," Dostoevsky feels, is an embodiment of this enthusiasm, "a passionate appeal, a prayer before the perfection of past beauty, and a hidden inner anguish for just such perfection which the soul seeks, but still must seek for a long time and for a long time must suffer birth pangs in order to find it."[31]

Dostoevsky's interpretation of the spiritual state of Fet's pagan goddess is of particular interest. The goddess has "already passed to the highest moment of life; she is already in eternity; for her time has stopped; this is the highest moment of life after which it ceases —Olympian tranquility draws near. The only thing that is endless is the future, eternally calling, eternally new, and there also is one's highest moment, which one must seek and eternally seek, and this eternal striving is called life."[32]

The aesthetic—and religious—character of Dostoevsky's mystical vision or anticipation of world harmony is very apparent in his interpretation of "Diana." Beauty in its visible expression in ideal form is immanent with a higher spiritual reality; the craving for beauty is a longing for a condition in which the formal aesthetic values of ideal form (*obraz*)—harmony, proportion, and repose —are realized on a spiritual plane. The craving for beauty is a craving for that highest moment of life which anticipates Olympian tranquility and eternality of time: it is a craving for transfiguration.

The most dramatic expression in Dostoevsky's writing of man's nostalgia before the infinite, his craving for beatitude, is to be found in Prince Myshkin's own description of the "highest moments" preceding his epileptic fits—moments filled with premonitions of universal harmony.[33] Myshkin describes these highest moments as a kind of "beauty and prayer," "a higher tranquility full of clear and harmonious joy and hope, full of reason and of [knowledge of] the final cause." Here he experiences flashes of the " 'highest mode of existence' . . . harmony, beauty of the highest order . . . a feeling . . . of completeness, measure, reconciliation, and ecstatic and prayerful fusion in the highest synthesis of life." "At that moment . . . I somehow or other began to understand the extraordinary saying that *there will be no more time*" (Pt. II, Ch. 5).

In Fet's poem the statue merely symbolizes to the observer the timeless beatitude toward which man strives; in *The Idiot*, however, subject and object merge: the observer (Myshkin) is assimilated, as it were, to the aesthetic object and experience itself. Here there is no Diana or Apollo of Belvedere or Venus of Milo: here for one moment there is only Myshkin in a state of transfiguration. What is striking about his moment of beauty and prayer is its plastic, almost kinesthetic character: this is an experience of classical form itself. For a moment Myshkin is transformed from the chaotic raw material of his dark spiritual reality into a work of art. And as with all transfiguration of reality in art, all creation of beauty, Myshkin's highest moment is one of profound moral purity and truth. In Myshkin's moment of beauty, truth, and revelation—and only in this moment—Dostoevsky approaches his ideal of depicting in Myshkin a "positively beautiful man," a perfect, sculptured embodiment of the good, the true, and the beautiful. The "chief beauty" of Pushkin's "positively beautiful Russian types," Dostoevsky wrote later in his *Diary of a Writer,* "is in their truth, an unquestioned and tangible truth, so that it is impossible to deny them; they stand as sculptured."[34]

Myshkin's experience of form, of beauty—the intensity of that experience aside—is not restricted, of course, to those brief moments preceding his epileptic fits. His entire stay in Switzerland, in contrast to his last days in Russia, is an experience of pure form and beauty in the classical sense. One of Myshkin's exchanges with the Epanchin women, early in the novel, is of considerable interest as an indirect formulation of Dostoevsky's whole concept of beauty as set forth in 1861. The prince has just mentioned the pleasant yet troubling feelings he always has when looking at scenes like the Lake of Four Cantons in Lucerne. Adelaida expresses a desire to see the lake and remarks:

"Find me a subject, prince, for a picture."
"I have no understanding of this sort of thing. I should think: one takes a look and paints."
"I don't know how to look."
"Now why are you talking in riddles? I don't understand anything!" interrupted the general's wife. "What do you mean you don't know how to look? You have eyes, and you look. If you don't know how to look here, then you won't learn abroad. You'd better tell us how you looked at things yourself, prince."
"Yes, that would be better," added Adelaida. "After all, the prince learned how to look abroad."
"I don't know; I only regained my health there; I don't know whether I learned to look. I was, however, happy almost all the time."

"Happy! You know how to be happy?" cried Aglaya.
"Then how can you say that you didn't learn how to look? You
probably could teach us."
"Teach us, please," laughed Adelaida.
"I cannot teach anything," laughed the prince. (Pt. I, Ch. 5)

Myshkin's response to the beauty of Lucerne's Lake of Four
Cantons, as well as to the other natural splendors there, is marked
by that same sense of anguish and yearning, happiness and sense
of alienation, that Dostoevsky posited as man's basic response to
beauty. This kind of beauty, obviously, is inaccessible, or at least
incomprehensible, to Adelaida; an amateur painter, she has been
engaged, significantly, "in copying a landscape she had already
begun from an engraving." She is obviously incapable of "looking"; she lacks the deeper spiritual—essentially artistic—insight
of Myshkin. What Myshkin sees, of course, is not on the surface of
reality; he perceives the inner idea of that reality. Myshkin, by nature an artist (as Ganya in the novel correctly notes), cannot explain "how to look" at nature. His simple remark—"I don't know;
I only regained my health there. . . . I was . . . happy"—echoes in
the context of the discussion Dostoevsky's general identification of
beauty, and health, the sense of higher beauty, and the feeling
of higher happiness. Aglaya's remark—"You know how to be
happy?" etc.—is entirely to the point: to be happy in the highest
sense is, in Dostoevsky's view, to know how to look at things, to
perceive beauty. The highest perception of beauty is revelation.
Aglaya instinctively grasps this and quite aptly remarks: "Teach
us, please." And Myshkin, indeed, remarks a moment later that
he is, perhaps, really a philosopher and "perhaps I really have the
intention of instructing people." Myshkin—artist, philosopher, and
sometime work of art himself, friend of donkeys and children—is
indeed projected in this scene and in the one that follows (the episode with Marie) as seer, holy fool, a tragic pseudo-Christ. The
whole novel turns on the tragedy of the incomplete, half-formed
Myshkin who leaves his European aesthetic paradise and plunges
unknowingly and with his premonitions of beatitude into the formless and disfigured hell of Russian life.

Art, then, transfigures not only reality; ideally, aesthetic reality
(whether in the form of an artistic masterpiece or a natural scene

like the Lake of Four Cantons) transfigures the person who comes in contact with it. A variation of Myshkin, in this respect, is the hero of "The Dream of a Ridiculous Man," who also passes through an aesthetic-religious experience equivalent to Myshkin's moment of ecstasy: his art experience is his dream-painting with its "real images and forms." "I saw, I saw, and the *living image* filled my soul forever . . . the living image of what I saw will always be with me and always correct and guide me." The Ridiculous Man's dream, both of earthly paradise and of his corruption of that paradise, is a dramatic experience from which he emerges purged of his self-destructive passions and profound guilt and transfigured by his memory of the forms and images of paradise.

There is every reason to believe, as we have noted earlier, that Dostoevsky in "Mr. —bov and the Question of Art" deliberately refrained from disclosing the deeply Christian content of his aesthetic. The concept of Christ as the supreme aesthetic-religious ideal had been suggested by Dostoevsky in his letter to N. D. Fon-Vizina. Dostoevsky's letters and notebooks in the 1860s give ample evidence of his deep Christian religious convictions. "Deism gave us Christ," he writes Apollon Maikov in 1867, "that is, a representation of man so sublime that it is impossible to understand him without veneration and it is impossible not to believe that this is the eternal ideal of mankind." And Dostoevsky angrily complains that the Turgenevs, Herzens, Chernyshevskys, and others spit on this "most sublime divine beauty."[35]

The Christian ideal, the ideal of the image of Christ, was a major inspiration in the final conception of Myshkin. Dostoevsky wanted to depict a "positively beautiful man," but he confessed that the "beautiful is an ideal, and the ideal is still far from being achieved either by us or by civilized Europe. In the world there is only one positively beautiful person—Christ, so that the appearance of this immeasurably, eternally beautiful person is actually, of course, an eternal miracle."[36] The Christian ideal is projected, though imperfectly, in the image of Myshkin; but the ideal of beauty proves impotent before the disaggregating force of Rogozhin's sensualism, his "monstrous passion" (*bezobraznaja strast'*).

The Christian religious ideal—we know from Dostoevsky's letter to his brother Mikhail on March 26, 1864—was clearly intended to point the way out of the "underground" for the defunct Schilleresque idealist, the man from the "underground."[37] The transition from the aesthetic idealism of the 1840s with its faith in the "beautiful and the sublime" to a faith in the Christian ideal is depicted by Dostoevsky in the figure of Stepan Verkhovensky in *The Devils*. "I really love Stepan Trofimovich and profoundly respect him," Dostoevsky wrote in his *Diary of a Writer*.[38] Stepan Verkhovensky is naïve, impractical, a dreamer charged with an ecstatic emotionalism; he is a tragicomic idealist divorced from Russian life and Russian reality, but he is the bearer of an aesthetic idealism which is nonetheless dear to Dostoevsky even in the brittle form in which it is expressed. Stepan Verkhovensky, apropos of his encounter with the nihilists of the 1860s, exclaims: "Oh, my friends! . . . you cannot imagine what sadness and anger seizes your whole soul when a great idea, long revered by you as sacred, is taken up by bunglers and dragged out onto the street to just such fools as themselves, as you suddenly encounter it now in the flea market, unrecognizable, filthy, stood up absurdly, at an angle, without proportion, without harmony, a plaything in the hands of stupid children! No! It wasn't like that in our time, and we didn't strive for that" (Pt. I, Ch. 1, Sec. vi). There is, in these observations of a befuddled aesthete of the 1840s, more than an echo of Dostoevsky's own angry distress at the utilitarian aesthetics of the radical democrats Dobrolyubov and Chernyshevsky, in the late 1850s and early 1860s. Dostoevsky most certainly included himself in the "we" of Stepan Verkhovensky.

It is against this same utilitarian aesthetic that Stepan speaks out at the literary quadrille. He announces the superiority of Shakespeare and Raphael over the liberation of the peasant, over nationality, socialism, the young generation, chemistry, over almost all humanity, "because they are already the fruit, the real fruit of all mankind and, perhaps, the highest fruit that there can be! The form of beauty already achieved, without the achievement of which I, perhaps, would not consent to live . . . without beauty it is impossible [to live] because there would then be absolutely nothing left to do in the world! All mystery is here, all history is here!" (Pt. III, Ch. 1, Sec. iv).

In *Notes from the Underground* Dostoevsky leads the Schilleresque dreamer to a despairing confrontation with reality.[39] In

The Devils he leads the idealist dreamer to a religious apotheosis. Stepan Verkhovensky rediscovers his revered and trampled aesthetic idea, his "great idea" in God. "The whole law of human existence," he declares, "consists merely of making it possible to bow down before what is infinitely great . . . long live the Great Idea! . . . Every man, whosoever he may be, must bow down before what is the Great Idea!" This is the heart of Dostoevsky's aesthetic thought in "Mr. —bov and the Question of Art." But the Christian God has replaced the idol, the pagan statue, the Venus of Milo as the infinitely great. "God is necessary to me if only because he is the only being whom one can love eternally." Stepan Verkhovensky embraces Christianity, partially, at least, because the "majestic ceremony of the administration of the sacrament awoke the artistic sensibilities of his nature."

In "Mr. —bov and the Question of Art" Dostoevsky raises the problem of material versus spiritual bread: "Physical bread I have," he cites the writer Nikitin, "but I have need of spiritual bread."[40] Stepan Verkhovensky declares firmly that "beauty is more useful than bread." And in 1876 Dostoevsky wrote in a letter that "without the ideal of Beauty man will anguish, die, go mad, beat himself, or plunge into pagan fantasies. And since Christ in Himself and in His Word carried the ideal of Beauty, thus I have decided: better to instill in the soul the ideal of Beauty; having it in the soul all will become brothers to one another and then, of course, working for one another all will also be rich."[41] The whole problem is reexamined on the tragic stage of Ivan's poem, "The Legend of the Grand Inquisitor."

"Society is moved by the aesthetic element," Shatov observes in a notebook to *The Devils*. "The aesthetic element depends upon religion. Upon religion directly, upon revelation and the direct intervention of God. The mystery of Christ."[42] It is in *The Brothers Karamazov*—in particular in the religious exhortations of Zosima —that the Christian foundation of Dostoevsky's higher aesthetic finds its purest expression. All beauty for Zosima is a theophany, a revelation of the divine infinite. Beauty is everywhere; it is immanent in nature and all its forms; it is only man who cannot see the beauty which lies before him. "Look around at the gifts of God: the clear sky, the pure air, tender grass, birds, the beautiful and sinless nature while we, only we alone, godless and foolish, do not

understand that life is paradise, because all we have to do is only
to want to understand, and immediately it will reveal itself in all
its beauty." It is man's sinful nature that prevents him from seeing
the truth. "Everything is perfect; everything, except man, is sinless." "I alone lived in ignominy," Zosima's brother declares at his
death, "I alone dishonored everything and simply didn't notice
the beauty and the glory." "But for the precious image of Christ
before us," Zosima declares, "we should perish and go completely
astray like the human race before the flood." "We will preserve the
image of Christ and it will shine like a precious diamond to the
entire world." The image of Christ will be preserved "in splendor
and without disfiguration, the purity of God's truth."

At the center of Dostoevsky's Christian aesthetic—as it becomes
more explicit in his notebooks and belles lettres in the last decade
of his life—is the image of Christ: here there are no teachings,
Dostoevsky insists, only occasional words; "the main thing is the
image of Christ from which comes all teaching. . . . From Christ
comes the thought that the chief acquisition and goal of mankind
is the result of achieved morality."[43] "The moral ideal is in Christ."[44]
Yet again, "not Christ's morality, not his teaching will save the
world, but precisely faith that the Word became flesh. This faith is
not alone intellectual recognition of his teaching, but direct attraction. One must believe precisely that this is the final ideal of man,
the whole embodied Word, God embodied."[45] If one does not believe that "the ideal was in flesh, then the ideal is impossible and
cannot be attained by mankind." Christ came so that mankind
might know that the human spirit can be in heavenly glory "in fact
and in flesh, and not only in the dream and in the ideal."[46] "Beauty
will save the world," Dostoevsky observed in the notebooks to *The
Idiot.* "The world will become the beauty of Christ," we read in the
notebooks to *The Devils.*[47]

The idea of the inseparability of the ideal (beauty) from its incarnation (Christ) is an aesthetic one for Dostoevsky. The ideal
exists in the abstract only in its *need,* but it is embodied in the
creative work, in the "image of beauty" before which man rever-
entially bows. The "utility" of a work (its moral element) is inseparable from the aesthetic element, from beauty incarnate, from
form. It is not the abstract idea or ideal of a beautiful life that in-

spires the Ridiculous Man, but the vision of the *living image,* the ideal in flesh. Myshkin's premonition of a higher life is a concrete aesthetic experience, a self-incarnation.

The aesthetic and religious elements merge in the *obraz.* Artistic and religious vision are ultimately one vision, reveal the same absolute reality. "The Holy Spirit," Dostoevsky observes in his notebook to *The Devils,* "is the direct understanding of beauty, the prophetic cognition of harmony and, therefore, a constant striving for it."[48] In turn, the artist, creating an image of beauty, gives intimations of the divine ideal lying beyond man's earthly existence. Art in the deepest sense is, like the Holy Spirit, prophetic, the incarnation of the Word itself, a premonitory symbol of the beauty of a transfigured humanity.

At the moment when Cleopatra, in her cruel, sensual, hellish ecstasy pronounces her vow—Dostoevsky observes in his interpretation of the improvisation in Pushkin's "Egyptian Nights"—the body grows numb and the spirit falters. "And you begin to understand the kind of people to whom our Divine Savior came at that time. You begin to understand also the word: Savior."[49]

Man's loftiest striving is to attain to the perfection of the image of beauty. But man strives on earth for an ideal which is contrary to his nature. He is tragically divided between his spiritual and carnal nature. His sinful nature prevents him from seeing divine beauty. At root it is "cruel sensuality"—we read in "The Dream of a Ridiculous Man"—that is the "only source of almost all the sins of mankind." The Ridiculous Man has seen in a vision the living image of that beauty which is truth. But Dostoevsky's pilgrim to primeval paradise corrupts it; before his eyes he witnesses, then, how man came to "love the lie and to know the beauty of the lie"; how, in his fallen state, love of the beauty of the lie passed to sensuality, and how "sensuality engendered jealousy, and jealousy—cruelty."

The statues of the Venus of Medici and Venus of Milo are embodiments of a divine beauty. Yet "one must be morally rather highly purified," Dostoevsky observes, "to look at this divine beauty without confusion." The Venus of Milo would produce only a "sensualistic impression on an undeveloped, lascivious heart."[50] "The chastity of an image will not save one from a crude and even obscene thought."[51] Myshkin recognizes the intrinsically chaste, Madonna-like beauty of Nastasya Filippovna precisely because *he* is innocent and chaste. Commenting on Fyodor Karamazov's interest in the "remarkable beauty" of the saintly mother of Alyosha and Ivan, Dostoevsky observes: "with a debauched man this can only be a sensualistic attraction." But while the debauched man is attracted to pure beauty in a sensualistic way, he may nonetheless have an awareness—perhaps a painful awareness (as in the case of Dmitry Karamazov)—of the purity of this beauty. Even more, the special piquancy of his sensual pleasure may consist precisely in the debauched man's awareness that he is violating pure beauty. Thus, Svidrigailov remarks of a young girl, a prey to his sensuality, that her face reminds him of the Sistine Madonna. The "incorrigible and uncontrollable sensualist" Totsky—seducer of Nastasya Filippovna—is a man of "refined character with an extraordinary delicacy of taste," we read in *The Idiot;* Dostoevsky adds, with a continuing touch of irony, that "he was an extraordinary connoisseur of beauty."

The moral-aesthetic spectrum of Dostoevsky begins with *obraz* —image, the form and embodiment of beauty—and ends with *bezobrazie*—literally that which is "without image," shapeless, disfigured, ugly. Man finds pleasure (he also calls it beauty) in *bezobrazie,* in the disfiguration of himself and others, in cruelty, violence, and, above all, sensuality—and "sensuality is always violence." Aesthetically, *bezobrazie* is the deformation of ideal form (*obraz*).[52] The humanization of man is the creating of an image, the creating of form (the verb *obrazit'*). God created man in His own image. All violence against man is a dehumanization—a deformation, finally, of the divine image. Zosima recalls how, as a young man, in a moment of "monstrous rage" (*svirepyj i bezobraznyj*), he struck his servant in the face, and he remembers how he then reproached himself for his act of violence against another being created, like himself, "in the image and likeness of God." The brutalization of men is at the center of *Notes from the House of the Dead;* the narrator of this work writes of the sensualists (akin, he notes, to the Marquis de Sade and Marquise de Brinvilliers) who obtain an aesthetic delight in flogging others, in inflicting the last degree of humiliation "upon another being bearing in himself the image of God." Such a sensualist is Lt. Zherebyatnikov who "passionately loved the art of execution and loved it solely for the art. He enjoyed it and, like some jaded Roman patrician of the Roman Empire, running out of pleasures, invented for himself various refinements, various unnatural variations, so as in some way to stimulate and pleasurably titillate his soul lapped in its fat."

In his profound despair over the brutalization of men, Ivan, symbolically, is prepared to discard Dostoevsky's vital distinction between *obraz* and *bezobrazie* in the definition of man; commenting upon man's bestial and supremely "artistic" cruelty to his fellowman, Ivan declares: "I think if the devil does not exist and, therefore, man created him, he created him in his own image." Here the dual nature of man vanishes, and the spiritual countenance of man (*obraz*) is replaced by the mask of moral *bezobrazie*. Ivan in his near-atheism posits the idea that man is created in the image of the devil.

The desecration of the iconographic image, the icon, or the religious painting quite understandably is symbolic in Dostoevsky's Christian universe of the deepest crime against man's humanity— murder. Peter Verkhovensky's desecration of the icon in *The Devils* parallels on the symbolic plane the murder of Stavrogin's saintly wife. Stepan Verkhovensky, outraged at those who would place a pair of boots above Shakespeare or Raphael, wishes to speak out at the literary quadrille against the "stinking and debauched lackey who first will mount the ladder with a pair of scissors in his hands and slash the divine countenance of the great ideal" (a reference to the Sistine Madonna which he reveres). Rogozhin's sensual *bezobrazie* ends up by his slashing Myshkin's "image of pure beauty"—the Madonna-like Nastasya Filippovna—with a knife. Fyodor Karamazov lasciviously blabbers (in "Over the Brandy") about his favorite topic—women—and concludes with a description of how he once spat on his wife's iconographic image of the Madonna. "Now look, you think it's a wonder working [icon]," Fyodor exclaims to his wife at that time, "but here and now I'm going to spit on it in your presence, and nothing will happen to me because of it." The theme of Fyodor Karamazov— desecration—finds its most dramatic completion in this symbolic violation of the Madonna. He pays for his defiling of the ideal in life and image, for his hubris, with his death.

Moral-sensual *bezobrazie,* as we have noted, is for Dostoevsky the central area in which man disfigures both himself and his ideal. The Ridiculous Man's corruption (through sensuality) of paradise with its beautiful forms and images is on the same plane as Stavrogin's rape of a young girl. In both cases "cruel sensuality" consists precisely in a disfiguration of the moral ideal (here innocent beauty)—the ideality of *obraz*. Ugliness disfigures, ugliness kills. After reading Stavrogin's "confession," Tikhon remarks that he finds something ridiculous in the "essence" as well as the "form" of the confession. "Ugliness will kill it," he whispers to Stavrogin. "Ugliness! What kind of ugliness?" asks Stavrogin. "Of the crime," answers Tikhon.[53]

The disfiguration of another is simultaneously a self-disfiguration—a loss of image, form, humanity. The body of Dmitry hunches up into a deformed position when he utters the terrible words: "Why is such a man alive?" (Dostoevsky significantly titles the tumultuous episode in which these words are spoken: "A Monstrous Scene"—"Bezobraznaja stsena".)[54] "Insane cruelty had long ago distorted this divine soul," Dostoevsky writes of Pushkin's Cleopatra, "and already frequently had degraded her to the likeness of a beast."[55]

The Underground Man's violation, both morally and physically, of the compassionate Liza, is in the deepest sense a despairing act of self-mutilation, a deliberate defacing of his own cherished ideal out of a feeling of its unattainability, a conscious laceration of his own nature, his own image. Man's being, then, is crucified by the opposite strivings of his divided nature: his corporeal self, with its destructive, carnal drives, and his spiritual self, with its higher strivings. The pleasure man finds in *bezobrazie*, in the ideal of Sodom, coexists in lacerating contact with his higher ideal; at the same time, the striving for that higher ideal is itself an effort to sublimate the forces of sensuality. (Fyodor Karamazov indirectly gives expression to this idea when he calls Father Zosima a "sensualist.") The drama of Dmitry Karamazov, of course, provides the most vivid example of this ceaseless interplay of opposites in man's nature as Dostoevsky conceives it.

The feeling of the beautiful that man experiences in the contemplation of higher beauty is for Dostoevsky aesthetically and morally of an entirely different order from the feeling of pleasure man experiences in his moral *bezobrazie*. There can be no fusion of these two orders of aesthetic sensation. Yet man in his degeneration may lose the perception of the difference between these two antithetical aesthetic experiences. "Is it true," Shatov asks Stavrogin in *The Devils*, "that you maintained that you know no difference in beauty between some sensual, bestial act and some worthy deed, for example, even the sacrifice of one's life for humanity? Is it true that in both extremes you found a coincidence of beauty?" Stavrogin finds this question "impossible to answer" and remains silent. Shatov continues: "I also don't know why evil is vile while good is beautiful, but I know why the perception of this difference is erased and lost in such gentlemen as the Stavrogins." "You have lost the distinction between evil and good because you have ceased to know your people" (Pt. II, Ch. 1, Sec. vii).

It is essential to note that Stavrogin does not experience two kinds of beauty. The "coincidence of beauty" is the obliteration of distinction between aesthetic categories; it signifies the loss of aesthetic criteria, of measure and feeling for healthy beauty. The faculty of taste in Stavrogin has atrophied: the feelings he obtains from both a good deed and an evil act, he confesses, are "too petty." He has fallen into indifferent debauchery, and it is on this level of moribund moral-aesthetic consciousness that he weakly registers aesthetic experience. His inability to answer Shatov's question is indicative of his central dilemma or void: he does not *know* what he feels (like a man who has lost the sense of taste). The distinction between the good deed and evil act is for him an academic one; he unquestionably knows (intellectually) that the feelings of beauty in these two different acts relate to two entirely different aesthetic categories. There is a certain fatal logic in Stavrogin: the same contradictions (of which he is fully conscious) that drive him to suicide compel him to silence in this critical exchange with Shatov.

Dostoevsky's conception of the normal and the abnormal, of moral health and moral sickness, turns not on a distinction between good and evil (evil is everywhere and in all men), but on a distinction between a spiritual condition marked by struggle and one marked by inertia. The cardinal sin in Dostoevsky's novelistic universe is inertia. "The teachings of true philosophy," Dostoevsky writes in his notebook, "[call for] the annihilation of inertness."[56]

He censures man not for the presence of vileness, evil, but for the absence of ideals. What is important to him, for example, is that the Russian peasant has "preserved . . . the beauty of his image" in the midst of barbarism. "I repeat," he continues in his *Diary of a Writer* in 1876: "judge the Russian people not by those vilenesses which it so often commits, but by those great and sacred things for which, even in its very vileness, it constantly longs. . . . Judge it not by what it is, but by what it wants to become. And its ideals are strong and sacred."[57] Dostoevsky, of course, does not justify abominations committed by people; he simply insists that —where there is striving for an ideal—man can be judged finally only in reference to his total, evolving being. "If a people preserve the ideal of beauty and its need," Dostoevsky writes in 1861, "that means there is also a need for health, for the norm, and therefore in this way the highest development of a people is guaranteed."[58]

Stavrogin is doomed because he has no ideals, because there is no creative tension or struggle in his existence. He is far from the "Prince"—that earlier version of Stavrogin whom we encounter in the notebooks to *The Devils*—who declares: "If I am imperfect, foul, and evil, yet I know that there is another ideal of mine which is beautiful, sacred, and blessed. . . . From the image of the one to whom I bow, I draw forth also his spirit and hence all my moral being. And therefore it is absolutely necessary to bow down."[59] Stavrogin has lost both the sense of higher beauty and his God. He bows to no one. In essence nothing is important to him. His face is the symbol of his stagnant inner being, a congealed mask of a triumphant sensualism—moral *bezobrazie*. Stavrogin, in all essential respects, has been literally "killed" by ugliness.

The chapter, "A Confession of a Passionate Heart: In Verse," in *The Brothers Karamazov,* concludes with Dmitry's dramatic (more accurately—melodramatic) peroration on beauty. This passage, although a logical extension, both thematically and structurally, of Dmitry's excited confession, has a unity and shape of its own.

> Beauty—this is a terrible and awful thing! Terrible because it
> is indefinable, and it cannot be defined because God has

posed only enigmas. Here all shores meet, here all contradictions live together. I, brother, am very uneducated, but I have thought much about this. There are fearfully many mysteries! Too many enigmas oppress man on earth. Solve them as you will, you will not emerge dry from the water. Beauty! Here I cannot bear the fact that a man, a man even with a lofty heart and with a lofty mind begins with the ideal of the Madonna, yet ends with the ideal of Sodom. What's even more awful is the person who, though already with the ideal of Sodom in his soul, yet does not deny the ideal of the Madonna, and his heart glows with it, and truly glows as in his youthful, sinless years. No, man is broad, far too broad, I would narrow him. The devil knows what it is all about! What to the mind is ignominious, is nothing but beauty to the heart. Is there beauty in Sodom? Rest assured that it is to be found in Sodom for the overwhelming majority of people—did you know this secret or not? What is awful is that beauty is not only terrible, but also a mysterious thing. Here the devil struggles with God, but the field of battle is the heart of men. But a man always talks of his own ache. (Bk. III, Ch. 3).

Two things are immediately striking about Dmitry's discourse on beauty: first, that he uses the word *beauty* in a way that Dostoevsky never uses it outside his belles lettres, that is, to define aesthetic experience in general, apart from moral context; and second, that he finds the phenomenon of beauty, in all its contradictory content, deeply disturbing, precisely in a moral sense. These two aspects of Dmitry's observations deserve comment.

Dmitry speaks emphatically of beauty as the source of man's woes. But he immediately posits what is in fact the ambivalence of beauty: here (in beauty) all shores meet; here all contradictions live together; here in man's broad soul the ideal of the Madonna coexists side by side with the ideal of Sodom. We encounter again, then, Dostoevsky's familiar distinction between two kinds of aesthetic experience. What is not familiar and is disorienting (against the background of Dostoevsky's formal aesthetic commitment to one higher beauty) is Dmitry's blanket use of the word *beauty* to cover several varieties of aesthetic experience. But Dmitry is not Dostoevsky, nor is he a philosopher viewing the problem from without; he is a direct, unsophisticated, untutored man who expresses his ache as he feels it and in the conceptual language at his command.

We cannot uncritically attribute Dmitry's ideas about beauty to Dostoevsky. Dmitry is tormented over what appears to him to be a lack of coordination in man between ethical judgment ("what to the mind is ignominious") and aesthetic feeling ("is nothing but beauty to the heart"). In other words, Dmitry complains that aesthetic feeling is indifferent to, and independent of, moral judgment. Is this Dostoevsky's view? Here we must reiterate a notion advanced at the outset of the discussion: to Dostoevsky it is not beauty that is ambivalent, but man who experiences two kinds of beauty—not only the true, higher beauty, but also a low order of aesthetic sensation ("beauty in Sodom") which *he* calls beauty. "Is there beauty in Sodom?" Dmitry asks. "Rest assured that it is to be found in Sodom for the overwhelming majority of people." The aesthetic confusion is in *man;* and this confusion is reflected in Dmitry's whole peroration on beauty and, first of all, in his broad use of the term *beauty*. Dostoevsky must not be confused with the Dmitrys: *their* aesthetic confusion is not his; on the other hand, his commitment to a conception of ideal beauty points in his novels to the ultimate solution of their dilemma, to man's ultimate salvation and transfiguration.

The possibility of Dmitry's salvation—concretely, a perceptive shift in the direction of control, order, form—is rooted in his active moral consciousness. Precisely in his keenly felt sense of ignominy (nonexistent in Stavrogin), in his moral despair at what he discovers in himself and in man, lies the measure of possibility for change. Consciousness of evil in self is the first step in the direction of purgation of evil. "That which seems to you to be foul within," Zosima observes, "is, by the fact alone that you observed it, cleansed." But Dmitry has his higher ideal. "I am a lover of Schiller, I am an idealist," he declares in the notebook to *The Brothers Karamazov*.[60] It is Schiller and his poetry that Dmitry recalls in the depths of his degradation. "I have always read that poem about Ceres and about man. Has it reformed me? Never! Because I am a Karamazov." But Dmitry nevertheless bows down. "Granted that I be cursed, granted that I be low and vile, but let me also kiss the edge of that veil in which my God is shrouded."

In the very depths of his ignominy—"and I consider this beauty for myself"—he begins his hymn to that luminous divine ideal "without which the world cannot stand or exist."

"I am not Silenus, but I am strong" ("Ne Silen, a silën"), Dmitry remarks, setting himself off by way of a pun from the aesthetically disfigured image of the father of the satyrs. The quest of Dmitry— the quest of man—is an aesthetic one: it is for form and, therefore, for moral structure.[61] It is not without significance that Dmitry's consciousness of a "new man" within himself is accompanied by an aesthetic awareness of himself as an "image and likeness of God." Dmitry will never be "re-formed," but in his denial of his disfiguration (even as he "follows after the devil") and in his recognition of his symbolic likeness to God (even as he senses his disfiguration) he maintains a creative tension toward the ideal.

There can be no mistaking the central Christian structure, with its classical foundation, of Dostoevsky's aesthetic thought—his unwavering commitment to the notion of ideal beauty. At the same time, we cannot fail to note in his writing and thinking a de facto recognition of another kind of beauty—one indifferent to moral context and experienced by man as pleasurable disharmony. Dostoevsky succeeded in harmonizing his commitment to ideal beauty with his recognition of "another ideal" in the framework of his dualistic view of man—his strict division between the material and spiritual nature of man. Man finds pleasure in the destructive drives of his corporeal nature yet simultaneously strives for a spiritual ideal, a tranquility and aesthetic integrity which is contrary to his nature. Dostoevsky recognizes only the beauty which is the object of man's higher strivings.

Yet in his critical writings Dostoevsky never succeeded in resolving the contradiction between a classical aesthetic which acknowledges only one beauty, and a practical poetics (his own) which seeks out the inner shape, rhythmic proportions, and dynamics of change of a disfigured reality. In the realm of fine arts Dostoevsky recoiled before the formulation of the aesthetic of the ugly. Yet one may discern in his recoil elements of uncertainty and conflict. The problem of an aesthetic of the ugly is raised in "The Exhibition in the Academy of Arts: 1860–1861"; it is the disquieting center of Dostoevsky's reflections on several paintings.

Dostoevsky raises the question of the depiction of the ugly in art in his discussion of M. P. Klodt's painting, "The Last Spring."[62] The subject of the painting, he reports, is a girl, dying of tuberculosis, who sits in an armchair opposite a window. She will not live beyond spring, and the servants know this. A sister is weeping; another kneels before the sick girl; father and mother are talking beyond a screen. This whole scene is illuminated by a splendid, vivid, spring sun. Dostoevsky obviously is drawn to this painting. It is "remarkable," "splendidly executed," but also "an unfortunate picture." "The artist has selected for himself . . . an extraordinarily difficult task: to present the repulsive in a beautiful way; nobody will ever succeed in doing this." Dostoevsky compares the impact of this picture to that of an actor dying on stage according to all the rules of pathology, in a display not of stage truth but of natural truth. The spectators would all run away from such a scene, the critic insists. Klodt also has presented the spectator with the agony of dying, an agony which will remain hanging on the wall eternally. No spectator could stand it; he would run away. "No, artistic truth is not that at all; it is something quite different from natural truth."[63]

Art, Dostoevsky believed, transforms reality—morally transfigures it. Klodt's painting presented an example of natural truth without transformation; aesthetically and religiously—death without transfiguration. ("Taken in itself," Dostoevsky wrote, "death is a repulsive business.") Dostoevsky recognizes a purely formal beauty of craftsmanship, but it is a beauty lacking in spiritual content. His judgment is summed up in the phrase: "The painting is done beautifully, irreproachably, but in sum the picture is far from beautiful."[64]

The criticism of Klodt's painting—the demand that the subject should be transfigured—finds an interesting parallel in Dostoevsky's orientation to Hans Holbein's painting, "Christ in the Tomb" —a painting which depicts the mutilated, dead body of Christ.

Prince Myshkin observes a copy of this painting in Rogozhin's house. The presence of this painting in the ancestral mansion of the Rogozhin's—a family whose faith in Orthodoxy already has been cracked—is itself anticipatory of a negative judgment of the painting. Myshkin remarks: "Why, some people may lose their faith by looking at that picture." Later, Ippolit Terentiev gives his opinion of this painting. "It aroused in me a kind of strange anxiety." Most painters of Christ, he observes, show Him as preserving some shade of his extraordinary beauty even in the moment of greatest agony. "But in Rogozhin's picture there was no trace of beauty . . . just nature alone." Holbein's picture gave expression to the idea of a dark, insolent, and senselessly eternal power that nothing can resist. "Here one cannot help being struck with the idea that if death is so horrible and if the laws of nature are so powerful, then how can they be overcome? How can they be overcome when even He did not conquer them?" "I think I stood before [the painting] about five minutes," Ippolit notes. "There was nothing good about it in an artistic sense" (Pt. III, Ch. 6).

Hans Holbein's painting is clearly bad art because it deeply disturbs man's moral and religious tranquility; it is the embodiment of an aesthetics of despair. The concomitant of its disfiguration of form in the realm of belief is atheism. "One's faith could be smashed by such a picture," Madam Dostoevsky reports her husband as saying at the time they viewed the Holbein painting in Basel. It appears her own reaction to the painting with its ugly detail was similar to Terentiev's: "Granted that it is strikingly faithful, but really, it is not at all aesthetic, and it awoke in me nothing but repulsion and a kind of horror." But the painting which horrified her "so deeply impressed Fedya that he pronounced Holbein a remarkable artist and poet." This painting with its "emaciated body, bones and ribs visible, hands and feet with pierced wounds, all blue and swollen terribly, as in a corpse which has just started to rot"—this painting, according to Madame Dostoevsky, filled Dostoevsky with "ecstasy," produced upon him an overwhelming impression.[65]

Dostoevsky's private judgment of Holbein's painting is extraordinarily revealing against the background of Ippolit's condemnation of it as poor art. Dostoevsky recognized both "artist and poet" in Holbein—the highest praise he could bestow upon a creator—but he was unwilling as novelist or critic to draw the conclusions—in the realm of aesthetic theory—that followed logically from his positive judgment of Holbein's painting. Can the ugly in art be beautiful? Dostoevsky quite obviously pondered this question. In *The Idiot* he poses it quite directly. At the conclusion of his discourse on Holbein's painting, when he informs his audience of that vision of a "dumb, dark, and senseless essence" which came to him "in a strange and impossible form," Ippolit Terentiev asks: "Can one perceive as an image that which has no image?" ("Mozhet li mereshchit'sja v obraze to, chto ne imeet obraza?") Ippolit's question—one of the central ones in modern aesthetics—is answered affirmatively by much of Dostoevsky's art, just as it is answered by Picasso's "Guernica" and other works of painting and sculpture in the twentieth century. But for Dostoevsky—committed as a matter of faith and philosophy to a Christian classical aesthetic—the very posing of this question is a contradiction in terms. The image (*obraz*) is beauty; "that which has no image," the formless, is *bezobrazie*. The dilemma for a classical aesthetician is even more apparent when we rephrase Terentiev's question to bring out its crucial moral emphasis: Can one realize in an image that which is ugly? Can that which is monstrous and evil, full of disharmony and discord, be depicted in an aesthetically attractive way? These questions in the sphere of pure aesthetics are paralleled by Dmitry's famous question: "Is there beauty in Sodom?" Dmitry's answer is that beauty *is* to be found in Sodom for the majority of people. It is obvious that as a private individual Dostoevsky counted himself among this majority; it is clear, too, that his aesthetic sense was sufficiently broad to find beauty in painting that did not court the senses with classical harmonies and moral ideals. But as novelist and philosopher-critic, as an artist desperately seeking a bulwark against the dissolving currents of scepticism, moral relativism, and despair, Dostoevsky declined to go beyond de facto recognition of another kind of beauty. Privately one might enjoy the lacerating beauty and poetry of Holbein's disfigured Christ (as one might enjoy beauty in Sodom), but in principle, in the sphere of aesthetic theory and religious convictions, one had to deny this kind of beauty all along the way.

" 'Le laid, c'est le beau'—here is the formula," Dostoevsky wrote in 1861, "with which self-satisfied mediocrity thirty years ago thought to sum up the idea and the direction of Victor Hugo's talent, falsely understanding and falsely transmitting to the public what Victor Hugo himself wrote to explain his thought."[66]

[Hugo's idea, according to Dostoevsky, is] the basic idea of all art of the nineteenth century. . . . It is a Christian and supremely moral idea. [The] formula [of this idea] is the restoration of the fallen man, crushed unjustly by the yoke of circumstances, by the stagnation of centuries and by social prejudices. This idea is the justification of the pariahs of society, humiliated and rejected by all. Of course, allegory is unthinkable in such an artistic work as, for example, *Notre Dame de Paris*. But to whom does it not occur that Quasimodo is the embodiment of the oppressed and despised French people of medieval times, dumb and disfigured, gifted only with fearful physical strength, but in whom there sleeps, finally, love and a thirst for justice and, at the same time along with it, a consciousness of its truth and its still untested, boundless strength.

Dostoevsky suggests that this "idea" will be embodied, perhaps, in a great work of art that will "express the strivings and characteristics of its time quite as fully and eternally as, for example, *The Divine Comedy* expressed its epoch of medieval Catholic faith and ideal."[67]

Dostoevsky's formula for understanding Hugo, then, is not "Le laid, c'est le beau." The ugliness (*bezobrazie*) of man to Dostoevsky is a disfiguration of the norm. Hugo, in his view, does not make the ugly beautiful. Rather he restores to man his true image, reveals the divine image behind the mask of caricature. " 'Le laid, c'est le beau,' " Dostoevsky not unexpectedly remarks, is a "stupid caricatural formula"; it caricatures the "Christian and supremely moral idea" of transfiguration.[68] Holbein's "Christ in the Tomb" was—from the point of view of Dostoevsky's Christian aesthetic —just such a caricature of the supreme symbol and embodiment of transfiguration, Jesus Christ; its message was death and disfiguration. Dostoevsky's commitment to the notion of ideal beauty is a commitment, in the most fundamental sense, to the ideal of ethical beauty. To give de jure recognition to Holbein's disfigured Christ, to call it beauty, would not merely destroy the notion of an aesthetic ideal—it would deny the notion of an ethical ideal, ultimately, the ideal of religious transfiguration, the reality of salvation.

Dostoevsky finally resolves the dilemma of two kinds of beauty in the manner of his pledge to Mme. Fon-Vizina in 1854; he af-

firms that even if it were proven to him that Christ, the symbol of
highest beauty and perfection, were outside the truth, he would
still prefer to remain with Christ. He *chooses* to remain with Christ,
though at the same time acknowledges the existence of "opposite
proofs" which plunge him into doubts. So also, in his aesthetic dilemma, Dostoevsky chooses to acknowledge only one higher, ideal
beauty, though without denying the existence of "another ideal,"
or without denying that men call the experience of this ideal,
beauty. Philosophical truth for Dostoevsky is contradiction, and
life the interaction of contradictory elements. As we have seen,
he structures his notion of two kinds of beauty, two ideals, in the
framework of a dualistic view of man's nature (corporeal and spiritual) and in terms of a dialectical interaction between the earthly
truth of man's nature and the spiritual truth that is revealed in his
strivings. It is the existence of one higher, ideal beauty—and the
reality of man's existential choice of that beauty—which saves man
from the destructive tensions of his earthly nature. "And thus man
strives on earth for an ideal which is contrary to his nature," Dostoevsky wrote in his notebook in 1864. "When man does not fulfill the law of striving for the ideal . . . he experiences suffering
and has called this condition sin. And thus man continually must
experience suffering, which is balanced by the divine pleasure in
fulfillment of the law, i.e. sacrifice. Precisely here, then, is earthly
equilibrium. Otherwise the earth would be senseless."[69]

"BY THE WORD REALITY we understand everything that is," observed Belinsky in 1840, "the visible world and the spiritual world, the world of facts and the world of ideas."[1] Belinsky's definition—which belongs to his middle or so-called Hegelian period of rationalization of reality—comes close to characterizing Dostoevsky's omnibus view of reality. We shall not encounter a single binding concept of reality in Dostoevsky's thought; rather, his notion of reality is a syncretism.[2] Reality for him embraces concrete, historical reality with its classes, its immediate problems and conflicts, and its social and national types which give expression to the life and development of society. But Dostoevsky's reality also encompasses the ideals and dreams that are part of social reality, and their embodiment in ideal types. These ideals and dreams, though they arise in a specific historical moment or context, relate ultimately to a universal spiritual reality; it is in this deeper, archetypal reality that Dostoevsky seeks the ultimate meaning of man's existence. Reality, then, is "all available human meaning"; but "we cannot exhaust the whole of a phenomenon, we can never reach its ends and beginnings. We are familiar only with the immediate, visible, current, and this only in its appearance, while the ends and beginnings—all this is still a realm of the fantastic for man."[3] But it is precisely this realm of reality without end—at its point of intersection with man's "immediate" present—that is the exploratory realm of art for Dostoevsky. Reality for him, finally, is *man:* the journey of his life. This journey, like that of Dante in the *Commedia,* is eminently real, concrete, and historical; yet at the same time, like Dante's, it is symbolic and imbued with a meaning and perspective that is transcendental and timeless.

In "Mr. —bov and the Question of Art," Dostoevsky writes that "one may know a fact, see it oneself a hundred times, and still not get the impression one would if somebody else, a particular person, stands beside you and points out to you that very fact, but of course in his own way, explains it to you in his own words, compels you to look at that fact with his own glance. A real talent is recognized by just this influence."[4] This is a very simple way of describing the role of the artist in the artistic representation of reality. The "particular person," the artist, distinguishes an ordinary fact; he gives it special shape or form (his own glance, his own words, his own way). The artist does not mirror reality (the ordinary observer performs this essentially unperceptive act a hundred times); rather he acts upon reality, "explains" it through the shaping he gives to it, through form; he gives us a unique "impression" of it. The artistic power, then, with which the artist compels us to view reality resides in the form that he gives to reality. We may note, finally, the basis here for a distinction between two kinds of reality: an apparent, everyday reality, and a real, or underlying, reality that is visible to the artist but hidden to the formless and unforming glance. The artist is the one who *sees* into life, perceives all its richness and complexity in depth. The image of the eyes—of sight and vision—is recurrent throughout all of Dostoevsky's discussion of the artistic representation of reality. "Really, examine some fact of real life, even one which at first glance is not very striking," Dostoevsky writes later in his *Diary of a Writer,* "and if only you are able and have the eyes you will discover in it a depth such as is not to be found in Shakespeare. But really here is just the whole point: *whose eyes and who is able?* Indeed, not only to create and write artistic works, but even just to note a fact, something in the way of an artist is also needed."[5]

The problem of the representation of reality in art and literature is at the center of "The Exhibition in the Academy of Arts: 1860–1861." Dostoevsky singles out for particular criticism a work of the painter V. I. Jacoby, entitled "Convicts at a Halting Point."[6] The picture is striking for its remarkable exactitude, he writes. "Everything is like that even in nature . . . if one looks at nature, so to speak, only from without." The spectator looks at the picture as though he saw it in a mirror or in an expertly touched-up photograph. But the photographic snapshot or mirror reflection is by no means an artistic work, Dostoevsky insists. "Not photographic faithfulness, not mechanical accuracy, but something else, larger, broader, deeper is demanded from art." Accuracy and faithfulness are needed only in a basic sense, as material "out of which the artistic work is then created; it is a tool of creation. In a mirror reflection one does not see how the mirror looks at the subject or, put another way, it is evident that it does not look at all, but reflects passively, mechanically." Dostoevsky insists that this is not the case with the true artist; whether in a picture, story, or musical work "he himself will be visible invariably; he will be reflected involuntarily; even against his will, he will speak out with all his views, with his character, in accordance with his development." When we overhear two people discussing an ordinary street incident, Dostoevsky observes by way of example, we often guess their age, the nature and field of their work, their level of development, and even their rank in the civil service.[7] The artist, then, cannot evade identification.

Dostoevsky does not elaborate upon the notion that a writer will be reflected in his art even against his will. Belinsky much earlier had advanced the view that the thought of an artist in his poetic creation may contradict his personal convictions.[8] The radical critic Dobrolyubov later elaborated on this view with his theory that social type in an artistic work may reveal an author's view independently of, and even contrary to, his conscious intentions.[9] Dostoevsky appears to be echoing Dobrolyubov's theory in the distinction he makes in "Stories of N. V. Uspensky" between the "preconceived view" of the artist and his "real view" expressed in social type.[10]

"There is not, and cannot be, any epic, indifferent tranquility in our time," Dostoevsky wrote in "The Exhibition in the Academy of Arts: 1860–1861." Only completely undeveloped, capricious, or mad people could manifest such tranquility. And since these "sad possibilities" are unlikely in the artist, Dostoevsky concludes that the artist's audience is right in demanding that he "view nature not as a photographic apparatus sees it, but as a man."[11] The representation of reality in art is a humanistic process.

Dostoevsky's concept of the artistic representation of reality is brought out in his criticism of Jacoby's painting. The subject of the painting—the representation of convicts—was one which could not but intensely interest the author of *Notes from the House of the Dead*. Jacoby's painting (we summarize Dostoevsky's description of it) represents a group of convicts surrounding a wagon; upon it lies a dead man and on his outstretched hand is a precious ring.

The figure of the dead convict suggests a person of gentry origin. Another convict, "with a repulsive face," reaches out from beneath the wagon and is in the act of removing the ring from the dead man's hand. He produces upon the observer the impression of a "reptile that is foul and at the same time dangerous, like a scorpion." An officer stands by the corpse, very indifferently smoking a pipe; he is holding open one of the eyes of the dead convict and calmly looking at it. His face expresses neither sympathy, nor compassion, nor surprise—absolutely nothing. Another convict dully examines a wound made by his chains.

In ancient times, Dostoevsky remarks, people would have said that the artist "must see with physical eyes, and, above all, with the eyes of the soul, or with a spiritual glance." Jacoby, in his opinion, lacks this second pair of eyes. There is not a trace of artistry in the painting. The figures of the convicts, he complains, all appear as scoundrels, monstrous. The dead man alone is an exception to this impression of monstrousness. A splendid youth in life, academic demands made it impossible to give him "more ordinary or less classical features: thus one sees a man of birth among a vile people, vile in the sense that he has understood it all his life." Dostoevsky acknowledges the hopeless condition of the convicts, but "at the same time it is impossible not to allow that they are people. At least present them to us as people, if you are an artist, and leave the photographing of them to the phrenologists and the judicial investigators."[12] But it is precisely man that Jacoby does not reveal.

Dostoevsky resents this caricature depiction of the convicts with its underlying class snobbism. But the basis of his criticism is aesthetic: the artist must go beyond surface reality. "We think it insufficient to set forth faithfully all the given qualities of a person; one must resolutely illumine him with one's own artistic vision," Dostoevsky writes in his *Diary of a Writer* in 1873. "A genuine artist should under no circumstances remain on one level with the person portrayed by him, contenting himself with the mere realistic truth of that person: the impression will carry no truth."[13] "Above all," Dostoevsky writes in his critique of Jacoby's painting, "one must master the difficulties of transmitting actual truth in order to rise to the heights of artistic truth."[14] Jacoby in his striving for photographic truth, in his play for effect, has depicted a lie. "This is melodrama and not reality," Dostoevsky insists.[15] The painting, in other words, appeals for its effect to the upper class view of the convict and of the people; it confronts the observer with his own luridly exaggerated and cliché notion of a "vile" people. Here there can be no true reality, no representation of deeper human reality, but only a crude caricature in which the surface, the face of reality as it were, is divorced from its meanings, from the deeper moral substratum of reality.

The faces of the convicts are disfigured; this is "actual" or surface truth. But surface reality, Dostoevsky points out in 1873, is deceptive. Why—he asks—does a portrait painter long scrutinize the subject of his painting before setting to work? "Because he knows in practice that man does not always resemble himself, and therefore he seeks out 'the main idea of his physiognomy,' that moment when the subject most resembles himself."[16] Versilov in *The Raw Youth,* obviously echoing Dostoevsky's views, observes that only on rare occasions does a man's face express his "main idea, his most characteristic idea." The painter guesses this idea, whereas "photography catches man as [he] is, and it is quite possible that Napoleon, at one moment, would have turned out looking stupid, and Bismarck—tender."

The "main idea" is the organizing principle in a work of art; on the other hand, when the detail, or aggregation of details, substitutes for the idea the result is not realism but caricature. Thus, the quixotic hero of "Bobok," discussing a portrait of which he is the subject, remarks that he believes the artist did his portrait "not for the sake of literature, but for the sake of my two symmetrical warts on my forehead: it's a phenomenon, so to speak. They have no idea, so now they go to town on phenomena. Well, but how well he succeeded with my two warts in the portrait—they're alive! They call this realism."

The unselected and unilluminated truth of detail—"mere realistic truth"—is caricature or, simply, ugliness. This idea is suggested indirectly in Dostoevsky's formulation of a remark by the young Arkady Dolgoruky in *The Raw Youth;* recalling a past incident, he writes: "I remember (for I remember that whole morning to the detail) that there followed between us a scene most disgusting in its realistic truth." The realistic truth here, like the realism of Bobok's portrait, has nothing to do with artistic realism; it is chaotic, detail-crammed reality of everyday life; it is untransfigured actuality. The writer Uspensky, Dostoevsky writes in "Stories of N. V. Uspensky," sets up his photographic machine on a plaza, without even selecting a point of view, and takes in everything "faithfully, *as is*. Naturally, everything that is absolutely unnecessary to this picture, or rather, unnecessary to the idea of this picture, will enter into the picture." Some laud this kind of approach for its accuracy. But is this accuracy, Dostoevsky asks, and does accuracy consist in this? "This is confusion, not accuracy."[17] "You needed chaos, disorder at all costs," Dostoevsky remarks apropos of Jacoby's arbitrary use of detail.[18] "Reality strives toward fragmentation," the narrator remarks in *Notes from the House of the Dead*. On the other hand, art imposes order upon reality—not mechanical order, but the order of organic form; and artistic form for Dostoevsky is inseparable from idea. There is little, he insists, that can be transmitted through the mere description of material. The playwright A. N. Ostrovsky, he observes, would have to be stretched out to two hundred volumes, and then these volumes would not convey what Ostrovsky gave us in two volumes. "Moreover, one cannot faithfully transmit even the material with only a daguerreotype."[19]

Dostoevsky's sharp criticism of Emile Zola's naturalism in the 1870s, in light of the above discussion, is not unexpected. In his *Diary of a Writer* in 1876 Dostoevsky speaks of the "so-called realist" Zola.[20] "In realism alone there is no truth," Dostoevsky observes in his notebook in connection with a reading of Zola's *Le Ventre de Paris*. "Photography and the artist. Zola overlooked in G. Sand (in the first tales) poetry and *beauty*. . . . Realism is the figure of Hermann [in Pushkin's "Queen of Spades"] (although to the eye he may be more fantastic)." In connection with Zola's naturalistic method, Dostoevsky writes: "He will describe every nail in the heel of a boot, and in a quarter of an hour, when the sun rises, he will again describe this nail in another illumination. This is not art. Speak to me one word (Pushkin), but let it be the most essential word."[21] "I can scarcely read him—what muck! And we scream about Zola as somebody famous, a torch of realism!"[22]

"I am terribly fond of realism in art," Dostoevsky wrote in his *Diary of a Writer* in 1877, "but there is *no moral center* in the pictures of some of our modern realists."[23] Jacoby's painting of Russian convicts lacked precisely a moral center. The criticism of his painting appears in sharper relief against the background of Dostoevsky's own canvas on convict life, *Notes from the House of the Dead*. The moral center in this work—the restoration of the image of the "lost people"—was reached through the aesthetic accomplishment: the penetration of surface, or naturalistic, truth. A "repulsive crust," the narrator observes, covered even the most decent convicts. Yet "one need only remove the outer superficial crust and examine more attentively the kernel itself, more closely, and without prejudice, and some of us will see things in the people that we never expected."[24] Here, of course, is a very simple and clear statement of Dostoevsky's notion of authentic realism. To be sure, he does not ignore the repulsive crust—the frightful details, the ugly actuality of convict life. But the multitude of raw details are never presented for themselves alone, for melodramatic effect. Reality, however chaotic and disfigured at first glance, yields to an inner, organizing idea—a moral idea. The ugly, the repulsive, the disfigured presents itself to the reader invariably as a deformation of a norm: that norm is the moral-aesthetic shape of man-created-in-the-image-of-God, a preeminently humanistic norm for Dostoevsky. Dostoevsky sought the truth about the convicts not only in the cross section of the moment; *Notes from the House of the Dead* is not a snapshot. "After all, the whole truth must be told: these were an exceptional people," the narrator remarks at the conclusion of his memoirs. "Indeed, they are, perhaps, the most gifted, the strongest of all our people. But mighty forces perished in vain, perished abnormally, wrongfully, irrevocably. And who is to blame? And this is just the point: who is to blame?"

The young Arkady Dolgoruky remembered an episode to the detail, remembered it in all its disgusting realistic truth. The narrator in *Notes from the House of the Dead* also recalls his past—but differently. "This was really long ago," he observes at the beginning of his memoirs, "it all seems like a dream to me." The passing reference to the dreamlike character of his recollections is not without significance. The dream here is artistic transfiguration; it is aesthetic distance between the writer and his material. Much later, in his autobiographical sketch, "The Dream of Marey" (1876), Dostoevsky indirectly provided the key to his artistic approach in *Notes from the House of the Dead*. He relates how, as a convict, he once had dreamed of a kindly peasant who had be-

friended him as a child. The dream came to an end. He got off his
bunk and looked around. "I suddenly felt that I could look at these
unhappy creatures with quite different eyes and that suddenly, by
some miracle, all hatred and malice had disappeared completely
from my heart." The dream here has both a psychological and
aesthetic character; it is both catharsis and revelation; it opens
what Dostoevsky calls the eyes of the soul. The miracle effected by
the dream is the miracle of artistic transfiguration.

Neither Jacoby nor Klodt illuminates his subjects from within,
looks upon them with the eyes of the soul. They give us "natural
truth" in place of "artistic truth." On the other hand, Dostoevsky
feels this artistic truth in the work of the Swiss painter Alexandre
Calame, entitled "The Lake of Four Cantons."[25] "The magician-
artist has put his soul into it." The person who views Calame's
painting profoundly and sweetly contemplates this picture "and
sees that the artist himself was steeped in a kind of sad meditation
as he looked off into the distant mountains, into the clear sky,
toward the misty remote."[26] The Lake of Four Cantons in Switzerland evokes in Myshkin the same sense of melancholy and sublime
that Calame's painting evoked in Dostoevsky. In the review of the
Academy of Arts exhibition, the artistic insight of Calame contrasts with the "daguerreotyping" of Jacoby and others; in *The
Idiot,* Myshkin's artistic insight into nature is juxtaposed with the
limited photographic realism of the young amateur painter, Adelaida Epanchin. Adelaida, a copyist, is incapable—as we noted
in the preceding chapter—of "looking" at things in a genuinely
artistic manner, of perceiving authentic beauty. Myshkin, quite
significantly, proposes to Adelaida ("You most of all!") a subject
for a painting which is entirely appropriate to her surface realism.
The subject for the painting—the face of a man about to be guil-
lotined—is imbued with precisely that sense of horror and despair,
that repellent mood of death, which Dostoevsky observed in Klodt's
painting and which Ippolit Terentiev finds in Holbein's canvas.[27]
The execution scene is clearly suitable for a painter like Adelaida
"who does not know how to look." No transfiguring insight is
called for here; there is no beauty, no hope, no divine ideal into
which a true artist could peer. Ordinary vision suffices for Myshkin's execution scene. "I must confess that I looked at it as though

rooted to the spot," Myshkin remarks apropos of an execution scene he witnessed in Lyons. "I could not take my eyes off it." "I couldn't have taken my eyes off it, either," responds Aglaya. The impact of the Klodt, Holbein, Myshkin paintings is not a liberating or edifying one; these works exercise a morbid, hypnotic, and fundamentally unhealthy attraction. Even Myshkin rebels against his interest. "As soon as you finished your story you seemed to be ashamed of what you said," Aglaya remarks to him at the conclusion of his idea for a painting. "Why is that?" (Pt. I, Ch. 5). Just as when he was confronted by Ippolit Terentiev's question: "What kind of beauty will save the world?"—so here, Myshkin, significantly, does not answer Aglaya's question. The conflict between the opposite sides of Myshkin's nature (manifested in his attraction both to the Lake of Four Cantons and to the execution scene—his idea for a painting) undoubtedly reflects Dostoevsky's own ambivalent reactions to the Holbein-Klodt type of painting. But most clearly expressed in *The Idiot* is Dostoevsky's conviction that authentic art must penetrate to the spiritual ideal of reality. The absence of faith in the aesthetic-religious ideal inevitably—in Dostoevsky's view—must be reflected in the artist's vision. The aesthetic concomitant of despair, he seems to say, is naturalism.

Dostoevsky writes with positive approval of another canvas observed at the Academy of Arts exhibition—François Diday's painting of the Reichenbach waterfalls in Switzerland.[28] The painter did not "worry about effect and did not paint a portrait of the waterfall, but transmitted the impression and disposition of spirit which Reichenbach produced upon him with its grandiose impact." How all this is conveyed in a picture—Dostoevsky writes again of the spiritual content of Calame's painting—is the artist's secret, but it is clear that he did not photograph nature, "but only took it as a means in order to imbue the spectator with his own, tender, peaceful, sweetly contemplative, spiritual disposition." Nothing would be easier, Dostoevsky observes, than to copy such a simple picture, but he considers it doubtful whether the "soul of the original would go into the copy."[29] "The point is that before us nature lies unconscious," he observes in his review of Uspensky's stories. "If the material is merely unconsciously described, then we know nothing about it." The same raw material of reality might evoke different responses in different artists, depending upon the

view of the artist. Uspensky, Dostoevsky observes, wrote his story
"The Cart" ("Oboz") in order to make fun of the peasants who
could not count. But Dostoevsky cannot believe that there was
nothing besides this in the reality, the material itself. There were
other things, he insists, but Uspensky "did not note those other
things that lay under his glance because he regarded as important
only what he wanted to write about." But if another person looked
he would have found something else; a third person would have
found still something different; "and each would be telling the
truth." What Uspensky found ridiculous, another would have
found tragic, "and both would have been right."[30] Different artists,
different consciousnesses, then, perceive different realities. We have
here an example of what Erich Auerbach has called "conscious
perspectivism." The notion of an indivisible, objective reality is
replaced by the conception of reality as a function of consciousness.[31] Dostoevsky in 1873 leaves no doubt as to the philosophically idealist character of his conception of reality. " 'One must
depict reality as it is,' they say, whereas there is simply no such
reality, and indeed such a reality never existed on earth, because
the essence of things is inaccessible to man, and he apprehends
nature as it is reflected in his idea, passing through his feelings."[32]

Dostoevsky defines the "idealist" character of his realism in a
letter to Apollon Maikov in 1868. He confides to his friend the
plan of a "huge novel" to be entitled "Atheism." At its center is a
Russian man who suddenly loses faith in God, gets involved with
atheistic groups, falls into the power of a Jesuit, but finally, in the
end, rediscovers Christ and the Russian land. At this point in the
letter Dostoevsky pauses to exclaim:

> Ah, my friend! I have completely different concepts about
> reality and about realism from our realists and critics. My
> idealism is more real than theirs. Lord! To relate intelligibly
> all that we Russians have experienced in the past ten years
> in our spiritual development—now wouldn't the realists shout
> that this is fantasy! Yet this is authentic genuine realism! Pre-
> cisely this is realism, only deeper, and they are swimming in
> shallow water. Now isn't Lyubim Tortsov [the central char-
> acter in Ostrovsky's play *Poverty Is No Crime*, 1854] really
> insignificant in essence—and yet this is all the ideal that their

realism allows. Deep realism—hardly! With their realism you won't explain one-hundredth of the real facts that have actually occurred. And with our idealism we have prophesied even facts. It has happened.[33]

Dostoevsky's point of departure for his defense of his idealism is his formulation of the drama of Russian man in terms of an immense moral and spiritual quest. But this is "realism, only deeper"; it is more real for Dostoevsky because it focuses the historical reality of the moment against a background of the permanent spiritual strivings and aspirations of man. Dostoevsky speaks of *explaining* real facts; he is proud that he even has prophesied facts, that he has grasped the inner dynamic of reality and anticipated its "facts." "They only understand what goes on before their eyes," he is reported to have said of his critics, "but because of nearsightedness they themselves are not only unable to look ahead, but cannot understand even how for another person the *future results of present events* can be crystal clear."[34] It is the cognitive function of realism that Dostoevsky values: in its most immediate action true realism captures social reality in movement; in its deeper action artistic cognition approaches religious revelation.

Dostoevsky's defense of his realism in his letter to Maikov had a definite purpose: it was to defend himself against the charge that his art (specifically, *The Idiot*) lacked verisimilitude as a depiction of reality, that his realism was fantastic. Maikov had written Dostoevsky apropos of the second half of Part I of *The Idiot*:

Here's my impression: an awful lot of strength, genius-inspired strokes (for example, when the Idiot is slapped, and what he says, and various other places), but in the whole action *there is more possibility and plausibility than truth.* The most real person, if you will, is the Idiot (does this seem strange to you?) but the others—all, as it were, live in a fantastic world; all of them have a strong yet fantastic, somewhat exceptional luster. One reads avidly, and at the same time— one doesn't believe in it.[35]

And in another letter Maikov comments:

Various reviews, the chief reproach being the fantastic quality of the characters; one gentleman even says that such country houses are not to be found in Pavlovsk.[36]

The charge that his artistic vision, or embodiment, of reality was "fantastic" certainly was not a new one to Dostoevsky. "As far back as the 1840s I was dubbed mockingly a fantasist," he observed in "Petersburg Visions in Verse and Prose" (1861).[37] "I am a frightful hunter after mysteries. I am a fantasist, I am a mystic, and, I confess to you, Petersburg—I don't know why—has always seemed to me something of a mystery."[38] Pushkin perceived and projected the historical-philosophical contradictions of Russian history, its social drama and pathos, in the complex image of a fantastic Petersburg; Gogol further contributed to this image through his Petersburg tales. The notion of the city as a vast, abstract, and impersonal entity, expropriating from man his humanity, threatening to transform him into a nonentity, making his whole existence strange, fantastic, unreal, finds embodiment in Dostoevsky's early stories, as well as in his later novels. The "fantastic titulary councillors" in the early tales—Mr. Proharchin, Vasya Shumkov, Golyadkin Sr., and others—are victims of their own involuted natures and, at the same time, real sacrifices of the Petersburg bureaucratic anthill state. Netochka Nezvanova, in Dostoevsky's work of the same name, writes: "I am not surprised that among such strange people as my father and mother I myself became such a strange, fantastic child." She is spoiled by her "fantastic, exceptional" love for her father. Her life and the world about her she compares with a "fairy tale," a "novel," a strange "dream." G. M. Fridlender has observed that these comparisons serve to emphasize precisely the strangeness, the fantastic and exceptional character of the reality around Netochka—a reality which appears to the reader of her notes and to Netochka herself not as stable and normal, but as extraordinarily unstable and abnormal.[39] Yet it is recognizably and vividly the real world in a picture that shows, in its distortion, how that world deviates from the ideal.

The criticism of his art as fantastic—to return to Maikov's observations on *The Idiot*—spurred Dostoevsky to a sharper definition and defense of his realistic method. He writes to his friend Strakhov:

I have my special view of reality (in art) and what the majority calls almost fantastic and exceptional, for me is sometimes the very essence of the real. The day-to-day aspect of phenomena and the cliché view of them, in my opinion, is still not realism; indeed, the very contrary. In every number of the newspaper you encounter a report about the most real facts and about the most complex facts. For our writers they are fantastic; and indeed, they are not concerned with them; and yet they are reality, because they are *facts*. Now who will note them, explain them, write them down. They are daily and of the moment, and not *exceptional*. . . . We let all reality . . . pass by our noses. Now who will take note of the facts and go deeply into them? . . . Is it possible that my fantastic Idiot is not reality, indeed even the most common! Why, just now there must be such characters in our strata of society that are divorced from the soil—strata which in reality are becoming fantastic.[40]

Dostoevsky, it will be noted, does not deny that certain phenomena, facts of reality, do indeed *appear* fantastic, improbable, exceptional. Indeed, as he affirms several years later, "true events, depicted in all their exclusiveness of their occurrence, nearly always assume a fantastic, almost improbable character."[41] Lebedev in *The Idiot* observes that "almost every reality, though it has its immutable laws, is always incredible and improbable." But the central question here is: fantastic, incredible, improbable from what point of view and to whom? Dostoevsky clearly answers that the facts of reality often appear incredible from the cliché viewpoint of the majority, appear fantastic to those who look at reality with merely surface, photographic eyes. A fact of reality from this viewpoint often appears fantastic (and, indeed, statically perceived, *is* fantastic) because it turns up in all its exclusiveness in a clutter of unrelated and haphazard detail; it appears fantastic, essentially, because it is unexplained (aesthetically—unformed), because it is unrelated to the underlying "immutable laws" which govern its appearance. "The aim of art," Dostoevsky writes, "is not the accidentalities of day-to-day life, but their general idea, sharply divined and correctly removed from the whole multiplicity of identical phenomena of life."[42]

Dostoevsky insists, as we have seen, that his "fantastic Idiot" is perhaps a part of even common reality, that there must be such characters in those strata of society divorced from the people. But it is not primarily upon faithfulness to common reality that Dostoevsky ultimately justifies his special realism (though he is proud that he has anticipated real facts in his art). He recognizes, for example, that a fact of reality may indeed be uncommon, exceptional, a rarity. A cruel monk, for example, beats to death a ten-year-old boy in a famous monastery. "Well, now isn't this a fantastic story at first glance?" Dostoevsky remarks. "And yet it is, it seems, wholly true." But if one were to write about it, he adds, people would shout that it was improbable, exceptional. "And they would be right, if the matter was judged only from the standpoint of faithfulness in depicting the ordinary run of life in our monasteries." Life in the monasteries, Dostoevsky freely acknowledges, is quite different, and the incident involving the evil monk will always stand out as an exception to the rule. "But for the narrator, for the poet, there may also be other tasks besides the ordinary run-of-life aspect; these are the general, universal, and, I think, eternally inexhaustible depths of spirit and human character."[43]

The ultimate test of verisimilitude of a fact, the test of "realism," then, is not in the identity of fact A to fact B to fact C and so forth; it is in the degree to which fact A, however isolated and exceptional, conducts us to the larger realities of society and the human spirit. An exceptional, seemingly strange or fantastic incident may open up a startling perspective of human evil or goodness. Realism in Dostoevsky's novelistic universe, as in Dante's *Commedia,* is vertical; the facts of our lives are starkly represented, sometimes even with naturalistic precision, but they are selected in such a way as to illuminate the hierarchical reality of the human spirit.

The facts of crime for Dostoevsky clearly were prime conductors to authentic reality. Evidence of his preoccupation with these "facts" and with their deeper significance may be found in his editor's note in his journal *Vremya* in 1861; here he informs the readers that his journal will carry accounts of criminal trials.

> We are thinking of entertaining the readers when, from time to time, we give accounts of famous criminal trials. Apart from the fact that they are more entertaining than all sorts of novels, because they illuminate these dark sides of the human

soul which art does not like to touch—and if it does then only in passing, in the form of an episode—apart from this, reading about such trials, it seems to us, will not be without use to the Russian reader. . . . In the trial we now present we are concerned with the personality of an extraordinary, enigmatic, terrible, and interesting man. Low instincts and weakness in the face of need made him a criminal, but he dares to present himself as the victim of his century. And all this with a boundless vanity. This is a type of vanity carried to extreme limits. The trial was conducted with magnificent impartiality, conveyed with the exactitude of a daguerreotype, of a physiological sketch.[44]

Dostoevsky does not conceive of the journalistic account of criminal trials as an art form. The account of the trial is offered to the reader as a fact of reality that has the exactitude of a daguerreotype. But in a few casual strokes Dostoevsky suggests that these facts have broad social and human significance. The daguerreotype is but the raw material of reality. He leaves it to the reader to perform, in effect, the act of artistic cognition which gives meaningful shape to the "exceptional" fact of reality.

The novel *Crime and Punishment,* of course, is that act of artistic cognition focused on an "exceptional" crime. Dostoevsky boldly "touches upon" the dark sides of man and society. The problem of the exceptional and fantastic character of Raskolnikov's crime (inseparable from his idea of the crime) is noted by the police investigator Porfiry. "Your article is fantastic and absurd," he comments to Raskolnikov. Raskolnikov's ideas on the relation of the superior man to the human herd, and the rights of crime which derive from this superiority, are indeed fantastic when seen from an everyday point of view. But Porfiry is aware of the deeper social import of Raskolnikov's ideas. "We are dealing with quite a fantastic affair, a somber affair, a modern one. . . . We are dealing with bookish dreams." Raskolnikov's crime has social reality (or typicality) for Dostoevsky not because students in the 1860s killed helpless pawnbrokers every day with axes, but because the syndrome of Raskolnikov's moral, psychological, and ideological being reveals in its roots deep imbalances within Russian society, profound spiritual disorder.

It was his critics, Dostoevsky wrote in his notebook around 1875, who were "ignoring facts. They do not observe. There are no citizens, and nobody wants to make an effort and compel himself to think and observe. I cannot tear myself away, and all the cries of the critics that I am not depicting real life have not dissuaded me." "There are no foundations to our society, no principles of conduct that have been lived through, because there have been none in *life* even. A colossal eruption and all is crumbling, falling, being negated, as though it had not even existed. And not only externally, as in the West, but *internally, morally*."[45]

"Does the fantastic have a right to exist in art?" Dostoevsky asks in a letter to Turgenev in which he defends Turgenev's story-fantasia, "Ghosts." "Now just who answers such questions! If there is anything that one might criticize in 'Ghosts' it is that *it is not quite fully fantastic*."[46] Dostoevsky has in mind here the use of the literally fantastic or unreal in art. Only art, obviously, can provide an answer to the question Dostoevsky raises. Know-nothing people demand "limited utilitarianism." "Write for them a most poetic work—they will put it aside and take something in which a thrashing of somebody is described. *Poetic truth* is considered nonsense. Only that alone which is copied from real fact is needed." It is the inner reality revealed in Turgenev's fantasy that interests Dostoevsky. The form of "Ghosts" will astonish people, he writes. But the main thing is to understand the real content. The real, here, is the "*anguish of an educated and conscious being living in our time,* a tangible anguish."[47] Dostoevsky clearly sympathizes with a nostalgic, melancholic element in Turgenev's story—an anguish which Dostoevsky, as we have noted earlier, considered a distinguishing mark of the human condition. Dostoevsky significantly singles out in Turgenev's stories images which hint at the "elemental still unresolved thought (that very thought which is in all nature) which it is unknown whether human intelligence will ever resolve, but now the heart only anguishes over it and is frightened even more, although it does not want to wrench itself away from it." And Dostoevsky concludes that "such a thought is precisely timely and such fantastic things are *extremely positive*."[48]

E. T. A. Hoffmann's fantasy is especially meaningful to Dostoevsky precisely because it is imbued with poetic truth. Hoffmann's art is thoroughly fantastic, full of magicians and spirits, and sometimes Hoffmann "seeks his ideal beyond the earthly world, in some kind of extraordinary world, regarding this world as the most lofty, as though he himself believed in the certain existence of a mysterious, magical world."[49] (We are not far, here, from Zosima's Christian vision of "another world" in *The Brothers Karamazov*.) Hoffmann above all has "an ideal." There is purity in this ideal —and most important to Dostoevsky—"there is beauty—real, authentic, indigenous to man."[50]

Dostoevsky's observations on Edgar Allan Poe's stories provide a further insight into his general conception of the uses of the unreal-fantastic in art. Poe's writing cannot be regarded as wholly fantasy, Dostoevsky observes in 1861, or, if his art is fantastic, it must be considered so only in an external sense, and then only initially fantastic. Poe allows for an improbable event, but then "in everything else he is completely faithful to reality." He might be called "not a fantastic but a capricious writer." "He almost always takes the most exceptional reality, places his hero in a most exceptional external or psychological situation, and with what power of insight, with what striking faithfulness does he not relate the spiritual condition of this man!"[51] The feature of Poe's realism that Dostoevsky so admires here is—or will become—an integral aspect of his own realistic method.

Dostoevsky gives expression to a similar theory of realism in his story "A Gentle One: A Fantastic Story" (1876). Dostoevsky comments on his story in a preface. The form of the story—the chief character speaks to himself and, as it were, to "some kind of judge"—is the fantastic element to Dostoevsky. "This supposition about a stenographer writing everything down (after which I polish up the notes) is just what I call fantastic in this story." Yet the story is "real in the highest degree." Victor Hugo, Dostoevsky adds, employed a similar method in his "The Last Day of a Man Condemned to Death." He assumed an even greater improbability, namely, that the condemned man could put down his notes right up to the last minute. "But had he not allowed for this fantasy, there never would have come into existence the work itself—the most real and most truthful of all the works written by him."[52]

Dostoevsky's interest in the unreal-fantastic in art reaches back to the earliest beginnings of his creative life. In his story "The Double" (1846) he strives to combine the wholly real phenomenon of Golyadkin Sr.'s moral and psychological ambivalence with the highly improbable existence of a "real" double, Golyadkin Jr. We have no record at that time of Dostoevsky's views on the fantastic in art. But in the final year of his life he did set forth his own view of the principles regulating the use of the fantastic in art. He criticizes a story sent to him by a correspondent, Ju. F. Abaza. The thought is a good one, he writes, "but God how impossibly you carried it through! The thought that a breed of people, having received an initial idea from their forebears and *having subordinated themselves to it exclusively* in the course of several generations, subsequently must necessarily degenerate into something peculiar to humanity . . . even . . . something hostile to humanity . . . this thought is correct and profound." But the "descendant" is "*impossibly* depicted." He should have been given only moral suffering. But the writer has invented "something crudely physical, some kind of block of ice instead of a heart. The doctors after curing him for so many years did not notice that he had no heart. Now how can a man live without a physical organ?" Dostoevsky's objection to the absence of a physical heart seems less an objection to an unreal element than an aesthetic objection: the detail, in the context of the story, obviously struck him as unintentionally grotesque—indeed, the whole story, to judge from Dostoevsky's account of it, was grotesque and entirely lacking in a sense of artistic measure. Dostoevsky continues in his letter to Abaza:

> Granted that this is a fantastic tale, but after all the fantastic in art has limits and rules. The fantastic must be contiguous with the real to such a degree that you must *almost* believe it. Pushkin, who gave us almost all forms of art, wrote "The Queen of Spades"—the pinnacle of fantastic art. And you believe that Hermann really had a vision, and precisely in accordance with his world view, and yet at the end of the story, that is, after having read it through, you do not know what to think. Did this vision emerge from the nature of Hermann, or is it really one of those [visions] which have touched on another world, full of spirits evil and hostile to mankind? (N.B. Spiritualism and its teachings.) Now this is art! Now in the place where the chemist creates a heart out of wine and communion bread—this you do so crudely that it even makes

one laugh. (As a writer I must confess, however, that this scene is daring and not lacking in the picturesque.)[53]

In this notion that the "fantastic must be contiguous with the real to such a degree that you must *almost* believe it," do we not have in all likelihood the ideal which Dostoevsky sought to achieve in his early stories, "The Double" and "The Landlady?"

One may distinguish in Dostoevsky's thought, so far, two formally distinct categories of the fantastic in art, or of so-called fantastic realism: the *seemingly* fantastic facts or phenomena which are represented in art and which find a real (even if sometimes rare) correlative in life, and the *actually* or literally unreal phenomena that we encounter in one degree or another, for instance, in Hoffmann and Poe. In the first instance, real phenomena (e.g. facts of crime, violence, eccentric behavior) serve to illuminate the larger reality of man and society; in the second instance, art, returning to its mythic root and function, either strives directly to illuminate the mystery of a deeper reality with purely imaginative elements or posits a fantastic fact or situation as a point of departure for an otherwise "real" representation of reality.

We have spoken of "actually or literally unreal phenomena" in defining the notion of the fantastic as it is exhibited, for instance, in Poe or in Turgenev's "Ghosts." But the very distinction—assumed here—between real and unreal phenomena or facts is obliterated, or at least seriously blurred, in Dostoevsky's Christian religious illumination of reality. We noted at the beginning of this chapter Dostoevsky's view that man is familiar only with the immediate and visible, "and this only in its appearance, while the ends and beginnings—all this is still a realm of the fantastic for man." The "fantastic" here, of course, is precisely ultimate reality in the philosophical or religious sense. The philosophically idealist understructure of Dostoevsky's thought on reality is evident at all stages of his career; it is strikingly visible, however, in the last decade of his life, a time when the Christian religious emphasis of his thought is most pronounced. Ultimate reality for the author of *The Brothers Karamazov* is the transcendent reality of the universal, Christian ideal. Much on earth is concealed from us, Zosima observes in *The Brothers Karamazov,* "but instead there is given us a mysterious, precious perception of a living connection with another world, with a lofty and sublime world, indeed the roots of our thoughts and feelings are not here, but in other worlds. That is why also the philosophers say that it is impossible to perceive the essence of things on earth." The assumption of a "connection" between an earthly reality and "another world," the affirmation of the reality of that other world, leads Dostoevsky to affirm the reality of "facts" which are not of earthly origin but which are manifest in man's earthly existence. Thus, we read in the notebooks to *The Brothers Karamazov:* "NB: If there is a connection with that world, then it is perfectly clear that it can and must be expressed *sometimes* by unusual facts which can be generated not only on the earth alone." We read further: "But the lack of faith of people did not disturb him at all; these people do not believe in immortality and in another life, hence also they cannot believe in miracles because for them everything is entirely on earth." "Much is inexplicable in this world without miracles."[54] Here we are concerned not merely with a "fantastic" spiritual reality (revealed, for example, in Myshkin's epileptic fits), but with fantastic *facts* (miracles) on earth. We cannot, therefore, maintain a distinction between "real" and "unreal" facts; we can only distinguish between the *origins* (earthly or transcendental) of observable facts and phenomena. After reading "The Queen of Spades," "you do not know what to think. Did this vision emerge from the nature of Hermann, or is it really one of those [visions] which have touched on another world?" Dostoevsky, to be sure, was concerned in this letter with the *art* of the fantastic, but the substantive question he raises demands attention in the light of his religious outlook.

The inaccessibility to man of ultimate reality, the lofty and sublime world which is revealed to Zosima, is the tragic fact of man's earthly existence. Man's blindness, Dostoevsky writes, is such that he would "rather believe in a miracle and in an impossibility than in reality, than in truth *which we do not wish to see.* And this is the way it always is in the world, herein is the whole mystery of mankind."[55] "The individual cannot divine completely the eternal universal ideal even though he be Shakespeare himself,"[56] Dostoevsky writes in 1861. Yet in the final analysis he believes it is the artist (and above all Shakespeare) who comes closest to divining this universal ideal, to disclosing the idea (the ideal) of reality. "This is not simply a reproduction of the everyday [world] with which, many teachers assure us, all reality is exhausted," Dostoevsky writes in his notebook to *The Devils,* apropos of Shakespeare. "All reality is far from exhausted by the everyday, because in great part it exists in the form of a subsurface, unexpressed, future Word. Frequently there are prophets who divine and express this integral Word. Shakespeare is this prophet sent by God to announce to us a mystery, about man, about the human soul."[57] The secret of man lies not only in the present. "The realists are wrong, because man is a whole only in the future and is by no means completely exhausted by the present."[58] The role of the artist, then, is ultimately that of seer; in him, imaginative (poetic) consciousness and religious prophetic consciousness are one; phenomena to him are not divided into real and unreal, actual and fictitious; he reveals man to himself in the completeness of his destiny, his timeless being.

It is not surprising, considering the syncretic nature of Dostoevsky's thought, that we should find in it a conscious striving to reconcile, indeed, to merge the notions of realism and idealism. Dostoevsky, unlike Belinsky, Chernyshevsky, and other radicals of his generation, stood permanently at the crossroads of German philosophical idealism. "The idealist and the realist, if only they are honest and highminded, have one and the same essence— love for mankind, and one and the same object—man; only the *forms* of the representation of the object differ," Dostoevsky wrote in his *Diary of a Writer* in 1876. "One has no reason to be ashamed of one's idealism: it is the same road to the same goal. So that idealism, in essence, is just as real as realism and can never disappear from the earth."[59]

It is in man that the real and the ideal merge. It is man, therefore, in the fullness of his material and spiritual being, who is both the center and circumference of Dostoevsky's "reality." The highest form of representation of reality, the most supreme realism for Dostoevsky, is inextricably linked with the revelation of man's quest for the ideal—with the revelation, finally, of that ideal itself.

What is artistic reality? "They say that the artistic work must reflect life, and so forth," Dostoevsky observed to his young friend, E. N. Opochinin. "All that is rubbish: the writer (the poet) creates life, a life in such full amplitude as did not exist before him."[60]

"Types, give us types, there are no types in our literature—these are the words which one has to say almost every day, which one also has to hear every time conversation turns on our contemporary belles lettres." These comments are from a review which appeared in 1873 in *Grazhdanin,* a journal edited by Dostoevsky. The reviewer continues:

> And really, the absence of types in literature is one of the many illnesses of our epoch. Our journals now abound with novels, stories, tales; but with the exception of such capital works as the novel of Count Tolstoy, Dostoevsky's *The Devils,* and Leskov-Stebnitsky's *Cathedral Folk,* are there many types in them? All these characters are statues, cast in the most ingenious poses, where one thing is lacking: a central living thought which permeates the whole work and unites all its constituent parts.[1]

These words—written either by Dostoevsky or with his direct participation—point to the primacy of type in Dostoevsky's thought on realism and the representation of reality in literature. Form and content, artistry and idea are fused organically in the artistic type. The artistic element, Dostoevsky insists, provides inner content in the highest degree. "Gogol in his 'Correspondence' is weak, although representative; but in those places in *Dead Souls* in which —ceasing to be an artist—he begins to reason straight from himself, Gogol is simply weak and not even representative; and yet his works, his 'Marriage,' his *Dead Souls* are the profoundest of works, the richest in inner content precisely through the artistic types delineated in them." Griboedov's "Woe from Wit," Dostoevsky adds, is "only really strong in its vivid artistic types and characters." "The whole depth, the whole content of an artistic work," he concludes, consists, therefore, only in types and characters. And this is almost always the case."[2]

The word *type* appears in Dostoevsky's vocabulary at the very beginning of his literary career. The young journalist and *flâneur* writes in 1845 of the powerful impression created upon him by Petersburg "with its glitter and luxury, thunder and clatter, with its endless types."[3] Dostoevsky's fascination with Petersburg and its endless types reflects the new interest of the "natural" school in all aspects of social reality; it echoes the then-current craze for the depiction of types—the pigeon-holing of individuals in terms of different classes or professional and administrative groupings. In 1842, at a time when the writings of Janin and other French writers were stimulating in Russia an interest in literary type, Belinsky wrote ironically that "all enlightened Europe knows that the 'ideal' [i.e. the type] is nothing other than a gathering in one figure of various features scattered in nature and reality—and by no means reality itself in its potential."[4] "We are all creating types now and consider ourselves typical writers," one observer commented in 1844.[5]

The self-consciousness over type extended to the typical heroes themselves; something of the novelty of the word *type* in the early 1840s can be felt in the manner in which the dreamer-hero of Dostoevsky's story "White Nights" (1848) introduced himself to his newly found companion, Nastenka:

> "Listen, do you want to know who I am?"
> "Why yes, yes!"
> "In the strictest sense of the word?"
> "In the most strict sense of the word!"
> "Well, then, I am a type."
> "A type, a type! What kind of a type?" exclaimed the girl.
> "... just what is a type?"
> "A type? A type is an original; it's an absurd person!" I answered. . . . "It's a character. Listen: do you know what a dreamer is?"*

The self-conscious dreamer is one of Petersburg's "endless types." Dostoevsky explores the tragedy of the dreamer as a social and psychological type in various writings between 1846 and 1849. The characters Dostoevsky creates in his early writings,

---

*There is a play on the Russian word *original* here: it means both original—as opposed to a copy, and also a queer person, a "character."

whether the hero of "White Nights," or Devushkin in *Poor Folk,* or Golyadkin in "The Double," are projected as social types. Dostoevsky considered revising "The Double" in 1859. "Why should I lose a splendid idea," he writes to his brother Mikhail, "the greatest type, in its social importance, which I was the first to discover and of which I was the prophet?"[6]

A concern with the justification of his major fictional protagonists as types pervades Dostoevsky's writing. The hero of *Notes from the Underground* is projected by Dostoevsky in an author's footnote as a social type of the 1840s. The man from the "underground" is, of course, "fictitious." But "such persons as the author of these notes not only can, but even must, exist in our society, taking into account those circumstances in which our society has been formed. I wanted to bring before the public, more vividly than usual, one of the characters of a still recent past." We have here a very simple and precise explanation of the relationship of the literary social type to reality: he does not actually exist, but people like him exist, though they do not turn up so "vividly." The man from the "underground" speaks for a whole range of Dostoevsky's social types when he observes that he "only carried to an extreme" what others "have not dared to carry through halfway."

We encounter a proliferation of types in Dostoevsky's criticism and belles lettres. He takes note of "national," "historical," and "negative" types like Pushkin's Eugene Onegin or Shakespeare's Richard III; "Petersburg" types like Pushkin's Hermann; completed historical types like Goncharov's Oblomov or some of Tolstoy's aristocratic heroes (the "lofty" and "beautiful type"); the "type from the stalk"—for example, a Stenka Razin or Danila Filippovich—the man from the masses "unconsciously troubled with his own typical strength, absolutely direct and not knowing where to find a foundation";[7] contemporary and emergent social types like Raskolnikov and the hero of *The Raw Youth;* "ideal" historical-national types like Pushkin's chronicler Pimen, or his Tatyana; quasi-social positive types like Myshkin; current ideal types like Zosima who are faithful to a still-to-be-realized spiritual ideal. All of these types are authentic because they are true to a deeper historical, social, moral, and spiritual reality; because they carry us beyond mere surface and local reality; because, finally, they are imbued with a unifying poetic idea. It is no accident that

Dostoevsky considered the defining characteristic of Russian literature to be its concern with poetic generalization of life. In the course of a discussion on the "positive types" from the Russian clergy appearing in Leskov's novel *Cathedral Folk,* Dostoevsky notes that the creation of this new type is the result of a combination of a careful, loving study of life with a powerful poetic inspiration.

> It is remarkable that of all European poets none more than precisely the Russians scorn to such a degree all that, which in composition, in a work, may be called in one word intrigue, i.e. chiefly the interaction, combination of forces and persons. A profoundly significant, characteristic fact! Really how simple is the structure of our tragedy, novel, and even lyric. How simple our tragedy in the immortal creations of Pushkin. How simple always the structure of Turgenev's novel, so simple that the West has called him the "master of the novella" (and not of the novel). And simplicity in the creation of Count L. Tolstoy—*War and Peace!* . . . How simple the genius-inspired verse of Fet, in depth and directness of talent (not in manysidedness) the first lyrical poet of new Europe! Strange: our poets take life not in its complexity, but in its depth. The form of the novel moreover is created precisely by the need for poetic idealization (typicalization) of the complexity of life—and the result? our poets least of all are novelists, while our novelists more than anything are poets, and after that, novelists![8]

The concept of art as philosophy and even the notion of realism as poetry are rooted in German romantic thought. René Wellek has called attention to Friedrich Schlegel's paradoxical assertion that "all philosophy is idealism and there is no true realism except that of poetry." Again, he cites one of the interlocutors in Schlegel's "Gespräch über die Poesie" (1800) who is praised for choosing Spinoza in order to "show the primitive source of poetry in the mysteries of realism." Schelling in his *Lectures on the Method of Academic Study* (1802) even uses the term *poetic realism.*[9] Dostoevsky's early romantic identification of art with poetic-philosophical intuition underlies his mature concept of realism, of artistic truth in art. We have forgotten, Dostoevsky writes in 1873, "the

axiom that truth is more poetic than anything in the world, especially in its most pure state; more than that, it is even more fantastic than anything the ordinary mind could fabricate or conceive."[10]
Dostoevsky's tendency to refer to himself as a "poet" and to his
works as "poems" has been noted.[11] "This . . . is a real poem," he
wrote of his projected spiritual-religious epic, "The Life of a Great
Sinner."[12]

Dostoevsky's identification of realism with poetry implies, then,
an infusion into reality of poetic inspiration, poetic idea and truth;
it implies if not a moral transfiguration of that reality, then a focusing of that reality in a poetic (for Dostoevsky always moral-aesthetic) perspective. "Poetic idealization" in the deepest sense
goes beyond indifferent typicalization. Dostoevsky refers to two
characterizations in Leskov's *Cathedral Folk* as "completely unmotivated, unauthenticated monstrosity." Dostoevsky regrets that
the "poet" (the novelist Leskov) scorned the truth that "even negative types exist only as poetic truth, i.e. if the negative type occu-
pies a chief role in the creation, then it must amaze us with its
living energy and force (the Covetous Knight, Richard III, etc.) so
that involuntarily the thought presses upon us: 'Lord, what an
abundance of life, and how vulgar all this is!' "[13] The artistic or poetic rendering of reality, then, is a shaping which is simultaneously
an ordering. There is no room for unmotivated, unauthenticated—
that is, uncontrolled—monstrosity in art.

Dostoevsky's first major statement on type appears in the context of his critique of photographic realism in "Stories of N. V.
Uspensky" (1861). In this essay Dostoevsky essentially affirms
that the photographic approach to reality excludes all possibility
of poetic idealization, generalization, representation of typical
phenomena in art. His essay is a more or less direct response to the
radical socialist Chernyshevsky's review of Uspensky's stories, "Is
It Not the Beginning of a Change?" (1861).[14] In his review Chernyshevsky noted the curious "accidental" quality of Uspensky's
narration; "as for tendency, better not ask anything about it." He
praises Uspensky's rigorously realistic portrayals of the people and
contrasts this picture with the more idealized and softened views
found earlier in Russian literature. The public, according to
Chernyshevsky, likes one quality in Uspensky: "He writes about

the people without any adornment."[15] Chernyshevsky's interest in Uspensky's stories, of course, is social and political, rather than aesthetic; his views accurately reflect the impatient, anti-aesthetic activism of the new generation of radicals. Chernyshevsky, as far as Dostoevsky was concerned, raised the specter of art without transfiguration, art without poetry, art without ideals.[16] Some people—Dostoevsky writes, alluding to Chernyshevsky and the radical critics—wish to see in Uspensky a

> *founder* of some kind of new view in the description of the life of the people, the inventor of some kind of new point of view from which one ought to look at the people. They say: "Mr. Uspensky approaches the people simply, without any prejudices and *previously* composed views; he analyzes a matter *directly, as it is,* because society is still not ready for a correct view of the people and even, at the present state, stands lower than the real concept of the people; and therefore any literary preconceived view will be mistaken. Let us satisfy ourselves with the material, and so on and so forth."[17]

Nature lies unconsciously before us, Dostoevsky points out, and it is just this fact that imposes upon the writer the necessity of presenting his own view of reality. Here Dostoevsky makes a distinction between the writer's "preconceived view" (admittedly "erroneous, although it is difficult for the writer to renounce it") and that view or idea of the writer which emerges from an examination of the accumulated material of reality: this is his *"real* view [*real'ny vzgljad*] which expresses, depending upon the force of the writer, sometimes even the whole of *contemporary* social thought about national life at a given moment."[18] Russian writers, according to Dostoevsky, after examining the material of reality have not feared to express their view of national life and have done so with great typicality and truth. A writer's "real view" is not preconceived; it is embodied in the type. The artist comes and

> conveys to us *his view* of this material [which lies unconsciously before us], and he will tell us what this phenomenon is called, and he will name for us the people participating in it, and sometimes name them so that these names pass into type, and, finally, when everybody believes in this type, then

its name becomes a synonym for all who relate to this type of person. The stronger the artist, the more faithfully and profoundly he will express his thought, his view of a social phenomenon, and the more he will help social consciousness. It goes without saying that almost more important than anything is how the artist himself is capable of looking, what is the substance of his own view—is it humanistic, is the artist himself, finally, perspicacious, a citizen? Herein lies the task and designation of art, and at the same time there is clearly defined also the role which art has in social development.[19]

It is through the type, therefore, that the artist speaks, interprets social reality, and exercises an influence upon social consciousness. This influence, Dostoevsky suggests, will not exceed the inherent artistic strength of the artist himself; on the other hand, the ultimate impact or stature of a work will depend upon *how* the artist is "capable of looking" (artistic vision is not indifferent looking), whether his view is humanistic. There is no contradiction in Dostoevsky's outlook here. Moral humanism for him is an organic attribute of aesthetic consciousness. The artist and the citizen are ideally joined. What he insists upon—as we shall note again—is that the artist function as an artist, in his own sphere of aesthetic consciousness and creation.

The photographic approach to reality results in a mechanical and quantitative approach to the creation of type. But reality resists clear-cut distinctions. "Here now I am striving to reduce our whole prison to categories," the narrator in *Notes from the House of the Dead* remarks apologetically. "But is this possible? Reality is infinitely diverse, compared with all, even the most shrewd deductions of abstract thought, and will never tolerate sharp and sweeping distinctions. Reality strives toward fragmentation" (Pt. II, Ch. 7).[20] The mechanical, cerebral approach to reality, the amassing, categorizing, and codifying of the surface details of reality, lead to what Dostoevsky calls "false and disproportionate typicality."[21] Here there is no question of any "real view" of the material of reality, only a concern with what Dostoevsky in 1873 terms "essences." He writes of the "author-typemakers" who engage in making essences; they mark off for themselves a specialty in literature (the depiction of merchants, peasants, etc.)

and go about with pencil and notebook, eavesdropping and writing down characteristic turns of speech. As soon as the typemaker has need of a merchant or priest in his novel, he selects his language from his notebook. The reader laughs and praises him, and it really seems truthful: it is taken from real life. But all this is worse than a lie, Dostoevsky observes, since the merchant or soldier in the novel speaks in essences, that is, as no single merchant and no single soldier ever speaks in real life. Dostoevsky does not deny the importance of the quantitative element in the creation of type, in the gathering of lexical material. "It is good and useful to write down bits of phrases and one cannot do without this, but one must not use them in a mechanical way."[22] Literal faithfulness to reality is not enough. In his review of Uspensky's stories, Dostoevsky notes, apropos of an exchange between two characters, that "their conversation is true to type [*tipicheski veren*], and you are taken by its reality." But he goes on to complain that at the same time "there isn't any sense in this conversation, there is no special focus, it does not bear on anything in particular and is even '*without any tendency*.' "[23] Indifferent, mechanical typicalization, then, lacking a central and unifying idea or focus, leaves raw, disaggregated reality essentially unchanged. Such typicality must necessarily be false and disproportionate. The rule that the spoken word is silver and the unspoken word golden, Dostoevsky observes in his discussion of author-typemakers, has long been unheeded by Russian artists. "There is little measure," he reflects sorrowfully, "the feeling for measure is fast disappearing."[24]

The formation of type is not a quantitative but a qualitative process. Authentic, poetic type embodies quintessential reality, truth "in its most pure state." In an early essay in 1839 Belinsky expounds a Hegelian view of the "ideal" and "idealization of reality." "The *ideal* is the general (absolute) idea, negating its generality in order to become an individual phenomenon, but once having become one, it again returns to its generality." To idealize reality is not to prettify it, according to Belinsky. "To 'idealize reality' means to express in the individual and finite phenomenon the general and eternal, not by copying accidental phenomena from reality, but by creating *typical* images, indebted in their typicality to a general idea which is expressed in them."[25] We find a similar concept of the "ideal" and of idealization in Dostoevsky's critique of Russian historical and genre painting in 1873. The modern genre painter, he observes, fears the ideal; when confronted, too, with a historical subject he senses he will inevitably have to "idealize" and therefore (in his opinion) to lie. " 'One must depict reality as it is,' they say." But Dostoevsky insists, as we have noted before, that such a "reality" does not exist, that man apprehends nature as it is reflected in his idea, passing through his feelings. "Hence it is necessary to give more leeway to the idea and not to fear the ideal." Dostoevsky cites the example of the portrait painter who scrutinizes his subject before beginning to paint in order to seek out the main idea of his physiognomy. What is the poet doing here, he asks, "if not trusting rather his idea (ideal) than the projecting reality? The ideal, after all, is also reality, just as legitimate as current reality."[26]

Dostoevsky's use of the word *ideal* here instead of *type*—the word he usually uses to connote an imaginatively formed construct or image of reality—reflects the strongly Hegelian roots of his view of the nature of the artistic representation of reality as well as his preoccupation at this point with the fine arts. But for Dostoevsky the Hegelian notion of the "ideal" (to be distinguished, though not really dissociated, from Dostoevsky's concept of the moral and spiritual "ideal") is applicable to literary representation of reality as well as that of the fine arts. "One talks about realism in art," Dostoevsky writes apropos of Javert in Victor Hugo's *Les Misérables*. "Javert is not realism but in the highest degree an ideal-type, but there is nothing more realistic than this ideal-figure."[27] Authentic realism, then, in the Hegelian sense, gives expression to the ideality or ideal of reality. It is in this context of the word and notion of "ideal" that we must understand Dostoevsky's assertion to Maikov (cited previously) that "my idealism is more real than their [realism]." Dostoevsky's criticism of Russian genre painting now comes into focus. Russian genre, he maintains, has "yet to reach the stature of Gogol and Dickens." Genre painting, he writes, is the art of depicting contemporary, current reality which the painter "sees with his own eyes": at this point Dostoevsky pauses with a nota bene. "We say—'saw with our own eyes.' But Dickens never saw Pickwick with his own eyes but only noted him in the diversity of the reality which he observed; he created a person and presented him as the result of his observations. Therefore, this person is just as real as one actually existing, although Dickens only took the ideal of reality."[28]

The relation of the type—whether social or ideal—to reality is indirect: a Pickwick or Onegin is not to be encountered literally in life. On the other hand, the literary type evokes a powerful sense of reality, of concrete, even local, actuality. The playwright A. N. Ostrovsky, Dostoevsky remarks in a letter, portrayed in one of his plays a corner of Moscow life "so typically that it was as though I were sitting and talking with Belotelova." But the mood here is subjunctive, contrary to fact. Of another character Dostoevsky remarks: "I have seen her a thousand times; I was acquainted with her; she came to our house where I lived in Moscow at the age of ten; I remember her." Of still another Ostrovsky character, Dostoevsky observes that he "came out somehow as just a private person. Only true to reality and no more."[29] "Reality" here is, of course, daguerreotype reality, lacking in the ideal.

We find a fairly detailed discussion of the relation of social type to reality in the opening chapter of Part IV in *The Idiot*. "Writers in their novels and stories for the most part try to take social types and to present them in an artistic and picturesque way—types extremely rarely encountered in reality in all their fullness, and which nevertheless are almost more real than reality." Gogol's Podkolesin ("The Marriage") "in his typical form is perhaps even an exaggeration, but by no means a fiction." People recognized their friends in Podkolesin; even before reading Gogol they knew their friends were like Podkolesin; they simply did not know his name. Dostoevsky concludes that "in real life the typicality of people is, as it were, diluted, and all these Georges Dandins and Podkolesins exist in actuality, dart and rush about us every day, but, as it were, in a somewhat watered-down state." Dostoevsky is, of course, quite ready to grant, for "completeness of truth," that an exact replica of Molière's Georges Dandin "might be encountered in real life, but then only rarely." He expresses a similar thought about Stavrogin in one of his letters. Though a Russian and a tragic figure, though belonging to a specific social stratum, though drawn from his own heart, Dostoevsky writes that Stavrogin is nonetheless "a character rarely appearing in all his typicality."[30]

The "Iliad of the ordinary man" who has done nothing in his life will be boring: Alexander Herzen quarrels with this notion, on various grounds, in one of his early works. But the problem is posed, if only in passing.[31] It is the problem of the depiction of precisely "ordinary" people that engages Dostoevsky's particular attention in his discussion of type in *The Idiot*. Podkolesins even in their watered-down state have noteworthy characteristics. But there are people, Dostoevsky observes in *The Idiot,* "about whom it is difficult to say anything which would describe them at once and in their entirety, in their most typical and characteristic aspect; these are the people whom one usually calls 'ordinary' people, the 'majority,' and who really compose the huge majority of any society." These people cannot be ignored without violating verisimilitude, for they are in the majority and form "a necessary link in the connections of human events"; moreover, it would be unreal to fill one's novels only with "strange and odd" people; hence the need, says Dostoevsky, to seek out "interesting and instructive nuances even among ordinary people." What are some of these nuances for Dostoevsky?

> When, for example, the very essence of certain ordinary peo-
> ple consists precisely in daily and perpetual ordinariness, or
> even better, when in spite of the most extraordinary efforts of
> these people at all costs to get out of the rut of humdrum life
> and routine, when they still end up by remaining unchange-
> ably and eternally pedestrian, then such people acquire in-
> deed a certain kind of typicality: as ordinariness which ab-
> solutely will not remain what it is and strenuously wants to
> become original and independent, without having the slight-
> est capacity for independence.[32]

The problem of the "ordinary" type is a fundamental one in Dostoevsky's works, and it touches upon major problem constellations in his thought on Russian man and society. It embraces the petty bourgeois Ganya Ivolgin in *The Idiot* and the narrator-hero of *The Raw Youth,* both of whom nourish ambitions to "rise" out of characterless anonymity; on a higher plane the problem of the "ordinary" type involves the man from the "underground" and the hero of *The Gambler,* both of whom may be taken as symbolic character-images of the educated Russian man divorced from

Russian life, feverishly craving "originality," yet inwardly disfigured by "Russian shapelessness" (*russkoe bezobrazie*). The
problem of featureless human reality broadens out into the problem of featureless—formless, characterless, imitative—Russian reality. The characteristic quality—original quality—of St. Petersburg for Dostoevsky is precisely "its whole lack of character and
impersonality."[33] Russia's "national landscape" is not the sights of
the Crimea or the Caucasus, Dostoevsky recognizes, but the northern and central parts of European Russia. "This 'gaunt nature,'
whose entire typicality consists, so to speak, in its lack of character, is nevertheless dear and precious to us."[34] But Russia's national
landscape—natural, urban, and human—precisely in its "breadth,"
its un-European form, its morally disfigured aspects, is also a
source of pain and distress to Dostoevsky.

The social type for Dostoevsky gives expression to fundamental
problems and aspects of man, society, the nation—problems perti-
nent not only to the moment, but also, sometimes, to the entire future life of the nation. Pushkin's Onegin, a "historical," a "national
type," fully expressed the life of his epoch. In him are expressed
"precisely all those features which might have been expressed only
by a Russian person at a certain moment in his life, precisely that
moment when civilization for the first time was felt by us as life."
But Onegin entered into Russian life and literature. "This type entered, finally, into the consciousness of our whole society and began to be reborn and developed with each generation."[35] Gogol's
artistic types, Dostoevsky wrote, "almost oppress the mind with the
most profound and unbearable questions, evoke in the Russian
mind most disturbing thoughts, with which—one feels this—it may
be possible to cope only in some far-off time; indeed, will we ever
cope with them?"[36] In the final analysis, Pushkin and Gogol, for
Dostoevsky, give expression to the whole problem content of nineteenth-century Russian society.

Dostoevsky's comments to the publisher Katkov on his use of
the actual Nechaev conspiracy in *The Devils* excellently illustrate
how he regarded—from the standpoint of literary type—the material of individual character and incident in real life. Dostoevsky
writes in his letter that one of the major incidents of his story will
be the well-known murder of Ivanov by Nechaev in Moscow. But

he hastens to add that apart from the newspaper accounts he has no further knowledge of Nechaev or Ivanov. *"And even if I did I would not be copying it,"* he writes. "I take only the completed fact. My fantasy may be in the highest degree different from former reality and my Peter Verkhovensky may in no way resemble Nechaev; but it seems to me that in my aroused mind there has been imaginatively created that person, that type which corresponds to this crime." What interests Dostoevsky, then, is not Nechaev himself. "In my opinion these miserable monstrosities are not worth literature."[37] It is rather Nechaev as a social type, as an emblematic anti-hero of his time, that interests Dostoevsky. "The face of *my* Nechaev, of course, does not resemble the face of the real Nechaev," he wrote later in his *Diary of a Writer*. "I wanted to pose the question, and as clearly as possible, in the form of a novel to provide an answer to it: how, in our transitional and amazing contemporary society, are possible, not Nechaev, but the *Nechaevs,* and how could it happen that these *Nechaevs* finally enlisted the Nechaevists?"[38] Dostoevsky's Nechaev, then, as a social type is a focal point for examining a broad social phenomenon in all its moral and spiritual implications for society.

Nechaev-Verkhovensky, of course, in Dostoevsky's final conception and characterization is an extraordinarily original and individualized creation; he is far from being any kind of simple reflection of this or that individual or group in Russian society. He carries in himself an element of nihilism rooted in Russian life, but "taken by himself," Dostoevsky emphatically states in his notebook, he is "still an *accidental and exceptional* being. (Only he considers others to be like him, like himself—and *in this he errs* to a degree of disgusting naïveté.)" This "last Russian conspirator" is "not a socialist, but a rebel, his ideal is rebellion and destruction."[39] Precisely in his weird embodiment of an almost abstract principle of negation, of irrepressible evil, of discord and chaos, Peter Verkhovensky emerges in *The Devils* as a kind of Russian Mephistopheles, an elusive and never-to-be-shaken-off demon. Thus, through the unique prism of the individual with all his socially typical feature and detail, the outlines of a universal archetype are limned. And this is always the case with Dostoevsky's major fictional types.

Dostoevsky's mind moves rapidly and instinctively from local particularity to broad generalization. We may consider as typical Dostoevsky's comments in the May-June 1877 issue of *Diary of a Writer* on two abusive anonymous letters he had received. He immediately takes the opportunity to "say two words in general"— never a sign of brevity in any language—about anonymous letters and about the people who write them. "The fact is that it has seemed to me for quite a while that in our time—so unstable, so transitional, so full of changes, and so unsatisfactory (and so it must be)—there inevitably must have appeared an extraordinary multitude of people who have, so to speak, been ignored, passed by, left without any attention and who are saying with irritation: 'why are *they* everywhere, and not I; why don't they pay attention to me?' "[40] Dostoevsky's analysis of the abusive letter writer has universal applicability. People who are—or who feel—ignored are to be found in all societies and all times. Dostoevsky is interested in the psychological makeup of anonymous letter writers, but his creative interest in the subject as a writer leads him to focus this phenomenon in a broad perspective. In his second installment on the abusive letter writer, Dostoevsky launches into an imaginative reconstruction of the anonymous letter writer as a social type. Such a person, he observes,

> can represent an extraordinarily important literary type in a novel or a story. The principal thing is that here one can and must look at the matter from quite another point of view, from a broad human standpoint, and coordinate it with Russian character in general and with the contemporary current causes among us of this type in particular. Indeed, no sooner do you get to work on this character than you immediately recognize that we cannot help but have such men at present, or, to be more precise, you recognize that it is this kind of man that we most must expect in our time.[41]

We have here a vivid example of Dostoevsky's striving for total focus, an illustration of the epic workings of his creative mind. The unity of the particular with the universal, the immediate problems of Russian man and society with the "broad human standpoint" is characteristic of Dostoevsky's art.

The social type, Dostoevsky suggests in *The Idiot,* is necessarily an intensification, perhaps an exaggeration, of that which is encountered normally in real life. "All art consists in exaggeration to a certain degree," Dostoevsky observed in his review of the Academy of Arts exhibit in 1861, "with the qualification, however, that one does not pass beyond certain limits." The portraitist knows this well. In order to give a strong sense of likeness to a person, the painter will slightly enlarge an already large nose, "but then if you add just a bit more, you get a caricature." Thus, poor portraitists never can cope with ordinary people whose noses are neither too large nor too small and whose mouths and chins are of moderate proportions. An average artist—"not a Gogol"—would never be able to create a successful portrait of Chichikov in *Dead Souls,* who lacks all angularities in character and behavior.[42]

Dostoevsky's remarks on caricature raise the question of the distinction between satirical type, which represents precisely exaggeration of reality to the point of caricature (for example, Gogol's landowners in *Dead Souls*), and artistic type, which represents only a normal degree of intensification (for example, Onegin). Dostoevsky directs himself to this question in some draft variants of his Pushkin speech in 1880. Here he uses the word *type* (though not the notion of typicality) in the sense of caricature, or, in any case, a severely stylized representation of an individual.

> In literature there are types and real persons—the latter representing sober and complete (as far as possible) truth about man. The type rarely consists in a real person, but a real person can appear thoroughly typical (Hamlet, for example). Gogol's Sobakevich is only Sobakevich, Manilov is only Manilov, we do not see real people in them, but we see only those features of these people which the artist wished to evoke. Now Khlestakov, for example, and Dmukhanovsky are already *in part* real persons in spite of all their typicality. And Chichikov is unquestionably a person, although once again not elucidated in his full real truth. . . . The type almost never contains in it full truth because it almost never represents full essence: the truth in it is what the artist wanted to express in this person, and what he wanted to point out. Therefore the type is quite often only half of the truth, and half of the truth

quite often is a lie. Oh, it is not to belittle such a genius as Gogol that I say this! In satire that is even impossible. If he had exhibited in Sobakevich and others purely human features, if Gogol had invested him with the whole real truth, types still would have emerged but would have been weakened and dissolved . . . what was necessary and precisely what Gogol wanted to point out as the typically bad features of Russian man. But to assert that Sobakevich is completely real, that there cannot be anything else in him besides what is shown—means directly to slander the real truth. There is nobody in the whole world who could be regarded as a scoundrel and nothing else.[43]

Despite his deep respect for, and understanding of, the satirical power of Gogol's art, it is clear that Dostoevsky as a writer was drawn to the "real person" in art who is "typical," to the art that expressed full truth as opposed to the art which presented partial truth. One senses this in his comparison of the character-types of the playwright D. I. Fonvizin with Captain Mironov and others in Pushkin's *The Captain's Daughter*. One finds truth in Fonvizin's play *The Minor* (1782), Dostoevsky affirms; the various characters are palpable, belong. Worse people could be found. "And yet you feel that all of them, however many of them there are, better or worse, all of them are truth as local cases, whereas in general, as types of Russian people, they are really falsehood. Why is this so?" Again, as in the discussion of Gogol's satirical types, Dostoevsky affirms that Fonvizin's types represent falsehood in the broader sense because "full truth remains unexpressed, because half a truth is a lie." Full truth would have exhibited Mrs. Prostakova and her family in a reconciling light. In words which express his own artistic ideal, Dostoevsky notes: "Because only in real truth can the artist set forth the whole essence of the matter and its truth, point out finally the source of the evil, compel you yourself to recognize the 'extenuating circumstances.' "[44] Dostoevsky finds the realization of this ideal in Pushkin. "The appointed purpose [of Pushkin] was to utter the *full* truth about Russian man, which we so rarely hear."[45]

In his discussion of Pushkin's *The Captain's Daughter* Dostoevsky emphasizes the full "truthfulness of the images, the truthfulness of the truth which they depict . . . a truthfulness before which all thought about idealization, about partiality or passion on the part of the poet, disappears, vanishes into nothingness; while on the other hand the Russian man, the Russian spirit is justified." Dostoevsky finds an authentic Russian type in Captain Mironov, as opposed to the Prostakovas. With reference to Captain Mironov's dramatic confrontation with the rebel chief Pugachev, Dostoevsky remarks: "And not for a single moment does the thought flash through your head that this is only a local instance and not the entire Russian common man in the huge majority" or "that all simple Russian people would not act in this way."[46]

Dostoevsky's preference for the "whole truth" of Pushkin's realism reflects his passionate idealism, his search for unity, form, beauty in life and art. He certainly did not find the whole truth embodied in Gogol's art. Gogol's art, as we have seen, evoked in Dostoevsky "disturbing thoughts," almost despair. (The troubled reaction of poor Devushkin to Gogol was a hint.) Whether Gogol believed in something finer than he depicted, whether he too, like Dostoevsky, passionately wanted to hear and utter the "whole truth" about Russian man is another question. What is certain is that in his art Russian man and the Russian spirit are not justified in the sense that Dostoevsky found them justified in Pushkin. The half-truth of Gogol's satirical types in *Dead Souls* remains for the reader—in his enchanted subjection to Gogol—the whole truth of Russian reality.

Type for Dostoevsky is the artistic medium through which the artist reveals the dynamics of reality, the configuration not only of the past, but also of the future, as it is disclosed in the indications of the present. But can we speak of a type in art if it has not already made its full appearance in reality, if it is not fully recognizable and identifiable in real life? These questions are raised by the writer Ivan Goncharov, author of *Oblomov* (1859), in an exchange of letters with Dostoevsky in 1874. Goncharov's critical interest is centered on Dostoevsky's portrayal of a priest in a sketch "Little Pictures," a version of which first appeared in an anthology, *Skladchina,* in 1874.[47] Dostoevsky's priest is portrayed so sharply and maliciously (in Goncharov's view) as to strike one as a slander:

It seems without verisimilitude, although, perhaps, there are such people (I hardly know anyone of this kind). You say yourself that "such a type is being born"; forgive me if I permit myself to note a contradiction here: if it is being born, then it is still not a *type*. You know better than I that a type is formed through long and numerous repetitions or accumulations of phenomena and persons in which the likenesses of various and sundry participate over a period of time, and finally [the type] becomes established, hardened, and grows familiar to the observer. A work of art (I mean the work of art of an objective artist such as you, for example) can only appear, in my opinion, after life has set; it does not harmonize with life that is coming into existence.[48]

Dostoevsky's letter of reply to Goncharov has not been preserved. It would appear from Goncharov's second letter, however, that Dostoevsky initially, at least, defended the actual existence of such priests. "Probably I didn't express myself clearly enough in my letter," Goncharov begins his reply. "I in no way wished to say that I had not seen this type and that therefore he did not exist or was unfaithfully drawn by you." Goncharov confesses that he doesn't get about and is unfamiliar with contemporary types of Russian society. He affirms that he took the priest for slander simply because he had all the marks of the nihilist whip, on the one hand, and appeared like a worldly Bourbon abbé, on the other. "You say that this type, perhaps, has been existing, but that we have not noticed it. But if we . . . that is, *all of us,* have not noticed him, then he is not a type." "By type I understand something very rooted, established for a long, long time," Goncharov reiterates, "and forming sometimes a series of generations." He cites the playwright Ostrovsky as an example of an artist who depicted only types of merchant-autocrats rooted in Russian life, while ignoring those in the process of formation, "because they are still not types, but new moons—and we don't know what will come of them, what they are being transformed into, and in what features they will take final form for a more or less extended time."[49]

Goncharov's peculiarly heavy emphasis upon the artist as a depictor of "established," "hardened," "set" forms is perhaps characteristic of an artist whose supreme artistic achievement lay in an extraordinary portrayal of a representative of the old social order, a type approaching—in a psychological and social sense—absolute stasis. Yet Goncharov's theory of the social type, with its solid foundation of sociological determinism, if accepted as dogma, would limit the scope of the writer to the role of historian of the fixed forms and imagery of society. The central focus of Dostoevsky's realism—even if we limit ourselves to a sociological perspective—is man and society in movement, in a state of social upheaval. Behind the opposition, here, of two theories of social type lie two different social realities, or rather, social reality viewed in two different perspectives. Of interest in this connection is Dostoevsky's comparison in his *Diary of a Writer* in 1877 of two episodes: one from Tolstoy's semi-autobiographical work, "Childhood and Boyhood," depicting a moment of childish despair and rebellion in the hero, and the other from a letter describing the suicide of a twelve-year-old boy, from a social background very different from that of Tolstoy's hero. The two episodes reveal certain elements in common, Dostoevsky acknowledges, but nonetheless in the latter episode "there are also features of some new reality, quite different now from that which existed in the tranquil and stable, long-established Moscow landowner's family of the middle-upper stratum, of which Count Tolstoy was our *historian*." Tolstoy appeared at that moment when the old Russian gentry order faced a "new, still unknown, but radical crisis, at least a tremendous rebirth into new and still future, almost quite unknown forms."[50]

Dostoevsky compares the reactions of the boy who committed suicide with Tolstoy's young hero. The latter could dream about suicide, but only dream, for the "strict order of the historically formed family of the nobility" would prevent him from moving from dream to action. But the other boy *"dreamed and then acted."* Dostoevsky stresses that he speaks not just about the present epidemic of suicides. And at this point he makes an appeal for the broadening of the Russian realistic novel.

> One feels that here something is wrong, that a huge portion of the Russian social order has remained quite without observation and without a *historian*. At least it is clear that the life of the middle and upper stratum of our gentry, so vividly depicted by our belletrists, is already a quite insignificant and

isolated corner of Russian life. But who will be the historian of the other corners which, it seems, are so frightfully numerous. And if in this chaos—in which for a long time, but now especially, there exists a social life—if in this chaos it is yet impossible even perhaps for an artist of Shakespearean dimensions to seek out a normal law and guiding thread, then at the very least who will illuminate at least a part of this chaos, even without dreaming about a guiding thread? Chiefly, it seems that nobody is at all concerned with the matter; it all appears premature for our greatest artists. We have among us, without doubt, a disintegrating life and, therefore, a disintegrating family. But there is, necessarily, also a life that is forming itself anew on new foundations. Who will note it, who will point it out? Who even in the smallest degree can define and express the laws of this disintegration and of that which is being created anew? Or is it too early? But of the old, too, of that which is past—has it all been noted?[51]

It was Dostoevsky himself, of course, who undertook in his art to express the new social chaos, to seek out its "normal law and guiding thread," its characteristic features, and its new emergent types; and he accomplished this task (perhaps he inwardly sensed this) in Shakespearean dimensions. His remarks that we just cited appear a direct response to Goncharov who had insisted in an essay in 1871 that "art, a serious and strict one, cannot depict chaos, disintegration." Goncharov again expressed the view that art can depict "only a life fixed in some image." Art must present "a constant, definite image of a form of life." Like Dostoevsky, Goncharov acknowledges that the old order with its people (types) has outlived itself, but he maintains that "the new paths have not yet been established." And he concludes, pessimistically, that "art has as yet nothing to rest upon."[52] The fundamental question that Goncharov raised here was, in substance, not a new one to Dostoevsky. He had asked that question through Ippolit Terentiev in *The Idiot,* namely: "Can one perceive as an image that which has no image?" But the question, though abstractly posed, is raised in the context of a discussion of visual representation or perception of phenomena (painting, dreams), not of literature. In the realm of the visual arts Dostoevsky tended to answer Terentiev's question with a (perhaps uncertain) no; in the realm of literature Dostoevsky's answer was certainly yes. And this yes is uttered first of all in his novels.

The chaos overtaking Russian society was, in Dostoevsky's view, apocalyptic in nature. We have noted his view—expressed in the notebooks to *The Raw Youth*—that Russian society was without "foundations," was being overwhelmed by a colossal eruption. "All is crumbling, falling, being negated, as though it had not even existed. And not only externally, as in the West, but *internally, morally.*" In these same notebooks he makes it clear that he considers the life depicted in his novels to be the central, the real reality of Russian life. To those who accused him of leading the reader into a "stuffy and gloomy underground" inhabited by unreal people, to those who attacked him for giving a "too exceptional and one-sided view of life," to those who saw in his work evidence of "a complete ignorance of real life," Dostoevsky answered in his notebook: "*My* life is the life that is the general rule. Future generations who will be more dispassionate will be convinced of this, *the truth will be mine, I believe this.*" "Tolstoy, Goncharov thought that they depicted the *life of the majority;* in my opinion, however, they depicted the *life of the exceptions.*"[53] The life of the majority —the life of those for whom "there has been no life"—was disfigured. In a revealing passage in his notebook, Dostoevsky points to the "underground" type as the embodiment of the morally and psychologically disfigured majority.

> I am proud that I was the first to bring forward the real man of the Russian majority and the first to expose *his disfigured and tragic side. The tragedy consists in the consciousness of disfiguration.* . . . Only I brought out the *tragedy of the underground,* consisting in *suffering, in self-punishment, in the consciousness of something better and in the impossibility of achieving it* and chiefly in the vivid conviction of these unfortunates that everybody is in this situation, and therefore it is not worth even trying to reform. What is there to support those who reform? A reward, faith? There are rewards from no one, faith in nobody. Another step from here, and one is at extreme debauchery, crime (murder). Mystery.

Such was Dostoevsky's own view of his supreme achievement. His art, he believed, was a profoundly truthful revelation—though without marring the ideal!—of disfigured Russian reality. "The underground, the underground, the poet of the underground!" he continues in his notebook. "The feuilletonists repeat this as something degrading for me. Fools, this is *my glory, because truth is here.*"[54]

Dostoevsky recognized the disfigured and chaotic character of the "new reality" and of the "Russian majority" forming that reality. He saw clearly that the typical hero of that world was different from the gentry heroes of Tolstoy or Goncharov. He recognized the need for a realism that would cope with a "disintegrating life." But how did Dostoevsky reconcile his classical higher aesthetic with the demands of a realism that essentially called for a new aesthetic of disfiguration? The evidence suggests that he was unable to resolve the dilemma raised by the conflict of two conflicting aesthetic philosophies. Of particular interest in this connection is the letter of Arkady Dolgoruky's former teacher at the conclusion of *The Raw Youth*. The letter brings into sharp focus Dostoevsky's special view of his realism and the problem of the representation of type in the new reality.

Arkady Dolgoruky, himself a "type," a representative of the disintegrating family in Russian society, sent his former teacher his "Notes"—the manuscript, essentially, of *The Raw Youth*. In the letter of reply his former teacher comments on the problems, in reality the dilemma, faced by the novelist who would depict the chaotic moral and social reality of the type from the "accidental" family. The problems of such a novelist are contrasted, at the outset, with the situation of the more conventional novelist who stays within the mainstream of the Russian novel, who confines himself to the depiction of the gentry family with its "family traditions and beautiful finished forms" and its "beautiful types."

"If I were a Russian novelist and had talent," writes the educator, "I would without question take my heroes from the Russian hereditary nobility, because only in this type of cultured Russian people is possible at least the appearance of beautiful order and the beautiful impression, so necessary in a novel for a refining impact upon the reader." Arkady Dolgoruky's teacher insists that he is not joking and observes that Pushkin long ago had noted the subject of his future Russian novels in "Traditions of the Russian family" (Ch. III, Stanza 13 in *Eugene Onegin*):

> And believe me, here is to be found everything that has ever been beautiful among us. In any case here is everything that has ever attained any sort of perfection among us. I don't say this because I am unconditionally in agreement with the correctness and truthfulness of this beauty; but here, for example, were finished forms of honor and duty which, outside the nobility, are not only not to be found in finished form anywhere in Russia, but have not even begun to take shape anywhere. I speak as a tranquil man and as one seeking tranquility. Whether this honor is the good kind and whether this duty rings true—this is a secondary question; but most important of all for me is precisely the finished quality of the forms, and at least some kind of order, and not prescribed, but lived through, finally, by ourselves. God, what is really more important than anything else among us is some kind of order, any kind of order, but let it be our own at last! Herein consists all hope and, so to speak, tranquility; at least something, finally, that is structured, but not this everlasting upheaval, not splinters flying everywhere, not rubbish and trash, out of which nothing at all has come in two hundred years. (Pt. III, Ch. 13, Sec. iii)

The letter writer is an educator: his concern is frankly moral and didactic; he seeks, above all, form, beauty, tranquility. Where can we locate Dostoevsky in these observations? It is certainly not Dostoevsky the novelist who desires to take his heroes from the aesthetically and morally formed world of the gentry. Yet we cannot but recognize Dostoevsky in the letter writer's characterization of the moral-aesthetic environment of the Russian "family" novel, in the importance he ascribes to Pushkin in the history of the Russian novel, in his positive evaluation of the role of aesthetic culture in Russian life, in his almost despairing aesthetic humanism.

The views of Dostoevsky, moreover, are fully reflected in the letter writer's candid recognition (for all his preference for the good and the beautiful) that the development of Russian society has undermined the foundations of the "beautiful type" (Tolstoy's "lofty type," as Versilov expresses it in a draft variant to *The Raw Youth*).[55] No longer does the trash gravitate to the upper class of people where it is absorbed, according to the letter writer, but, on the contrary, the "beautiful type" is disintegrating and pieces are falling into the disorderly mass below. The Russian social-economic order is in a state of profound upheaval. "The beautiful type no longer exists in our time, and if fragments remain, then, according to prevailing opinions now, they bring no beauty with them." In an obvious reference to Tolstoy's *War and Peace,* the letter writer observes that one still might write in the historical genre and depict a multitude of "extraordinarily pleasant and joyful details." "Such a work, if executed by a great talent, however, would belong not so much to Russian literature as to Russian history. It would be a picture, artistically finished, of a Russian mirage, but one which really existed, until people guessed what it was—a mirage." The "grandson of these heroes" (a clear reference to Levin in *Anna Karenina*) could be depicted in his "contemporary type no other than in a somewhat misanthropic, solitary, and unquestionably melancholy aspect." But such a hero would be without a field of action. "Looking further ahead—even this grandson-misanthrope will disappear; new persons will appear, still unknown, and a new mirage; but just what kind of people? If they are not beautiful, then the distant Russian novel is impossible. But alas! Will it only be the novel that will be impossible then?"

The mood of this letter writer varies from poignant hope to poignant pessimism. The bell tolls not alone for the classical Russian novel, but for the whole society with which it is intimately associated; it tolls, perhaps, for beauty, for form itself. A widening abyss lies between Russian culture with its beautiful forms and the unstructured existence of what Dostoevsky calls the "Russian majority." The letter writer speaks of this tragedy of Russian culture. Boris Pasternak's *Dr. Zhivago* is in many respects the bitter epilogue to this tragedy. Dostoevsky believed fervently, at least in one part of his deeply divided being, in the creative power of the people who inhabited the abyss; he believed that the peasant had preserved the image of beauty even in the midst of his degradation. Pasternak looks at the people, the masses, without illusions. In *Dr. Zhivago* old Russian culture with its beauty and forms vanishes in the "everlasting upheaval" of Russian life.[56]

The path of the old realism of the nests of gentry folk, then, leads to a dead end. But the novelist who would depict the new reality and the type from the disintegrating family faces special problems. His task is not an enviable one.

> The type of this accidental family is shown, in part, even by you in your manuscript. Yes, Arkady Makarovich, you are *a member of an accidental family,* in contrast to our still recent gentry types who had a childhood and youth so different from yours. I confess that I would not like to be a novelist of the hero of an accidental family! It would be unrewarding work and without beautiful forms. And what is more, these types in any case are still a matter of current reality [*eshche delo tekushchee*] and therefore cannot be artistically finished. Great mistakes are possible, exaggerations, oversights are possible. In any case, one would have to guess at far too much. But then what else can the writer do who does not want to write in the historical genre alone and who is gripped by a yearning for the current? Guess and—make mistakes.

These lines are of extraordinary interest when examined in the light of Dostoevsky's polemic with Goncharov on the question of type. The letter writer affirms that the type of the "accidental" family—precisely a transitional, emerging type—cannot be "artistically finished," can have no beauty of form. Is Dostoevsky parodying Goncharov's views here—the Goncharov who believed that the notion of a transitional type is a contradiction of the very idea of type? In part, yes.[57] But is not Dostoevsky also expressing, though obliquely, various elements of (and contradictions in) his own point of view? Is there not a recognition here that Goncharov was not *entirely* wrong in maintaining that an emergent type must necessarily lack full verisimilitude? Truth in art, Dostoevsky insisted, is inseparable from form, artistry; an image or type that is artistically unfinished cannot be a full type, a total embodiment of truth. In the case of the transitional type like Arkady Dolgoruky in *The Raw Youth,* the image (type) is unformed both in an aesthetic sense (it has not had time to take full shape) and in a moral sense (it partakes of the current disorder). It follows that the representation of the transitional type in literature cannot be "artistically finished."

The letter writer further suggests—and here too we may ask whether he is expressing Dostoevsky's views—that from the vantage point of a writer in the future the beautiful representation of such a disfigured type as Arkady Makarovich would be possible. Such "Notes" as yours, the educator writes at the conclusion of his letter, "might serve as material for a future artistic work, for a future picture of a disordered but by then long-vanished epoch. Oh, when the frenzy of the present passes and the future arrives, then the future artist will seek out beautiful forms even for the depiction of past disorder and chaos." The writer, in other words, looking back on the accidental type that is *now* emerging, necessarily will see that type in the perspective of its full development, in its completed form. The writer will then be a historian of social reality in the Goncharov sense. He will be dealing, essentially, with *historical* reality. In the novel of the future—the historical novel about the type from the disintegrating family—everything will be explained, everything will be commensurate, proportionate with the future, and the writer will be in a position to seek out and embody with artistic perfection what Dostoevsky termed the "ideal of reality." We are pursuing here the logic of Dostoevsky's own thought.

"But . . . what else can the writer do who does not want to write in the historical genre alone, and who is gripped by a yearning for the current? Guess and—make mistakes."

Artistic perfection in the depiction of transitional or emergent types, Dostoevsky appears to concede, is unattainable; but in that spirit of contradiction that pervades so many of his fervent beliefs, he insists that no other choice is open to artists of the contemporary but to "guess and—make mistakes." All art—we must remember—from one point of view for Dostoevsky is a guessing, a divining of the "subsurface unexpressed future Word." The notion that the authentic artist reveals hidden types was expressed directly by Dostoevsky in his critique of author-typemakers in 1873.

Our artists (like any group of ordinary people), [he wrote,] begin clearly to note the phenomena of reality, to give attention to their characteristic features, and to work out a given type in art only when for the most part it is passing and disappearing, being reborn into something else in accordance with the course of the epoch and its development. . . .

> Only the writer-genius, or at least a very strong talent, guesses
> a type *on time* and presents him *in time,* whereas mediocrity
> only follows in his footsteps more or less slavishly and works
> according to prepared patterns.[58]

Nonetheless, Dostoevsky's final position on the question of the
depiction of transitional type would appear to be a somewhat more
complex or compromising one than is evident in his observations
of 1873. In this connection we may inquire whether Dostoevsky's
oblique apology for the absence of "artistic finish" and "beautiful
forms" in the depiction of transitional type is not rooted in his failure to resolve the contradiction between his classical higher aesthetic, with its deeply moral conception of form, and his practical
writer's aesthetic, which sought out the inner form and rhythms of
a "reality [which] strives toward fragmentation." Privately in his
notebooks Dostoevsky proclaimed the special achievement of his
realism to be the representation in art of the disfigured "underground." At the same time his higher aesthetic made it difficult for
him to acknowledge beauty or form in disfiguration. His own
strange feeling of insecurity as an *artist* (here contrasted with
poet) was undoubtedly deepened by his tendency to identify artistry with the values of classical form. For no matter how successfully
he conveyed images of a disfigured and disintegrating reality, the
beauty symbolized by the sculptured images of antique art, of Raphael or Pushkin, remained for him the norm of artistic perfection,
the sublime ideal in art. It is not surprising, therefore, that Dostoevsky gave so much thought to the creation in art of positive
types—both sacred and lay figures which might embody the lofty
ideals of the past and prefigure their fulfillment in the future.

" 'Positive' types are almost never successfully conceived by our
poets," Dostoevsky observed in 1873.[59] "The beautiful is an ideal,"
he noted at the time he was working on the image of Prince Myshkin in *The Idiot,* "and the ideal is still far from being achieved
either by us or by civilized Europe."[60] The absolutely good and
beautiful is beyond man's reach, but man expresses his passion for
that ideal in art and religion. Dostoevsky writes Apollon Maikov
in 1870 that he wants to introduce into one part of his proposed
work, "The Life of a Great Sinner," the person of Tikhon Zadon-

sky (a religious figure of the eighteenth century noted for his great humility), "of course under another name." Dostoevsky hopes that he will "bring forth a grand, *positive* sacred figure. This is no Konstanzhoglo and not the German [Stolz] (I forget his name) in *Oblomov*. Who can tell: perhaps precisely this Tikhon here is our Russian *positive* type which our literature is seeking, but not a Lavretsky, not a Chichikov, not a Rakhmetov and the others."[61] Dostoevsky's Tikhon, obviously, is a rare person in real life. How is it possible to speak of him as a type? What is Dostoevsky's concept of ideal (i.e. spiritually positive or beautiful) type?

Dostoevsky touches on the question of the ideal type in one of his articles on Russian literature in 1861. Here he attacks as false the point of view that Pushkin's monk-chronicler Pimen in *Boris Godunov* has nothing of the national spirit because he is an invented, made-up personality, because such humble truth-loving chroniclers allegedly did not exist in the period depicted. Dostoevsky insists that even if this were true the Pushkin chronicler would not cease to be an authentic old Russian personage. "Can we really say that there are no elements of Russian life and nationality in him because he is historically inauthentic? What about poetic truth?" Truth is always poetic for Dostoevsky. "Is it possible that the *Iliad* is not a national ancient Greek poem because all the personages in it obviously are re-created from folk legends and even, perhaps, invented?"[62] The notion of poetic truth is opposed here to concrete historical truth in the same way that artistic truth in the discussion of Jacoby's painting is opposed to "actual" or "natural" truth. Literal or surface reality, whether contemporary or historical, therefore, does not necessarily reveal concrete embodiments of national spirit or ideal.

The character of Tatyana in *Eugene Onegin,* according to Dostoevsky, is true, if not to literal historical reality, then to Russian spiritual reality. Tatyana, the chronicler Pimen, and other figures in Pushkin's works, Dostoevsky observed at the end of his life, are "artistic types of Russian beauty which came directly from the Russian spirit."[63] Dostoevsky was wont to defend the *actual* existence in reality of counterparts to his heroes (e.g. Myshkin); in the case of Tatyana and some of the heroines of Turgenev and Tolstoy, Dostoevsky insisted on one occasion that "if the ideals of such beauty were incarnated in art, then they were taken from somewhere, not composed out of nothing. Hence, such women also exist in reality."[64] But the reality of these ideal types is ultimately a question of poetic truth for Dostoevsky. It is ridiculous, he writes in 1861, to ask: " 'where now is the Russian family which Pushkin wanted to depict, wherein is its Russian spirit, just what was there Russian that he depicted?' The answer is plain: one must have at least a little understanding of poetry."[65]

In Dostoevsky's view the ideal or positive figure is a type in that he embodies a universal ideal, spirit, or striving in the heart of man —but in the heart of Russian man, the Russian people in particular. The universal spiritual and religious ideal for Dostoevsky is national in form. This idea is expressed particularly succinctly by Shatov in *The Devils*. "Do I reduce God to the attribute of the national?" he asks; "on the contrary, I raise the people to God. The people—this is a divine body." The characteristic of all great peoples (Jews, Greeks, and others), he believes, consists in their having their own special God to the exclusion of others.

Versilov's concept of an élite Russian cultural type (consisting of perhaps no more than a thousand people), though an aristocratic one, reflects certain elements in Dostoevsky's conception of ideal type. "Among us has been created through the ages a kind of lofty cultural type never seen anywhere, and the like of which is not to be found in the whole world—a type [marked by a feeling] of a universal compassion for all. This is a Russian type. . . . It preserves in itself the future of Russia" (Pt. III, Ch. 7 Sec. iii). Alyosha Karamazov would seem to belong to—or at least have characteristics of—this type. Dostoevsky describes him in his foreword to *The Brothers Karamazov* as "a strange man, even an eccentric [*chudak*]." He admits that "in the majority of cases an eccentric is a local and isolated instance." But he insists that this is not always the case and that it often happens that the eccentric "carries in himself sometimes the very heart of the whole, while the rest of the people of his epoch, everybody, have for some reason been torn from it temporarily as if by some gust of wind." Alyosha lives in his epoch, is nourished by national religious ideals, but is in essence an ideal type, a type of future Russian man.

Zosima in *The Brothers Karamazov* was Dostoevsky's supreme effort to embody the ideal type in literature. He wrote that he took the "person and figure [of Zosima] from ancient Russian monks and saints: in profound humility [and filled with] naïve, bound-less hopes about the future of Russia, about its moral and even its political destiny."[66] Dostoevsky recognizes that Zosima is a poetic creation, yet he is very much concerned with convincing the reader of the reality of that creation. Here both art and religion are put to the test. Christ's teaching alone will not save us, Dostoevsky had written in his notebook earlier, but rather the belief that the Word will become flesh, that here is the final ideal, the whole em-bodied Word, God embodied. It is this kind of embodiment that Dostoevsky strives to achieve in his creation of Zosima; if he suc-ceeds with Zosima, he writes, he will *"compel* people *to admit* that the pure, ideal Christian is not an abstract matter but real in image, possible, ready to present itself to the eye, that Christianity is the only refuge for the Russian land from all its evils."[67]

Dostoevsky felt considerable uncertainty over his creation of Zosima. In 1879 he writes K. P. Pobedonostsev that he must rebut the atheistic propositions advanced in his novel, not point by point, but indirectly, in the form of an artistic picture. But he is troubled: will he be understood? "And here, moreover, there are still the obligations of artistry: it was necessary to present a humble and grand figure, whereas life is full of comedy and only grand in its inner sense, so that willy-nilly because of artistic demands, I was compelled in the biography of my monk to touch upon some of the more banal aspects so as not to violate artistic realism."[68] We have here, of course, an indirect acknowledgment of the im-possibility of creating a worldly image of ideal goodness and beauty. "The most lofty beauty is not without, but within," Do-stoevsky jotted down in his notebook to *The Brothers Karamazov*, adding: "Cf. Goethe, *Faust,* Part II." "Artistic demands," of course, did compel him to present Zosima in terms of some natural evolution from a secular to a wholly spirit-oriented existence, but the element of compulsion which entered into Dostoevsky's creative endeavor (directed at both the image of Zosima and the reader) attests to a certain unnaturalness, perhaps, in the whole enterprise. Artistic realism is served—but served mechanically. Dostoevsky —to borrow from his own critique of Gogol the raisonneur—is here "simply weak, and not even representative." He is carried away by the moral-religious didactic element in Zosima. Yet even in this realm Dostoevsky defends himself in a characteristic way.

"There are several didactic discourses of the monk over which people will shout out that they are absurd, because they are too ecstatic. Of course, they are absurd, in the everyday sense, but in another sense, an inner one, they seem truthful."[69] Truthful in an abstract sense, yes—but not "real in image," not artistically compelling.

"In the world there is only one positively beautiful person—Christ," Dostoevsky wrote in 1868.[70] In Christ the notion of the "ideal" as model or archetype perfectly coincides with the related notion of ideal as the embodiment of absolute moral or spiritual perfection. Dostoevsky recognizes with Renan that Christ is an "inaccessible type," one that can never be repeated.[71] The conception of Christ as a type lies at the basis of Dostoevsky's critique of N. N. Gué's portrayal of Christ in his painting, "The Lord's Supper." In his critique—in his *Diary of a Writer* in 1873—Dostoevsky distinguishes at the outset between two kinds of reality in art: contemporary, current reality (that of genre painting) and historical reality. "Historical reality . . . in art, of course, is not the same as current (genre)—precisely in the sense that it is completed and not current." In imagining a past event, and particularly a distant, completed, historical event, "the event *unfailingly* presents itself in its completed form, that is, with the supplement of its whole subsequent development which has not been taking place at that precise historical moment when the artist is trying to imagine the person or the events." It is for this reason, Dostoevsky maintains, that the artist cannot depict the event precisely as it occurred. Many artists, according to Dostoevsky, fearing that they will have to idealize—which in the artist's view means to lie—seek a way out by fusing the current and the historical realities. But the result of this is worse than any lie.

Such a lie, Dostoevsky feels, is Gué's painting. This is genre painting: here is depicted an ordinary quarrel between most ordinary people. "Here sits Christ, but is this really Christ?" Dostoevsky asks. He might be a very good young man, upset by a quarrel with Judas, but all this is not the Christ whom we know. "Where now are the succeeding eighteen centuries and what have these to do with the matter?" The painting does not explain how it was possible that from this ordinary quarrel between such ordinary people —as depicted by Gué—something so colossal could take place.[72]

Dostoevsky, of course, is offended by what appears to him to be a secular treatment of a religious subject. But the heart of his criticism, as in the case of his critique of Jacoby's painting, is aesthetic: the painter attempted to depict Christ outside the idea (ideal) of Christ. Gué's Christ, very simply, is not typical; he is not the Christ we know through the centuries, because He is divorced from His idea. "Here nothing at all is explained," Dostoevsky complains, "here there is no historical truth; here there is not even any genre truth." Dostoevsky sums up his critique with the extraordinary words: everything "comes out quite incommensurate, quite disproportionate with the future." Everything is false and "all falseness is a lie and far from being any kind of realism." "Mr. Gué," Dostoevsky concludes sarcastically, "was chasing after realism."[73]

When we attentively examine Dostoevsky's critique of Gué's painting we recognize that his demand for fidelity to the future (in the depiction of Christ) is in fact no more than his usual insistence that an event or person, ideological or spiritual phenomenon be portrayed in the context of a dynamically conceived reality—both concrete Russian social reality and that universal "subsurface" reality whose beginnings and ends are a mystery to man. The artist of a "historical" subject *knows* his subject in the entirety of its development (idea); Dostoevsky demands, as we have seen, that the artist of the contemporary scene approach his theme in its development; such an artist cannot know the future, but he must, artistically, *guess,* capture a social type "on time" and "in time." Dostoevsky in this sense imposes a most difficult task upon the artist: he must be a historian of the future.

"I have come to the irrefutable conclusion," Dostoevsky wrote in a letter in 1876, "that a writer of belles lettres, besides the poem must know to the tiniest detail (historical and current) the reality depicted by him."[74] But the details of reality, as we have noted, cannot substitute for the "poem." The poetic idea forms and organizes the material of reality. Type for Dostoevsky is the fruit of this forming, of "poetic idealization"; it embodies the quintessential idea of reality. Its function for Dostoevsky is first of all cognitive, and its social usefulness wholly resides in its cognitive function. The problem content and the spiritual ideals of reality, poetically visualized (formed) by the artist, come back to reality in type and serve, in turn, to educate and re-form man.

"Is THERE SOMETHING absolutely useful on this earth and in this life where we are?" doubtfully asks Théophile Gautier in the preface to his novel *Mademoiselle de Maupin*. And he replies: "joy seems to me the end of life and the only useful thing in the world." "The truly beautiful in life serves nothing"—he flings out at the crude utilitarian spirit of his age.[1] Dostoevsky also guards beauty against crude utilitarianism (though of a different kind), but nothing is more uncharacteristic of him than a detached epicurean or purely "aesthetic" view of life or beauty; nothing is more alien to him than a disjunction between beauty and humanism. Art and beauty are inseparable from man, he insisted in "Mr. —bov and the Question of Art." Historical facts indicate, he wrote, that "from the beginning of the world to the present, art has never left man, always has answered his needs and his ideal, always has helped him in seeking out this ideal, was born with man, developed together with his historical life, and died together with his historical life."[2]

The historic function of art for Dostoevsky—a function which wholly derives from its nature as beauty, form—is the aesthetic education of man. Art embodies man's highest ideals, gives order and form to reality; in turn art forms man, gives moral culture to both individual and nation. The universal, historic function of art is also the immediate, practical function of art. Dostoevsky recalls approvingly the last period of Belinsky's life when literature organically entered into life, "brought splendid fruits," educated "a whole new generation." The present time, he writes in 1861, is "a most literary one: in a word, a time for growth, education, self-consciousness, a time for moral development which we still lack too much." "I have always believed in the force of the humane, aesthetically expressed impression," Dostoevsky continues. These impressions accumulate and with education penetrate into the heart itself, "into the very essence, and form man. The word—the word is a great enterprise! And other forms of education take better hold in the man who is formed, more humane. But just this man is still not quite formed among us—this is the misfortune!"[3]

Form and humanity for Dostoevsky are interchangeable concepts. Man finds in art the symbol and embodiment of his own completion, ideal form, humanity. The road of aesthetics—as Schiller observed in his philosophical letters *On the Aesthetic Education of Man*—must be pursued, because man makes his way to freedom through beauty (Second Letter). True freedom, as Dostoevsky indicates in his representation of Myshkin's highest moment of "beauty and prayer," is achieved not outside of form but precisely in form and through form. The highest freedom is thus coincident with structuring. Art in this sense is embodied freedom.

Dostoevsky's concept of the aesthetic "usefulness" of art is first developed in "Mr. —bov and the Question of Art." Dobrolyubov had, in effect, placed a time limit on the usefulness of beauty, declaring the vanity of all efforts to evoke the beauty of a person who is but a naked skull. "The gods of the Greeks may have been beautiful in ancient Greece, but they are disgusting in French tragedies and in our odes of the past century."[4] Dostoevsky's position is simple. "Beauty is always useful." "Beauty is useful because it is beauty."[5]

But Dostoevsky is at pains to relate the aesthetic "usefulness" of art to the concrete world and to the contemporary affairs of men. The "lofty beauty" of the Apollo of Belvedere, he suggests, could perhaps have such a powerful impact upon a young man that it might have an unconscious influence upon him during some great social event in which the young man played a leading role. Historical facts, according to Dostoevsky, suggest that Corneille and Racine made their influence felt at decisive moments in the historical life of the people. Going back even further into the past, Dostoevsky ventures that even *The Iliad* might be useful in resolving contemporary questions. In modern times, times of strivings, struggles, hesitations, Dostoevsky believes *The Iliad* with its "eternal harmony" might have a decisive influence on the soul. "Our spirit is now highly receptive, the influence of beauty, harmony, and strength might act on it in a grand and beneficial way, *usefully* act on it, instill energy, support our strength."[6]

Dostoevsky placed great stress in his various critical writings on the role that literature played in Russian national development. "Is it possible . . . that the Marquis de Posa, Faust, and the rest were useless to Russian society in its development and will not still

be useful?" he asks in his critique of Dobrolyubov. All this literature, Dostoevsky believed, brought Russia to "contemporary questions."[7]

Dostoevsky viewed Russian literature, in turn, as "one of the
chief manifestations of Russian conscious life," the only truly organic manifestation.[8] It was Russian literature that gave Russia the
"right to concrete participation in universal European life," that
brought into Russian life from the West the "universal elements."[9]
Russian literature was deeply responsive, in Dostoevsky's view, to
the appeal for universality in the heritage of European culture; this
responsiveness to universality, to other literatures and cultures he
considered a national Russian attribute.

Russian writers, he wrote in 1861, "consciously declared in literature the new idea of the upper classes of society about the
people. . . . Indeed, in these views is our all: our development, our
hopes, our history."[10] But Dostoevsky does not cast Russian writers
in the role of givers of culture. Their idea of the people is closely
linked with the ideals of the people. Everything that is "truly beautiful" in Russian literature, Dostoevsky wrote again in 1876, is
"taken from the people, beginning with the humble, simple-hearted
type of Belkin, created by Pushkin. Indeed, with us everything
comes from Pushkin." Russian writers recognized the people's
ideals as the truly beautiful ones, and, Dostoevsky suggests, this
was more a case of the "influence of artistic sensibility than good
will."[11] But whether it was a question of artistic sensibility or of
moral consciousness, Dostoevsky believed almost every significant
talent in Russia had ended up by turning to the "national feeling";[12]
contrariwise, he believed that Russian literature must cease when
the "real Russian and authentic word" dries up.[13] What is truly
artistic is national.[14]

Victor Hugo in his *Notre Dame de Paris,* Dostoevsky notes, revealed the true image of the French people of medieval times.[15]
Essentially, Dostoevsky views Russian literature—and above all
Pushkin—as performing the same task for the Russian people:
confronting Russian man in his degradation with the beauty of his
true, inwardly preserved image. The preservation of the ideal of
beauty in the heart of a people, Dostoevsky maintained, guarantees
that people's highest development. "The people is always right in
the basic core of its feelings, desires, and strivings," he wrote in

1861 in the context of some remarks on Pushkin as a national poet, "but many of its paths are sometimes incorrect, erroneous, and, what is most sorrowful of all, the form of the people's ideals often directly contradicts that which the people is striving for, indeed, monumentally contradicts."[16] But in the end Dostoevsky is convinced that the "people will understand Pushkin. It will understand him later on and from his poetry will learn to recognize itself."[17] The national poet, then, embodying the popular ideal, must necessarily stand on a higher level of development and consciousness than the people; he elevates the people to its own ideal, recreates the form of that ideal (sometimes misshapen in real life) in all its purity.

Dostoevsky allows that an authentic folk poet might appear in the very midst of the people, one who might express his milieu, "but without in any way rising above it, and accepting the whole surrounding reality for the norm, for the ideal." The poetry of such a poet would be comparable to the oral folk song. A poet might appear, Dostoevsky even allows, who might reject reality as the norm, might in part even negate it, might depict some moment or movement or wish in the people's life. Such a poet might be a strong one, but he would not be profound; his horizon would still be narrow. Pushkin would still be immeasurably higher than he.[18] Higher consciousness, the perspective of universal culture—here is what Dostoevsky considered the mark of the great national poet. He repeatedly calls attention to the universal scope of Pushkin's artistic consciousness, to the Russian poet's capacity to give expression not only to the national ethos but to the characteristic features of other cultures.

The people will recognize its ideals in Pushkin. But is not Russian literature, the gentry-based Russian novel with its perfect forms and "beautiful types," fearfully distant from the misshapen reality of Russian man? Is not the contradiction between the ideal projected in literature and the concrete actuality really "monumental" in a tragic sense? These troubling questions are posed, as we have seen, in the letter of Arkady Dolgoruky's former teacher in *The Raw Youth*. Pushkin set forth in his "Traditions of the Russian family" "everything that has ever been beautiful among us"; but all this is strikingly unlike chaotic Russian reality. Yet in this beauty, this formed and structured culture, rests "all hope." Do we not perceive—behind the exaggerated, even somewhat priggish, aestheticism of the letter writer—Dostoevsky's own aesthetic optimism, his belief in art as an awakener of human culture, his conception of Russian literature as the embodiment of Russia's ideal of moral truth and beauty?

Perhaps no other Russian writer, except Gogol, experienced more painfully and explored more deeply than Dostoevsky that quest for form which lies at the center of Russia's national awakening in the first part of the nineteenth century. The raw material of life, as Dostoevsky finds it, is shapeless, disfigured; precisely Russian man, he felt, was still not quite formed. The problem of the chaos of Russian society—the absence of firm moral and social forms and norms—is at the center of Dostoevsky's great novels. The problem of Russian "breadth" was posed in an archetypal way by Gogol in the character of Pirogov ("Nevsky Prospect"). Pirogov's bland and indifferent acceptance of the beating he received at the hands of the locksmith Schiller, the absence in him of all self-inquiry or shame, Dostoevsky insists, points to "such a facility to accommodate oneself to anything whatsoever and, at the same time, to such a breadth of our Russian nature that, in the face of these qualities, even the unlimited pales and fades away. The two-hundred-year divorce from the slightest independence of character and the two hundred years of spitting upon our own Russian face had expanded Russian conscience to such a fatal boundlessness from which—well, what might be expected, what do you think?"[19] The importance of Pirogov for Dostoevsky lies in the fact that he embodies—in his shapelessness—certain fundamental negative traits of a Russian type. "The public, i.e. the exterior, European appearance, the law once and for all which is derived from Europe—this public produces on every Russian a crushing effect: out in society he is a European, a citizen, a knight, a republican with a conscience and with his own firmly established opinion. At home, to himself: 'Eh, what the devil do I care about opinions, let them go ahead and whip me.' " Pirogov, Dostoevsky believes, was a "terrible prophecy, a prophecy of a genius who had so frighteningly guessed the future—because the Pirogovs turned out to be immeasurably many, so many that you can't thrash them all."[20]

The phenomenon of European culture and its forms is illuminated here in a different light. There is, for Dostoevsky, besides the form of beauty achieved in the monuments of European art, another kind of "form": empty pseudoculture, the elegant veneer or style of European civilization early seized upon by sections of the Russian upper classes. This pseudoculture, this European form, however, lacked a positive moral equivalent. "Yes, of course, at that time Europe came to us easily—in its physical aspects, it goes without saying," Dostoevsky writes in *Winter Notes on Summer Impressions* (1863). "But naturally, as for the moral aspects, the whip remained." Captain Gvozdilov (a character in Fonvizin's play *The Brigadier-General,* 1766) still beats his wife, perhaps with even greater ease than before. But now that "we are complete Europeans," Dostoevsky remarks, Gvozdilov "maintains a certain decorum when he has to nail somebody, observes propriety, and he is becoming a French bourgeois, but a little time will pass and, like the North American of the southern states, he will begin to defend the necessity of the Negro [slave] trade with texts."[21]

Dostoevsky, of course, was only one among many Russian writers in the late eighteenth and nineteenth centuries who called attention to the disjunction in Russian life between much superficial European culture and forms and the morals of a slave order. But for Dostoevsky, more than any other Russian writer, the problem of form in Russian life served as a focus for central questions of Russian moral and spiritual development. For him the problem of form was nothing less than the problem of the formation of Russian man. Here the need to arrive at, and distinguish, real form or beauty as opposed to pseudoform was central.

"He is a formalist," Dostoevsky writes in 1873 apropos of a character in a Russian drama. "Feeling that content is slipping away, he stands all the more firmly for form."[22] Dostoevsky's remark defines his attitude toward European culture as mirrored in the taste of the French bourgeois and his Russian imitator. Some of Dostoevsky's most important ideas on this question are expressed by the gambler, Aleksey Ivanovich, in *The Gambler* (1866). The Frenchman, Aleksey remarks to his English friend Astley, is "completed, beautiful form. . . . The national form of the Frenchman, that is, the Parisian," Aleksey continues (after referring to Racine as a "great poet" despite all his posturing), "began to take shape into a refined form when we were still bears. The revolution was the inheritor of the nobility. Today the most vulgar little pipsqueak of a Frenchman can have manner, style, expressions, and even thoughts of a thoroughly refined form, without participating in this form either on his initiative or in spirit or heart; all this came to him by inheritance." "It is only among Frenchmen," Aleksey remarks, "and, I dare say, among several other European peoples, that form has been so well defined that it is possible to appear with extraordinary dignity and yet be quite a scoundrel."

The problem of "inherited" form raised here is acute for the Frenchman, but far more serious for the Russian. The Frenchman inherits the cultural forms of an earlier period in French life, but he remains nonetheless within the mainstream of his own culture; the dress fits. The Russian, on the other hand, is alien to the very style; starting out at a late date in his quest for cultural identity, the Russian, Dostoevsky suggests, all too often is impressed by spectacular but false beauty or form. This whole problem is adumbrated in Aleksey's view of the way a Russian girl responds to the Frenchman de Grieux's pose. He appears in a "role," "masked": "He has a refined form, Mr. Astley, and the girl takes this form for his own soul, for the natural form of his soul and heart, and not as the clothing which he has inherited." But to distinguish beauty of soul and originality of personality, one needs "independence and freedom." The Russian girl Polina (in *The Gambler*) is attracted to the handsome Frenchman de Grieux, according to the gambler, even though this beauty is only part of her imagination. It will be a long time, he insists, before Polina prefers the Englishman Astley to de Grieux. "Now look at it this way, Mr. Astley: on the one hand, a sugar boiler, and on the other—Apollo of Belvedere; all this is somewhat incongruous." The Apollo of Belvedere, in Aleksey's ironic frame of reference, is no longer Dostoevsky's embodiment of "lofty beauty"; it is, rather, a parody of that beauty; here, form has lost its spiritual interior essence and degenerated into a kind of elegant, mannered, and, above all, artificial stylization. Nonetheless, even the artificial form of the Apollo of France—de Grieux—contrasts strikingly with an "awkward and inelegant" Englishman or a morally shapeless Russian gambler—such at least is the view of the envy-ridden gambler, Aleksey Petrovich himself. It is interesting to note, in this connection, that the gambler is unable to free himself from the triumphant aesthetic spell of the

French Apollo in spite of a very keen intellectual understanding of the falseness of that kind of form. The external form of the Frenchman, as Aleksey observes, is "no form at all." Yet we may ask: is not the reason for Aleksey's obvious envy of de Grieux, perhaps, a secret and painful realization that even the external inherited form of the Frenchman is better than complete formlessness?[23] Do not the residual forms of a vanished aesthetic reality still point to that reality and so retain a certain positive value?

The classical ideal certainly entered into Dostoevsky's conception of the ideal Russian man. His representation of Alyosha Karamazov suggests an Apollonian physical type; Grushenka's body, Dostoevsky says directly, recalls the form of the Venus of Milo; Myshkin's highest moment is the incarnation of the classical ideal. Yet Dostoevsky recognized that the moral-aesthetic structure of the new Russian man would have to be national; it would have to emerge from the essentially "broad" character of Russian man (the line of Dmitry Karamazov) and of the Russian language. "Well then, why don't you speak more clearly. . . . You don't know any grammar," Marie remarks to Shatov in *The Devils*. "It's in the spirit of the language, Marie," Shatov replies. Arkady Dolgoruky in *The Raw Youth* suggests that "in no European language is writing so difficult as in Russian." The Russian language, Dostoevsky observed in his *Diary of a Writer,* lacked the precise form of European languages. Greek and Latin were the "two most finished forms of human thought" which, through their "moral-educative force," had brought "the one-time barbarian West to the highest degree of development and civilization." The European spirit is expressed "in a more finished and precise way" than the Russian; "still one cannot but admit with hope and high spirit that the spirit of just our language is unquestionably full of diversity, rich, many-sided, and all-embracing, because [it exists] in still unstructured forms—and it can already convey the pearls and treasures of European thought, and we think that they are conveyed precisely and exactly."[24]

A slight wavering, perhaps insecurity, seems present in Dostoevsky's thinking on the question of the virtues of the unstructured "breadth" of the Russian language; latent here, quite likely, is the conflict between his own admiration for pure classical form, on the one hand, and his own creative sense of form which grew out of his desire to come to terms with, and give expression to, Russian reality.

As for the "breadth" of Russian character and of man in general, Dostoevsky clearly pondered its positive and negative potentialities. The problem of Russian "breadth" is posed in a striking way in *The Raw Youth*. "A thousand times I have been amazed at this capacity of man (and, it seems, chiefly Russian man)," remarks Arkady Dolgoruky, "for cherishing in his soul the most lofty ideal side by side with the most extreme vileness, and all this absolutely sincerely. Whether this is a special breadth in Russian man which will lead him far, or simply vileness—that is the question!" (Pt. III, Ch. 3 Sec. i). Dmitry Karamazov was Dostoevsky's attempt to lead the "broad" Russian man out of his chaos and disorder into a new realm of moral form and freedom, a new synthesis of form and being. Dmitry is pulled in the direction of the luminous ideal of the Madonna, but he himself is the test creation of a new "broad" Russian aesthetic reality.

In the last decade of his life Dostoevsky places increasing emphasis on the need for the expression of the ideal in Russian life, literature, painting, and education, for all that evokes emotion for the "good and the beautiful." "I am an incorrigible idealist," he writes in his *Diary of a Writer* in 1876. "I seek sanctities, I love them, my heart thirsts for them, because I am so constituted that I cannot live without sanctities."[25] Memories of the lofty idealism of the 1840s arouse in him the question: did we keep the faith? And he insists in his moving tribute to George Sand that the "preservation of this faith [in a lofty ideal] to the end usually is the lot of all lofty souls, all true lovers of man."[26] Dostoevsky fervently longs for a broad transformation of the conditions of Russian life. "I do not wish to think and live other than with the faith that all our ninety million Russians . . . will someday all be educated, humanized, and happy."[27] But his central emphasis is upon moral development, upon cultivating lofty strivings in man, for "without ideals, that is, without at least some kind of defined longings for the better, no good reality can ever ensue."[28]

Characteristic of Dostoevsky's increasing concern for the depiction of positive aspects of Russian life is his short note, appropriately entitled "A Wish," in the journal *Grazhdanin* in 1873. He complains that "we know too little of what is good in Russia and show too little sympathy and encouragement for the honest laborer." In 1861, we may recall, Dostoevsky recommended journalistic accounts of criminal trials to the reader on the grounds that they illuminated "the dark side of the human soul which art does not like to touch." In "A Wish" Dostoevsky notes that an "example of courage and a splendid life can bring to society a hundred times more use than a tale of scandals and monstrosities which we love so much and with which, to pander our taste, our newspapers are so rich." The story of a beautiful life or a heroic act, he suggests, is the best weapon against all Russia's social ills.[29] His wish appears to have been realized in Leskov's *Cathedral Folk*. In the same issue of *Grazhdanin* in which "A Wish" appears, Dostoevsky anonymously reviews Leskov's novel; here he welcomes the fact that Leskov brings before the reader "positive types" from the Russian clergy. He calls Leskov's archpriest Savely Tuberozov a "miraculous, superb figure," an embodiment of "that great, 'huge' spiritual strength which from time immemorial has been, is, and will be the motive force of our history." Dostoevsky applauds this creation of a new, "almost central type (in its closeness to the heart of life)" as a great accomplishment.[30]

In a discussion of techniques and materials in popular education in 1861, Dostoevsky maintained that good reading for the people must first of all make "pleasant and entertaining reading," must first bring pleasure. Proper reading materials (the kind he proposes), he notes at one point, would help people to recognize poor literature, for "the attribute of good works is to cleanse taste and judgment, and this attribute is natural."[31] Purification of taste for Dostoevsky is inseparable, of course, from moral purification and edification, and it is the latter which Dostoevsky aims at when he thinks of the education of the young. Russian children, Dostoevsky writes later on in his *Diary of a Writer* in 1876, are brought up to behold repulsive pictures, such as a peasant whipping a helpless, overburdened horse across the eyes. Reformers and educators must enter into struggle with these terrible impressions, root them out, and plant new ones. In this connection Dostoevsky recommends that "a series of pure, holy, beautiful pictures would have a strong impact upon souls thirsting for beautiful impressions."[32]

For the young people of the educated classes Dostoevsky places much importance upon the great classics of literature. "I will only make a general observation," Dostoevsky writes in 1880 in response to an individual's request for information on reading for children. "Take and give only that which produces *beautiful impressions and gives birth to lofty thoughts.*" Among various authors recommended (Pushkin, Schiller, Goethe, Shakespeare, and others), Dostoevsky particularly advises that the letter writer's son read Turgenev and Tolstoy.[33] "Leo Tolstoy must be read in his entirety," Dostoevsky advises the father of a girl in another letter. Precisely the impressions of the *beautiful* are necessary in childhood, he stresses again. And he recalls that the "many beautiful and lofty impressions" he gathered from a reading of Walter Scott, for example, constituted in his soul "a great force in the struggle with impressions that were tempting, passionate, and corrupting."[34]

It is noteworthy that Dostoevsky did not include his own works in the lists of those he considered suitable for young people. It was not modesty, apparently, which motivated Dostoevsky in this connection. "My own works would not at all be suitable for her," Dostoevsky wrote to the father who requested information on suitable reading for his daughter.[35] And indeed, in Dostoevsky's works there is little of the positive beauty that he so admired in Tolstoy. The Dostoevsky novel does not plant a "beautiful impression" in the soul. His works are full of passionate idealism and striving, but the human reality he depicts is for the most part disfigured through conflict and suffering; his novels are without those beautiful forms and types, those embodied values of love, the family, nature, found in Pushkin, Turgenev, and Tolstoy. Dostoevsky's art in the deepest sense disturbs: it is a perpetual and mocking challenge to all philistine complacency, to all routine and inertia, to all binding orthodoxy or simplistic visions of man and reality. But it disturbs in an even more radical sense: it threatens to replace the universal and containing order—the given in Pushkin, Turgenev, or Tolstoy —with a *perpetuum mobile,* with a permanent philosophical instability. Dostoevsky, to be sure, wishes to believe in a Christian-ordered universe, and we recognize his deeply Christian outlook; but he is largely unable, in embodied character, to create a convincing countervision (except fleetingly in poignant but still very abstract glimpses of beatitude) to his primary vision of reality "striving" toward fragmentation. There is only a passionate desire for the ideal, for form, for beauty: this is the organizing principle of his world view. Beauty does not transfigure any significant part of Dostoevsky's reality—as it does in Tolstoy's universe; but it establishes a tension, a balance, an equilibrium in man which permits, ideally, a creative utilization of energies. Art in Dostoevsky's concept is profoundly religious; yet paradoxically, and in the highest sense, it enables man to live without God. In the final analysis, it is art, beauty, form, which orders reality. It is Dostoevsky's supreme sense of form that artistically structures fragmenting reality for us, brings it aesthetically under control, measures, limits, and contains that which by its nature is a perpetual challenge to order.

9 Critique of Utilitarian Aesthetic

"BEAUTY IS LIFE," N. G. Chernyshevsky stated in his dissertation, "The Aesthetic Relations of Art to Reality," in 1855. He concludes from this that "the true, the highest beauty is precisely the beauty that man meets with in the world of reality and not the beauty created by art."[1] Chernyshevsky's dissertation, essentially an application of Ludwig Feuerbach's materialist philosophy to the sphere of aesthetic, aimed at the destruction of Hegelian idealist aesthetic. In a practical sense, his dissertation sets the stage for the downgrading of art in radical criticism in the 1850s and 1860s. The literary theory and criticism of N. A. Dobrolyubov rests firmly on Chernyshevsky's materialist aesthetics. Dostoevsky's major statement on art and literature in 1861, "Mr. —bov and the Question of Art," is a direct response to the materialist and utilitarian challenge of Chernyshevsky and Dobrolyubov.

Chernyshevsky flatly rejects what is indeed a fundamental assumption of idealist aesthetic: the notion that the "idea of the beautiful, not realized in reality, is realized by works of art." Art, Chernyshevsky objects, cannot be deduced from a general striving on the part of man for beauty. Beauty is life, and man's striving for it is satisfied by reality; whoever is dissatisfied with real beauty will be even less satisfied with the beauty created by art.[2]

Man prefers real beauty, Chernyshevsky asserts; art is essentially a "surrogate": the sole aim of the majority of works of art is simply "to give those people who have not been able to enjoy beauty in reality the opportunity to acquaint themselves with it at least to some degree."[3] Thus, a man in the Siberian tundra might dream of magic gardens with wondrous fruits, but given a real garden with apples, grapes, and pears he will forget about his magic garden and will choose the "real apple" as opposed to diamond and ruby fruits.[4] From all this Chernyshevsky concludes that the first purpose of all art is to reproduce nature and life. But art "must not even think of comparing itself with reality, let alone of excelling it in beauty." Art must content itself with being a substitute for reality. "Reality is higher than dreams, and essential purpose stands higher than fantastic claims." In the last line of his dissertation Chernyshevsky observes that works of art often have the purpose of "explaining life" and of "pronouncing judgment on the phenomena of life."[5]

Dostoevsky's aesthetic outlook, of course, is the diametrical opposite of Chernyshevsky's materialist and utilitarian aesthetic. Dostoevsky, it is true, acknowledged that reality continually gives evidence of a richness and complexity which is incomparable with anything that imagination and observation could create. This fact, Dostoevsky noted in his *Diary of a Writer* in 1876, had impressed him even before he began writing. "And this fact struck me many times and made me wonder about the usefulness of art in the face of its apparent impotence." We have cited earlier Dostoevsky's view—expressed in the same essay—that even a small "fact of real life" may reveal to the eye a depth not to be found even in Shakespeare. But whose eye, and who is able? asks Dostoevsky. Reality, then, may be superior to art in richness and complexity, but it takes precisely an artist, that is, art, to make accessible even in a small degree the richness and complexity of reality.[6] For all practical purposes, then, the superiority of reality over art is purely academic.

In considering Dostoevsky's view of the relation of art and reality, one must also bear in mind that his view of reality extends far beyond Chernyshevsky's materialist concept of reality: it embraces the absolute reality of the idea, the ideal reality of Christian perfection and beatitude. This ultimate reality, this perfection that is ineffable beauty, cannot be fully rendered in art; at the same time art alone for Dostoevsky provides intimations of that reality; art alone is the symbol and substance of man's unrealized aspiration.

Dostoevsky directly responded to Chernyshevsky's materialist aesthetics in his satirical sketch, "Excerpt from the Novel 'Shchedrodarov,'" in 1864; here he sharply attacks Chernyshevsky's crude utilitarian approach to art. In his sketch Dostoevsky projects a scene in which the editors of a radical journal hire a well-known writer, Shchedrodarov, as critic. He is given a basic aesthetic upon which to base his literary criticism. "Instill in yourself the rule that a real apple is better than a painted apple, all the more so since one can eat a real apple, while it is impossible to eat a painted apple. Consequently, art is rubbish, a luxury, and can serve only to amuse children. This 'new idea,' tremendous in its simplicity, henceforth must replace all courses in aesthetics for you and immediately give you the proper point of view for evaluating all so-called 'artistic works.' " Shchedrodarov, Dostoevsky remarks at this point, lacked the courage to say here "that, in the first place, a real apple and a painted apple are two entirely different things, which cannot in any sense be compared; and in the second place, that, let us grant, a real apple can be eaten, but a painted apple is painted precisely so that one can *look at* it and not eat it. That, after all, one cannot eat everything there is in the world, and one cannot therefore limit the usefulness of things and works to their edibility alone."[7]

In his sketch Dostoevsky—through the figure of Shchedrodarov —indicts radical criticism for debasing art with purely utilitarian criteria, for disregarding the "moral ideal," the "historical course of events," "all life."[8] The aesthetic of the stomach leaves no room for people who might say: "I want to think; I agonize over unresolved eternal questions; I want to love; I am tormented over what to believe in; I seek a moral idea; I love art."[9] All this is metaphysics and dreams to utilitarian criticism. But the real task of criticism, Dostoevsky affirms through Shchedrodarov, is not to "prescribe the laws of life, but to study life and from life itself to extract law."

Dostoevsky's article, "Mr. —bov and the Question of Art," is the writer's first major critique of the utilitarian aesthetic and materialist outlook of the radical democrats led by Chernyshevsky and Dobrolyubov. It anticipates his later polemic with the radicals in *Notes from the Underground* (1864). The problems of the nature of art, of its general and specific "usefulness," of "tendency" in art, and of the responsibility of the artist to society—all fall within the scope of Dostoevsky's ranging discussion. The central and unifying motif in the essay is his insistence on freedom in artistic creation. But he does not attack the utilitarian aesthetic with the purpose of withdrawing art to lofty and inaccessible positions; rather he wishes to affirm the organic unity of art and man's needs. "We stand for literature, we stand also for art," Dostoevsky wrote several years after his critique of Dobrolyubov. "Only the most extreme theoreticism and, on the other side, the most vulgar lack of talent can deny this force. . . . We do not stand for art for art's sake."[10] But Dostoevsky's stress in his critique of Dobrolyubov upon the broad and universal aesthetic usefulness of art unquestionably led many to believe that he advocated a more quietistic role for art. In his essay, "Stories of N. V. Uspensky," which appeared less than a year after the critique of Dobrolyubov, Dostoevsky rejects outright the criticism that his journal wishes to "understand and study the contemporary world by art alone and by some kind of ecstasies of artists and poets. We never talked such rubbish; we have always and only insisted upon and proclaimed the independent significance of art, the naturalness of its independence, and, therefore, its complete necessity in the cause of social development and consciousness, but by no means its exceptional position."[11] Dostoevsky's critique of Dobrolyubov, in the final analysis, is an effort to synthesize or establish a dialectic of the idea of the absolute freedom of the artistic process (and of the artist) with the idea of art (and the artist) as essentially a servant and service to man and society.

Art can help a cause a great deal because of its tremendous resources and strength, Dostoevsky wrote in "Mr. —bov and the Question of Art." "We repeat: of course, one can only desire this, but not demand, if alone for the reason that people demand chiefly when they want to compel by force, while the first law in art is freedom of inspiration and creation. Everything that has been brought forth by demand, everything drawn out, from time immemorial has not succeeded, and instead of benefit has brought only harm."[12]

Two interrelated thoughts are contained here: first, that the artistic process, by nature free, cannot be coerced without violating the integrity of art; second, that "demand" itself conceals the threat of real, violent compulsion from without. The raising of the problem of demand in the double aspect of violence to both art and man points to Dostoevsky's deep fear of a coefficient of compulsion in radical utilitarian and utopian socialist theory. He significantly compared his life in prison to a "compulsory communism."[13] Later in *Notes from the Underground* he cast his hero in the role of a despairing prisoner rebelling against socialist utopia and the walls of his own rationalistic consciousness. Apollon Grigoriev, Dostoevsky's associate on the journals *Vremya* and *Epokha,* wrote in a literary essay in 1864 of his hostility to everything that emerges from the "naked logical process, that is, to theory with its narrow grasp of life and with its despotism ready to pass to terror."[14] Dostoevsky's almost obsessive concern with compulsion becomes more comprehensible in the light of a literary theory which projected a brand of social realism as the literary concomitant of ineluctable historical forces driving to a new, socialist society. Dobrolyubov was the leading exponent of this new social realism.

In theory Dobrolyubov made no demands upon literature. The function of the "realistic critic" in his view was to study literary works in order to determine their characteristic or typical features. "We do not feel called upon to *'cultivate the aesthetic taste of the public,'* " he wrote in an essay on the dramatist Ostrovsky. "We only set forth here those results which we have obtained from a study of Ostrovsky's works from the standpoint of the reality he depicted."[15] The writer cannot deal with problems or issues before they have matured in reality. "Literature answers the questions of life with what is in life."[16]

But who determines what is in life and whether literature is responding properly to the questions raised by reality? Dobrolyubov assumes this function; in practice, the prescriptive character of his criticism takes its point of departure here. "This environment has now reached the point when it itself can facilitate the appearance of such a man," wrote Dobrolyubov in reference to the Bulgarian hero of Turgenev's novel *On the Eve* (*Nakanune*, 1860).[17] Proceeding from this premise Dobrolyubov could criticize the writer A. Pleshcheev for offering to the reader, instead of men of action, dreamers and feeble armchair philosophers who make no contribution to the public cause. "Why, now, should one write touching stories about their dreams and inner sufferings, which lead to nothing useful?" "Yes, we attach no practical importance to the beautiful strivings of the soul as long as they remain only strivings; yes, we value only facts; we recognize the worth of people only through actions."[18] "We do not demand heroism but want only more consciousness and definiteness of strivings in the good youths."[19] The demand, of course, falls upon the writer. The prescriptive character of some of Dobrolyubov's criticism is particularly evident in his review of the poetry of I. Nikitin. "Life," Dobrolyubov declared, "now is affirming its rights on all sides; realism is invading everywhere."[20] Dobrolyubov criticized Nikitin for writing about his personal discord with the world around him and calls upon him to turn to the "depiction of those interests and phenomena of life which are close to him."[21]

In his critique of Dobrolyubov, Dostoevsky remarked that such prescriptive criticism is impermissible—"to be a despot is impermissible; and really, for example, you, Mr. —bov, dealt almost despotically with Mr. Nikitin. 'Write about your needs, describe the needs and requirements of your class—down with Pushkin.' " " 'But after all I myself am one in need, [exclaims Mr. Nikitin], physical bread I have, but I have need of spiritual bread.' "[22]

The juxtaposition of physical and spiritual bread points to fundamental philosophical and social issues which underlie the entire debate in aesthetics between Dostoevsky and Dobrolyubov: the problem of materialism and of its social solution to the problem of man and society. Here in this debate, as later though somewhat ambiguously in "The Legend of the Grand Inquisitor," Dostoevsky insists on the choice of spiritual bread with its coefficient of freedom. Those "unsolved historical contradictions of human nature," which serve the Grand Inquisitor as cause for lifting from man his burden of freedom, serve Dostoevsky, in his debate with Dobrolyubov, as the bulwark for his central postulate on the nature and significance of beauty and art, on art as an organic need of man.

The imposition of any demands upon art, Dostoevsky maintains, is based on a misunderstanding of the basic laws of art and of its chief essence—freedom of inspiration. Art is an organic whole with its own organic life and, therefore, fundamental and unchangeable laws for this life. The need for beauty is inseparable from man. Dostoevsky's idealist view of art and beauty, which we have already discussed in detail, is pivotal in his debate with Dobrolyubov. It comes as a clear response to Dobrolyubov's materialist and utopian theory of poetry—the aesthetic concomitant, one might say, to that social utopia which Dostoevsky attacks in *Notes from the Underground* in 1864. In his review of Nikitin's poetry, Dobrolyubov had characterized the function or sphere of poetry as "life, living activity, its eternal struggle and the eternal striving of man to achieve harmony with himself and with nature." Poetry has long depicted man's discord with his surroundings. But the reasons for this discord, according to Dobrolyubov, have been sought erroneously "either in the mysterious forces of nature or in the dualistic structure of the human organism, and in accordance with this poetry treated the external nature and psychological antagonism of man." Dobrolyubov, however, envisages a social solution to the phenomenon of discord in man and art. Attention, he continues, is being directed nowadays to the "distribution of goods of nature between people, to the organization of social relations." Poetry has taken up this subject, but only in a general way; it is the novel, however, the "creation of the new time," which has "stemmed directly from this new view of the structure of social relations as the cause of the universal discord."[23]

The theoretical roots of Dobrolyubov's scorn for poetry are disclosed here. In its practical aspects, poetry—particularly the poetry of sentiment, mood, and nature with its myth, fantasy, allegory, and historical themes—was remote and of no use to Dobrolyubov in the immediate struggle. In its theoretical aspects, poetry was the main camping ground of his chief enemy: philosophical idealism. Here were gathered all those "ideologists" beginning with Plato who rise up against realism, insist upon dualism, and believe that only pure ideas have reality;[24] here, also, were to be found Dobrolyubov's opponents in the "aesthetical" camp who imagine that beautiful works are the beginning of all good and who think that literature, especially poetry, "makes history . . . remakes even moral and national character."[25]

These same opponents support the contemporary poet in the conviction that social activity is not his affair and that he must stand apart when the "change and reconstruction of the social building" occurs. But sooner or later, Dobrolyubov insisted, poetry will undertake a study of "social inequities," following its discovery that "man agonizes and anguishes, is carried away and falls, rises and rejoices not from the power of dark forces and from inevitable fate, and not because two opposing elements sit within him, but simply from one or another measure of inequity in social relations."[26]

Dobrolyubov's theory of poetry was objectionable to Dostoevsky on two grounds: first, its frankly materialist character; and second, its concept of a definitive social solution to the problems of man, its rejection of the principle of permanent conflict, or dialectic, in man and history. In this connection the most crucial feature of Dostoevsky's own concept of beauty is, of course, the notion that the "need for beauty develops most at the moment man is in discord with reality, in disharmony, in struggle." Dostoevsky —in complete contrast to Dobrolyubov's purely historical and materialist understanding of the element of discord in human existence—views man's discord with reality as a permanent attribute of the human condition. This concept of conflict, of ambivalence within man and permanent discord between man's ideal and reality, has the character almost of a formal creative principle in Dostoevsky's art.

The view of ambivalence as suffering, yet as constituting the essence of consciousness, the view of man's eternal struggle for the ideal as the very essence of creative being form the most decisive argument, in *Notes from the Underground,* against the idea of a rational and harmonious social utopia. This view of man's condition, taken from its aesthetic side, plays a similar role in demolishing Dobrolyubov's aesthetic utopia. Indeed, at the point at which Dobrolyubov visualizes a socially motivated end to all discord in man and poetry, at the point at which he projects a new role for the poet in the "reconstruction of the social building," Dostoevsky postulates disintegration and chaos in the aesthetic—and, for Dostoevsky, therefore moral—sphere. There can be no vital life or healthy creation outside conflict. Man lives most when he is striving. But when man achieves the ideal of his desires, according to Dostoevsky, his aesthetic pleasures become unhealthy, inharmonious, and disfigured, a condition reflected in the simultaneous breakdown of morality and taste.

Dostoevsky does not characterize in his critique of Dobrolyubov the features of an art which succumbs to "another ideal"; he limits himself to the observation that just as "man in his life can deviate from normal reality, from the laws of nature," so "art will deviate along with him."[27] Dostoevsky's remarks about Alexandre Dumas-père, in his review of the Academy of Arts exhibit, suggest the view that decadence in art is accompanied by a loss of a sense of measure, a striving for sensation, exaggerated effects.[28] Much later, in his *Diary of a Writer,* Dostoevsky expressed himself on this question through the figure of a fictitious "paradoxicalist." Affirming the necessity of war as a revivifying element in the life of a people, Dostoevsky's paradoxicalist observes that periods of prolonged peace shift the emphasis to everything "bad and crude in man—chiefly to wealth and capital," bring about the death of all magnanimity, produce cynicism, boredom, apathy, a decline in thought, a dulling of feeling, and debauchery. The impact of prolonged peace and stagnation is felt in the arts—in "a galloping after effect, after some subtlety. The simple, clear, magnanimous, and healthy ideas will no longer be in fashion: something far more coarse will be needed; the artificiality of passions will be in demand. Little by little the feeling of measure and harmony will be lost; there will appear distortions of feelings and passions, the so-called subtleties of feeling which in essence are only their vulgarization."[29]

Moral breakdown in society, then, is reflected in art by a concomitant disintegration of aesthetic values—values which for Dostoevsky are the very essence of moral experience: specifically, the classical elements of balance and control, "measure and harmony," and with them the healthy informing notions of the simple, clear, and magnanimous. The loss of a healthy, structured and structuring idea (ideal) leads to melodramatic display, artificiality, distortion, a preoccupation with the presentation of emotional experience for itself alone (the "so-called subtleties of feeling")—in short, to a vulgarization of human experience, aesthetically, to the breakdown of form.

Art in Dostoevsky's view is not divorced from the fundamental moral condition of society, but it responds to that condition in different ways. It may participate in moral decadence, or it may counteract it. Authentic art, he writes in a discussion of war in his *Diary of a Writer* in 1877,

> alone supports in society the higher life and awakens souls who have fallen asleep in periods of long peace. . . . *True* art develops precisely in times of prolonged peace because it is opposed to the ponderous and corrupt slumber of souls . . . evokes the ideal, gives birth to protest and indignation, stirs up society, and frequently compels people to suffer who are thirsting to wake up and get out of the stinking pit. As a result, it turns out that the long bourgeois peace, nevertheless, in the end almost always gives birth itself to the demand for war.[30]

It is no surprise to hear Dostoevsky's paradoxicalist insist that the loftiest ideas in art have been contributed by war and struggle:

"Turn to tragedy, look at the statues: here is Corneille's *Horace,* there is the Apollo of Belvedere striking the monster."[31]

Dostoevsky, then, views true art as the embodiment of the principle of movement, of conflict, and, as such, as the implacable enemy of all stasis in man and society. Dobrolyubov, as we have noted, envisaged a social solution to the misunderstanding between poet and society. In Dostoevsky's view the idea of such a solution was anti-aesthetic—it ignored the fundamental essence of art; at the same time the very idea of such a solution implied to him an extremely simplified, utopian view of man and society. Dostoevsky viewed the life of man and society as a kind of systaltic movement, a continual opening and closing of the spirit. In this process true art played an essential and vital creative role.

Art, Dostoevsky believed, could play a socially useful, even direct, role in society. His principal emphasis in "Mr. —bov and the Question of Art," however, is upon the fundamentals of his aesthetic philosophy and, specifically, upon the concept of the aesthetic usefulness of art. From the standpoint of the general aesthetic usefulness of art, the contemporary moment is dissolved in the timelessness of man's striving for the ideal. To the question of why art does not always correspond in its ideals with the universal and contemporary ideal, why art is not always faithful to reality, Dostoevsky answers that the question is not correctly posed. *"Art is always contemporary and real, it never was otherwise and, chiefly, cannot exist otherwise."* And he adds that those who think art deviates from reality do so, first of all, out of an ignorance of the paths of usefulness of art.[32]

Can a writer ever lose contact with reality? Dostoevsky obviously believed that this was possible. And, by way of an apparent concession and in an abrupt shift of criteria, Dostoevsky remarks in his critique of Dobrolyubov that we sometimes think art deviates from reality because "there really are mad poets and prose writers who break all connection with reality . . . who are transformed into some kind of ancient Greeks or into medieval knights and who ferment in anthologies or in medieval legends." These artists, however, are fully mad and therefore few in number, he observes. On the other hand, "our poets and artists really can deviate from the real path." And Dostoevsky enumerates various causes of such deviation: absence of a social sense, misunderstanding of civic duty, immaturity, misunderstanding of reality, certain historical reasons, or an imperfectly formed society. In regard to all this Dostoevsky finds the "appeals, reproaches, and explanations of Mr. —bov in the highest degree respectable. But Mr. —bov really goes much too far." The works that Dobrolyubov calls "rattles and album playthings" Dostoevsky finds normal and useful.[33]

Dostoevsky's concession to the Dobrolyubov point of view suggests the complexity of his own view on the role of the artist in society. In the final analysis, he differs with Dobrolyubov not on the question of *whether* art should respond to contemporary reality, but on *how* it should respond; and central to his position is his insistence that art must remain art in this response regardless of its ideological orientation.

Dostoevsky attacked Dobrolyubov for refusing to recognize the primacy of artistry. An inartistic work cannot in any sense achieve its goal, he maintained, and the utilitarians only ruin their cause by refusing to recognize this truth. To demonstrate the self-defeating character of utilitarian aesthetics Dostoevsky analyzed, in "Mr. —bov and the Question of Art," Dobrolyubov's lengthy review of Marko-Vovchok's "Stories from the Life of the Russian Folk" ("Rasskazy iz narodnogo russkogo byta," 1859). "The task of literature is now to pursue the remnants of serfdom in public life," Dobrolyubov had written in his review, noting that Marko-Vovchok "in his simple and truthful stories is practically the first really masterful warrior in this field."[34]

Dostoevsky underlined the central contradiction in Dobrolyubov's analysis: affirming at the beginning of his review that these stories were not artistically finished works and that therefore there was no need to determine their absolute literary merit, Dobrolyubov had concluded his review by the remark that the truthfulness of the stories formed a basis for admitting the high merits of the literary production. The substance of Dostoevsky's criticism of Marko-Vovchok (he dwells on one story in particular) is that her art was so bad as to make a mockery of her ideas. The central failure of Dobrolyubov, on the other hand, was that he did not recognize the unity between the artistic idea of a work (the problem of "truthfulness") and form. How do we recognize artistry in a work of art?

In the fact that we see a harmony, as close as possible, between the artistic idea and the form in which it is embodied. Let us put it even more clearly: artistry, for example, even in a novelist, is the ability to express one's thought so clearly in the personages and images of the novel that the reader, reading the novel, understands the thought of the writer just as the writer himself understood it when creating his work. Therefore, in short: artistry in a writer is the ability to write well.[35]

There can, of course, be no harmony of artistic idea and form, no truth in art, if any idea, a purpose, a "tendency" is imposed upon a writer from without or imposed by the writer upon himself, in violation of his own particular artistic temperament. "I am terribly afraid of 'tendency' if it masters a young writer, especially at the beginning of his career," Dostoevsky writes in his article, "Apropos of the Exhibition" (*Diary of a Writer*, 1873). He expresses a concern over the type of modern young poet who to please social pressure "suppresses in himself the natural need to express himself in his own images," who out of fear that he will be condemned for "idle curiosity" "suppresses, erases images which make themselves felt in his soul, leaves them without development and attention, and drags out of himself, with feverish convulsions, a theme which satisfies the public, uniform liberal and social opinion." Many promising talents have been so consumed by tendency that the latter "clothed them in a kind of uniform." Of course, Dostoevsky acknowledges that a particularly strong talent could survive such tendency at the beginning of an artistic career.[36]

Dostoevsky's strong conservative political bias is in evidence, of course, when he attacks the "crude mistake" of people who believe that the "exposure of vice (or what liberalism has come to consider vice) and the awakening of hatred and revenge is the only path for the achievement of a goal." But he makes an aesthetic criticism of radical writing when he maintains that "any artistic work, without a preconceived tendency, executed solely out of artistic need, and even on a quite extraneous theme, without even hinting at anything 'tendentious' . . . will turn out to be far more useful for [our critic's] *own purposes* than, for example, all the songs of the shirt (not of Hood, but of our writers), though it may on the surface resemble that which other people call 'satisfaction of idle curiosity.' "[37] Thus, Dostoevsky expresses delight with Repin's depiction of the river haulers in his famous painting. They do not cry out to the spectator: "See how happy I am and how much you are indebted to the people." Repin does not make them "think about their social condition." And Dostoevsky insists that "just this humble innocence of thought of this miserable peasant achieves a goal incomparably more than you think—precisely more than your tendentious liberal goal!" (Dostoevsky is addressing himself to an unnamed critic.)[38]

In his attacks on utilitarian aesthetics and criticism, Dostoevsky naturally placed particular emphasis upon the aesthetic usefulness of art and upon the primacy of artistry in art, in contrast to his opponents who concerned themselves chiefly with the social direction or tendency of a work of art. Yet Dostoevsky's preoccupation with tendency both as belletrist and critic was no less passionate than, for example, that of Dobrolyubov. "Mr. —bov is not so much a critic as a publicist," Dostoevsky wrote with considerable justification.[39] But Dostoevsky himself was a determined publicist. "Without doubt every literary critic must at the same time be a poet himself," Dostoevsky wrote in 1864.[40] (His notion of the "poet" here is precisely that of a militant humanist and citizen.) " 'I am a critic and not a publicist,' " Apollon Grigoriev, Dostoevsky's associate on his journal *Vremya,* used to say with reproach to him. "But every critic," Dostoevsky retorts, "must be a publicist, in the sense that it is the duty of every critic not only to have firm convictions but *to be able* also to put his convictions across. . . . But Grigoriev, judging the word 'publicist' with prejudice—because of certain local examples offered by our past publicists [a reference clearly to Dobrolyubov and Chernyshevsky, among others]—did not want to understand what was wanted from him."[41]

Dostoevsky knew what he wanted from himself as an artist: a full commitment of his being, all his faculties of aesthetic and moral judgment, feeling and reason, to reality. He did not entertain any belief, as we have seen, in the possibility of pure objectivity in the artistic judgment of reality. Even in the area of nonartistic assembling of facts he did not seem to believe it was possible to escape tendency. Dostoevsky's views may certainly be discerned in a short exchange between Shatov and Liza in *The Devils.*

Shatov, on hearing Liza's proposal to publish a book in which the facts of a whole year would be classified, remarks: "That means something will come out with a tendency, a selection of facts with a well-defined tendency." When Liza objects that she does not want any tendency—"impartiality alone—that's the tendency" —Shatov retorts: "But there's nothing wrong with a tendency . . . and anyway, it's impossible to avoid it as soon as it comes to any selection. The selection of facts will show the way they are to be interpreted. Your idea is not bad" (Pt. I, Ch. 4, Sec. ii).

Not surprisingly, the idea of telling an artist to content himself with analysis and accumulation of material and not to dare to think and draw conclusions is as repugnant to Dostoevsky as imposing an alien tendency upon the artist. "Such advice," he wrote in "Stories of N. V. Uspensky," "is the same as saying: 'don't look with your eyes, don't smell with your nose.' In such prescription there will be violence, and all violence is unnatural, abnormal, criminal."[42] The reality of violence, it may be noted in passing, is always fresh on the consciousness of Dostoevsky.

Dostoevsky gave expression to the real character of his artistic nature when he wrote in "Mr. —bov and the Question of Art" that "in spite of our love for artistry and pure art, we ourselves yearn for, thirst for, a good tendency and highly value it."[43] Nothing is more characteristic of Dostoevsky than his love for artistry, pure beauty; indeed, we are not surprised that he expressed a desire in the last decade of his life to write a treatise on "Pure Beauty";[44] yet the "poet" in him is exploding with tendency, intoxicated with the sense of purpose and mission; his ideal may lie in another world, but he is committed to transforming, teaching, educating this one. By "good tendency" Dostoevsky certainly meant, first of all, moral tendency. "We thirst for moral conviction, tendency," he wrote in an article in 1861.[45] He expresses himself on this question with particular vigor and frankness, privately, in his notebook. "What is needed in poetry is passion; what is needed is *your idea* and without fail a pointing finger, passionately raised. But indifferent and real reproduction of reality is worth absolutely nothing and, chiefly, means nothing. Such artistry is absurd: a simple but barely perceptible glance will note more in reality."[46]

Moral tendency is projected here almost as a condition or function of true (as opposed to naturalistic) "reproduction" of reality.

But it is clear from Dostoevsky's formulation of the question that moral tendency is also something that the artist brings (or should bring) to the work of art, something that precedes it. Dostoevsky, as we noted earlier, distinguished between the "real view" of the artist, embodied in type, and his "preconceived view" from which, he acknowledges, it is difficult to free oneself completely. Now precisely preconceived views, driving moral and social "tendency," enter into Dostoevsky's own creative process. Art for him, as his letters amply attest, was not only an end in itself, but a means of putting across his ideas—ideas expressed in an extraordinary range of preachment and polemic in social, political, economic, and philosophical realms. His goal is to "speak out on everything even if I die from it," he writes Apollon Maikov in 1868 in connection with his idea for a novel to be entitled "Atheism."[47] He writes in a letter to Maikov in 1870 of a "rich idea" he is working on. "I am not speaking of the execution, but of the idea. One of those ideas which has an unquestionable effect in public. Something in the nature of *Crime and Punishment*, but still closer, still more vitally connected to reality and directly touching upon a most important contemporary question."[48] "What I am writing is a tendentious piece," he writes in March, 1870 about *The Devils*. "I want to speak out as passionately as possible . . . I want to speak out to the last word."[49] "I have great hopes for the piece," he writes again, "but not from the artistic side, but from the tendentious side; I want to express several thoughts, even if my artistry perishes in this connection . . . but I will speak my mind."[50] These sentiments are deeply characteristic of Dostoevsky's idea-centered creative drives. "Without a doubt I will write badly," Dostoevsky writes again in 1870. "Being more of a poet than an artist I eternally have taken themes beyond my strength. And therefore I will botch things up, that is for sure. The theme is too strong."[51]

The theme was never too strong for the artistic forces of Dostoevsky. He records his surprise in his *Diary of a Writer* in 1877 at encountering, in the sixth part of Tolstoy's *Anna Karenina*, a scene which responded to a "real 'topic of the day' "; he stresses, however, that it appears in the novel "not intentionally, not tendentiously, but precisely from the very artistic essence of the novel." In like manner Dostoevsky succeeded in absorbing into his artistic universe his most tendentious, preconceived views, as well as the most diverse and politically potent topical material. These plunges into "topics of the day," one may note here, were for Dostoevsky (as they were for Tolstoy) vital means of focusing upon the major phenomena of his time. For some reason, he writes in connection with Tolstoy's topical scene, he had not expected the author to lead his heroes to such "pillars." "True, in precisely such pillars, in this extremity of conclusion is to be found the whole meaning of reality, and without it the novel would even have taken on an indefinite character, in no way responding to either current or essential Russian interests: some little corner of life would have been depicted, with a deliberate ignoring of the major and most alarming [element] in just this life."[52]

A final problem deserves some consideration. What is Dostoevsky's attitude, in his critique of Dobrolyubov, toward the problem of the social responsibility of the artist? The problem in one sense is eliminated by his theory that all true art is useful and contemporary. Yet what about the artist's responsibility to society in the face of a grave social or national crisis? Here the problem obviously takes on special moral dimensions. How free, after all, is the writer from his civic responsibilities? Dostoevsky's resolution of these problems is curiously ambiguous and represents an attempt to synthesize, or establish a dialectic of, opposing points of view.

The problem of responsibility is posed by three examples in his article on Dobrolyubov. The first—advanced by the utilitarians in an imaginary debate staged by Dostoevsky—involves a hypothetical battle: you are in the midst of a battle, but instead of helping your comrades, you (an artist in soul) suddenly want to paint a picture of the battle. You throw down your weapon, pick up a pencil, and begin to draw. "Of course, you have a full right to give yourself over to your inspiration, but would your artistic activity at such a moment be reasonable?" remarks Dostoevsky's spokesman for the utilitarians.[53]

The example very effectively poses the problem in the radical democrats' context of a revolutionary, or potentially revolutionary, crisis. Dostoevsky provides another example of the same order—partly drawn from the memoirs of I. Panaev: a circle of artists and writers maintained that the artist should not busy himself with anything vital or current, politics, domestic or international affairs;

artists should concern themselves only with *"lofty art."* Dostoevsky completely rejects this point of view, remarking that it might
lead—say in the war of 1812—to some writers and poets pre-
ferring to busy themselves with a Greek anthology when all Russian society was busy saving the fatherland.[54]

As though the examples of the battlefield and the war of 1812
were not enough to demonstrate to the reader the moral obloquy
of withdrawing into lofty art at a time of crisis, Dostoevsky sets
before the reader a third hypothetical situation. On the morning
after the terrible Lisbon earthquake, the citizens of the city, hop-
ing to find information on the victims of the disaster, open their
newspaper and—in the most prominent position in the paper—
read the poem of a famous Lisbon poet. The poem that Dostoevsky quotes in full at this point is, in fact, one of the most beautiful
lyrics of the Russian poet Fet (a poet for whom both Dobrolyubov
and Chernyshevsky had little use).

> Whispers, timid breathing,
>   A nightingale's trill
> Silver and swaying
>   Of a sleepy brook,
> Night light, night shadows,
>   Shadows without end,
> A series of magical changes
>   On a dear face,
> In the misty clouds—purple of a rose.
>   Glistening of amber,
> And kisses, and tears,
>   And the dawn, the dawn!

The Lisbon poet, Dostoevsky observes, attached to his poem
the "well-known poetic rule that he is not a poet who cannot leap
headlong from the fourth story."[55]

Dostoevsky declares that the inhabitants of Lisbon would probably en masse execute their famous poet in the square, not at all
because he wrote a poem without a verb, but because in view of
the disaster of the preceding night the act of the poet would be
considered "offensive and unbrotherly." Of course, Dostoevsky relates, after executing the poet—also a very unbrotherly act—they

would without fail rush to Doctor Pangloss for wise advice, and Pangloss would immediately assure them that all was for the best.

At the same time, Dostoevsky asserts, these same Lisbonites thirty or forty years later might erect a monument to their beloved poet precisely for his amazing verse in general and, in particular, for the "purple of a rose." The poem for which they executed the poet might even have been of some use to the people of Lisbon, Dostoevsky adds, "awakening in them an aesthetic ecstasy and a feeling for beauty, and laid like beneficial dew on the soul of the young generation."[56]

What is Dostoevsky's own view of the responsibility of the artist before society in the three examples he sets before the reader? In the first two examples he certainly places the asocial artist in a negative light. It is in his third example that the ambiguity of Dostoevsky's position becomes apparent. Here there is a surprise reversal: the extreme asocial and irrational act of the poet (the publication of the poem with its devil-may-care footnote) is justified by the fact that, in the end, the poem turned out to have an elevating influence upon men. But it is the poem that is justified, not the poet. It turns out, Dostoevsky observes, "that art was not guilty on the day of the Lisbon earthquake . . . not art, but the poet who had abused art at a moment when it was not the time for it. He sang and danced at the grave of a dead man . . . but once again he, and not art, was guilty."[57]

The poet Nekrasov, expressing that profound sense of civic responsibility that characterizes so much of the nineteenth-century Russian intellectual consciousness, gave the most extreme interpretation to the concept of the poet's responsibility to society. His well-known lines read: "You may not be a poet / But you are obligated to be a citizen" ("Poetom mozhesh' ty ne byt' / No grazhdaninom byt' objazan," from "Poet i grazhdanin," 1856). The poet who wrote this about himself, Dostoevsky remarked in his *Diary of a Writer* in 1877, "thereby as it were recognized that he could be judged by the people as a 'citizen.' "[58] Dostoevsky, like Nekrasov, recognizes that the artist is both citizen and poet. But —and this seems the essential meaning of the Lisbon example— he prefers to remain with this ambivalence; in the final analysis he will censure the artist as citizen but not as poet. Whereas Nekrasov in the lines cited gives priority to the citizen over the poet,

Dostoevsky accords special status to the poet: in his conception of a situation in which the poet finds himself at cross purposes with the demands of the citizen, with the exigencies of the moment, he projects the poet essentially as a solitary and tragic figure.

Dostoevsky's support of the Lisbon poet may be more complete than it appears at first glance. It cannot be forgotten that Dostoevsky's opponents in 1861 were the same rationalists and utopian socialists against whom the man from the "underground" inveighs in *Notes from the Underground* in 1864. In the face of critics who, he felt, threatened to compromise the freedom of the artist with utilitarian demands and literary determinism, Dostoevsky brings into the foreground the Lisbon poet, a figure who can best be described as a poet-paradoxicalist or literary "underground" man. In what can only be taken as a deliberate challenge to society and justification of his poem, the Lisbon poet proclaims the "well-known poetic rule that he is not a poet who cannot leap headlong from the fourth story." At this point Dostoevsky remarks parenthetically and with a deceptive simplicity: "(For what reason? —I don't know to this day; but then let's assume that this is absolutely necessary in order to be a poet; I don't want to argue.)"

Dostoevsky advances here—quite cautiously to be sure, and reserving for himself a loophole—a conception of the poet that finds its analogue in some of the reflections of the man from the "underground" on free will as an expression of man's nature. The condition of being a poet embraces the poet's relation to reality; it involves—according to the poetic rule cited—the readiness to act irrationally. Dostoevsky suggests that the irrational element may be absolutely essential to being a poet. The condition of being a poet, it follows, is not an affair of reason; the act of creation becomes an act of will, and will, as the man from the "underground" observes, "is a manifestation of the whole of life, I mean the whole of human life, including reason."

In his defense of artistic freedom Dostoevsky[59] writes not of will but of *tvorchestvo*—here, "creativeness" or "force of creation." "Creativeness—the basic element of every art—is an integral, organic attribute of human nature and has the right to exist and develop if only because it is a necessary part of the human spirit. . . . As something integral, organic, creativeness develops out of itself, unsubordinated to anything, and it demands complete free-

dom; mainly, it demands complete freedom in its development."
To limit or stifle the creative and artistic needs of man is to cramp
the human spirit in its work and development.[60]

Dostoevsky acknowledges that the freedom of the artist may result in an abuse of art in certain circumstances (e.g. the Lisbon
earthquake or any time of great national crisis), but he posits this
freedom as inseparable from the action of creation, the condition
of being a poet. He does not support the Lisbon poet in his asocial
act, but he suggests—and this would seem to be the leitmotiv of
the Lisbon episode—that the justification of the poet consists in
the fact that he *is* a poet, that the poet by his very nature is in
tension with society, that without the irrational leap he would not
be a poet.

The appearance of Voltaire's Dr. Pangloss at the scene of the
earthquake with his rationalization of the poet's execution indicates the antirationalist direction of Dostoevsky's thought. Pangloss epitomizes in his whole philosophy precisely the kind of
abstract reasoning that Dostoevsky loathed. The facility with which
reason can compromise freedom itself is amusingly illustrated by
Voltaire at the conclusion of the chapter in *Candide* devoted to
the Lisbon earthquake.

> "Monsieur ne croit donc pas à la liberté? dit le familier.—
> Votre Excellence m'excusera, dit Pangloss; la liberté peut sub
> sister avec la nécessité absolue, car il était nécessaire que nous
> fussions libres; car enfin la volonté déterminée***" Pangloss
> était au milieu de sa phrase, quand le familier fit un signe de
> tête à son estafier, qui lui servait à boire du vin de Porto ou
> d'Oporto.

The episode of the Lisbon poet in Dostoevsky's critique of
Dobrolyubov would seem to suggest, on its deepest level, precisely
the impossibility of any compromise between freedom and absolute necessity.

Strakhov, Dostoevsky's close friend and collaborator on *Vremya*
in the 1860s, wrote in his memoirs that Dostoevsky was devoted
to the notion that literature must serve social needs. "But while
firmly adhering to this notion of service to the moment, and while
constantly probing contemporary phenomena and priding him

self on grasping them in his work, Fyodor Mikhailovich was ready to place above everything the strict demands of art."[61] There is no reason to believe that Dostoevsky's position, as set forth by Strakhov, was any different in the 1840s than in the 1860s and 1870s. He believed in both periods that narrow utilitarian and didactic tendencies were alien to art. But in the 1840s, politically he was a radical and an activist (however ill-defined and rootless the political program); his differences with Belinsky, Petrashevsky, and others over the function of literature in society could only have been minor in comparison with the broad areas of agreement in the realm of political and social goals and ideals. In the 1860s, however, Dostoevsky stood in opposition to the radical revolutionary movement. In the context of this basic political shift, his idealist outlook and basic theory of the aesthetic usefulness of literature could not but acquire a principled significance in his polemics with the radicals who sought to use literature for revolutionary and socialist ends.

But Dostoevsky never abandons the notion that literature should serve society; in practice always harnessing the impulse to serve with the "strict demands of art," he gave himself up in both art and criticism to passionate, and often frankly tendentious, commitment. He believed that the artist had to be absolutely free, but he wanted him free to commit himself organically to serving society and a lofty moral purpose. The main thing is "not to cramp art with various goals, not to prescribe laws for it, not to confuse it, because even without this it has many submerged rocks, many temptations and deviations, inseparable from the historical life of man. The more freely it develops, the more normally it will unfold, the sooner it will find its real and *useful* path."[62]

In the deepest human sense Dostoevsky defended the freedom of the beleaguered artist unconditionally, as a *man*. "Of course, we agree that there could exist a kind of foul, anthological worm who really had lost all sense of reality," Dostoevsky wrote, in the ironical manner of the man from the "underground," in his critique of Dobrolyubov. "But, in the first place, even a worm, after all, must live."[63] Yet in the realm of aesthetic theory, Dostoevsky defends the artist because he believed that the artist exercises his freedom as a creator of timeless beauty, of all that is precious and necessary to man in his moral evolution; though he may abuse this freedom as a citizen, yet as an artist he points out to man—in Schiller's words—the "direction of the good." To Dostoevsky this was the supreme service of the artist, a service which redeemed all human error.

CREATIVENESS, Dostoevsky believed, is an organic attribute of human nature and the basic element in all art. But creativeness itself is not the work of art as we perceive it in its final unity of form and idea. Without the poet's creativeness, or force of creation, no poem will emerge; on the other hand, the presence of creativeness in the individual is no guarantee that a poem will be born. The work of art, Dostoevsky recognized, is the end result of a difficult and, in many respects, quite uncertain creative process within the creator on both conscious and subconscious levels of being.

Dostoevsky gave some attention to the problems of artistic creation—and particularly to the problem of the disorder and failure of creative consciousness—in two of his early writings, "The Landlady" and *Netochka Nezvanova*. His interest in these questions must have begun with the earliest awakening of his own artistic consciousness. The youthful romantic Dostoevsky believed that the artist divines transcendental reality in a "burst of inspiration." But in a letter to his brother Mikhail in 1839, cited earlier, he dwells on the difficulty in giving expression to one's inspiration and ecstasy, in executing the idea of a creative work. "The spirit," he insists, "always hides more than can be expressed in words, colors, or sounds."[1] Dostoevsky's observation on the disparity between the abundance of spirit and the limitations of artistic means anticipates in some ways his later distinction between the functions of "poet" and "artist" in the creative process, as well as his complaint that he always had difficulty in mastering artistically the surge of poetic idea. There are echoes later on in his writing of the idea that we contain more than we can express. "Infinitely more remains hidden within than comes out in words," remarks the memoirist, Arkady Dolgoruky, in *The Raw Youth*. "Your thought, even if it is an evil one, is always deeper while it is within you; it becomes more ridiculous and dishonorable when it comes out in words."[2] The visionary hero of "The Dream of a Ridiculous Man" complains of the inadequacy of "our weak words" to convey his dream of beatitude. Here, of course, Dostoevsky is concerned with another, related problem: the difficulty of transposing visual images—in this case, images of pure beauty and moral perfection —into verbal images. At root, however, the problem faced by the Ridiculous Man is the same as that posed by the young Dostoevsky: how to give expression, in words, colors, or sounds, to one's ecstasy, inspiration, to a lofty vision of beatitude, to the ineffable world of the spirit. The context in which Dostoevsky first raises this problem is a romantic one, but the problem outlives the context.

In a general sense, of course, the idea that we contain more than we can express points to the whole philosophically idealist foundation of Dostoevsky's thought—his belief that the ends and beginnings of reality remain essentially unknowable. Even our personal, interior reality, Dostoevsky believed, in large part defies expression. "However much you have written about [your secret]," he writes to a correspondent in 1880, "there still remains a whole sea of the unexpressed which you yourself are unable to express and I cannot understand";[3] and in another letter of the same year: "I feel that within me more is hidden than anything I could have expressed up to this time as a writer." He confesses with pain that he has not expressed "literally one-twentieth" of what lay in his heart. It is in this letter that Dostoevsky cites the "profound" words of the philosopher Vladimir Soloviev: "Mankind, it is my profound conviction . . . *knows far more* than it has till now succeeded in expressing in its science and in its art."[4]

The tragedy of creative consciousness in the self-enclosed "dreamer," the man of heightened spiritual sensibility, is a major theme in Dostoevsky's writings in 1846–49. In a feuilleton in 1847 he describes the gradual etherealization of the world of the dreamer, his loss of all sense of time, place, and space. The reader has the uncanny feeling of being transported into a Proustian world—but it is the world of an abortive Proust, of unrealized creative potentiality. There is a repeated cycle in the dreamer: the world of fantasy is followed by an "awful awakening," and then, once again, "a book, a musical motif, some distant recollection, an old one, from real life, in a word, one of the thousands of causes of the most insignificant kind, and the poison is ready, and again fantasy vividly and abundantly spreads out across the patterned and whimsical canvas of a quiet, mysterious dreaming." The loss of contact with real life is accompanied by a dissolution of reality in the mind of the dreamer. Everything takes on the aspect of the fantastic. "His imagination is tuned up; immediately a whole story, tale, novel is born." The consequences to moral and aesthetic consciousness of this withdrawal from life are catastrophic. The dreamer loses that "moral sense with which man is capable of evaluating all real beauty." He begins to fear life, becomes apathetic, and "does not want to know that human life is an uninterrupted self-contemplation in nature and in actual reality." Such a life, Dostoevsky observes at the end of his feuilleton, is a "tragedy."[5]

On the social plane, Dostoevsky seeks the tragedy of the dreamer in the failure to make contact with reality, to steep himself in it. Man's most natural need is to "become conscious of, to realize, to give shape to, his I in real life."[6] "Life is a whole art," Dostoevsky remarks in another feuilleton, "and to live means to make an artistic work out of oneself." But only in contact with common interests, only "in sympathy with the mass of society and its direct, immediate demands, and not in drowsiness, not in indifference— from which the mass disintegrates—not in solitude, can man's treasure, his capital, his good heart be refined into a precious, inimitable brilliant diamond."[7]

The failure of the dreamer to realize self-image, form, in real life is manifested on the plane of consciousness in an inability to master creative fantasy, to synthesize the variegated discrete elements of imagination into a complete image, and to realize that image in concrete form. Dostoevsky illuminates the elementary movements of creative consciousness in his story, "The Landlady." The artist-dreamer Ordynov is disclosed as adrift in the womb of creation, "in his internal artistic world." "There was more unconscious inclination in him than logical, clearly defined motive to study and know," Dostoevsky writes of his hero. There was no order or definite system in his work.

> Right now he had only the first ecstasy, the first fever, the first delirium of the artist. He was creating for himself a system; it was being lived out within him for years, and in his soul already little by little there was rising a still dark, unclear, but somehow miraculously joyous image of an idea, embodied in

a new, clarified form, and this form wanted to emerge from his soul, was lacerating his soul; he still timidly felt its originality, truth, independence: a creative work [*tvorchestvo*] was already manifesting itself in his energies; it was being formed and gathering strength. But the moment of embodiment and creation [*sozdanie*] was still distant, perhaps very distant, perhaps quite impossible! (Pt. I, Ch. I)

The whole process of artistic creation, as Dostoevsky will later define it in various letters, is outlined here in the movement from the semiconscious, feverish state of inception, or forming of the "image of the idea," through the final stage of "embodiment and creation." But for Ordynov this final stage is, in fact, quite impossible. The peculiar tragedy of Ordynov's creative consciousness is dramatized in one of his dreams at Murin's. His encounter with reality, his experiences with Murin and Katerina have overwhelmed him, and he sinks into a delirious dream world where he anguishes under the "yoke of impressions." Prophetically, he realizes that "he was condemned to live in some kind of long, endless dream, full of strange, fruitless agitations, struggles, and sufferings." In his delirium his whole life, all his experiences, reading, dreaming, "came to life, everything took shape, became embodied, arose before him in colossal forms and images, moving and swarming about him." He saw magnificent gardens, the building and destroying of towns, the dead arising from cemeteries, the birth and death of whole tribes and peoples. At last he saw himself thinking "not in disembodied ideas but in whole worlds, whole creations; he saw himself carried along like a speck of dust in all this endless, strange, inescapable world; and he saw how all this life in its mutinous independence would crush, oppress, and persecute him with its eternal, endless irony; he heard himself dying, dissolving into dust and ashes, without resurrection, forever and ever."

The powerful dynamics of creative consciousness—the surge of imagery, the epic scope of imagination, the evocation of a universal, timeless reality—are revealed in Ordynov's dream; here there is poetry in the sense that Dostoevsky frequently uses this word. But Ordynov's dream also points to the tragedy of the creative consciousness which remains unmastered, which vanquishes the artist. The moment of highest creation for Ordynov is a moment of dissolution, of "dying." But there is no birth of creative work. "Reality strives toward fragmentation," we read in *Notes from the House of the Dead*. Dostoevsky's portrayal of the tragedy of the artist-dreamer suggests that man's inner reality, his mind and imagination, may be subject to the same internal dynamic, the same "striving" toward fragmentation under certain circumstances. Creativeness, Dostoevsky believed, develops out of itself and demands complete freedom in its development, but this is freedom for form, for development toward an aesthetic ordering of reality. The successful creator masters the "mutinous independence" of his fantasy, the poetic charges of his imagination. But Ordynov, like Prince Myshkin, only has a premonition of a "new, clarified form" within himself and, like Myshkin, fails to realize this form in art, science, or life.

Ordynov's inability to cope with real life, his collapse before Murin, delivers a final blow to an already seriously disordered creative consciousness. Ordynov, Dostoevsky writes at the end of "The Landlady," now laughed at his dream of becoming "an artist in science" and "did not take a step forward." "Thought did not pass into work. Creation ceased. It seemed as if those images deliberately grew into giants in his mind and laughed at his impotence, at their creator." Creation in Ordynov is stillborn. Nowhere has Dostoevsky more vividly dramatized the nightmare of creative impotence.

Inspiration, intuition, poetry are the germinal elements in artistic creation, but these elements must be supported and developed by conscious effort, work, artistry. The romantic cult of inspiration and genius can be fatal to the artist. The sick egotism of the artist-dreamer, the violinist Efimov (*Netochka Nezvanova*, 1849), has deep psychological roots, but it is nourished by romantic assumptions about the nature of artistic genius. Efimov regards himself as an "unrecognized genius" and behaves in such a way as to create the impression that "an artist was a special sort of man, unlike other people." Efimov has a much finer instinctive feeling for music than his friend "B." But his tragedy lies in his inability to combine his "instinctive understanding of music" with the discipline of an artist-craftsman. He has an inadequate knowledge of the techniques of his art; in his constant fantasy, constant dreaming about his genius, Efimov does not follow up his talent. The less talented

"B," on the other hand, early accepted the limitations of his talent, accepted the role of a "laborer in art." He attributes his success to "constant, ceaseless labor, to a clear consciousness of [his] forces, to voluntary self-subordination, and to eternal enmity toward conceit, premature self-satisfaction, and laziness which is the natural consequence of this self-satisfaction." Pushkin in "Mozart and Salieri" exalted the natural genius, Mozart, while contrasting him with the tragic figure of the rational, hard-working, but divided man of talent. Dostoevsky reverses this pattern in *Netochka Nezvanova*. It is the "genius" who emerges as the divided, embittered, and tragic figure—a victim of his own illusions, of romantic self-deception; on the other hand, the simple, striving, limited man of talent receives a firm nod of respect from Dostoevsky.

The young Dostoevsky, as his letters as well as some of the memoirs of his contemporaries suggest, may have shared some of the psychological problems of Efimov. But, unlike Efimov, he recognized from the beginning of his writing career the transcendent importance of work, craftsmanship, artistry. "Raphael painted for years, polished, revised, and the result was a miracle," Dostoevsky wrote in 1845 at the time he was working on *Poor Folk*.[8] And a few months later, apropos of his own revisions of *Poor Folk,* he remarks that the "fate of the best works is always such that one revises them endlessly." Chateaubriand, he notes, revised *Atala* seventeen times, and Pushkin "made similar revisions even with minor poems. Gogol polishes his miraculous creations two years in a row."[9]

"You obviously confuse inspiration, that is, the first, momentary creation of a picture or a movement in the soul (which always happens this way) with work," Dostoevsky wrote to his brother Mikhail in 1858. He asks his brother where he got the idea that a picture must be painted right away and comments that "work and a tremendous lot of it" is always necessary. He adds that the "light, elegant poem of Pushkin of several lines seems written at one stroke because it went through quite long pastings and scorings by Pushkin. These are facts. Gogol wrote *Dead Souls* for eight years. Everything that he wrote down at first turned out to be unripe." But there must be inspiration, Dostoevsky insists. "Without inspiration, of course, there will be nothing."[10]

Dostoevsky's deep concern with artistic craftsmanship as well as his view of the early stages of the creative process is disclosed again in some views on the Russian writer A. T. Pisemsky. Pisemsky writes quickly and too much, Dostoevsky wrote to his friend Maikov in 1856. The writer should have "a little more of a sense of his own worth, a little more respect for his talent, more love for art." Ideas ought not to be rushed into expression. "It is better to await more of a synthesis, to think a little more, to wait until the many small elements expressing one idea gather into one large, one major image [seen] in relief. Colossal characters created by colossal writers are often created and worked on stubbornly for a long time."[11]

The whole problem of creative inspiration and artistic embodiment is reexplored in a letter to Maikov in 1867. Dostoevsky comments on what an agony it is to have to write something on commission. "Do you know what it means *to compose?* No, thank God you don't know!" Dostoevsky had, at this time, accepted a large advance on his next work; at the beginning of the year he had hoped that "poetry would not leave [him], that the poetic thought would flash and develop artistically to the end of the year." He felt that this would be probable, since "many kernels of artistic thoughts always flash and make themselves felt in my head and soul. But then [they] only flash, and what is necessary is a full embodiment which always occurs unexpectedly and suddenly, but it is impossible to calculate when precisely it will occur; and then, having received in one's heart a complete image, one can pass to artistic fulfillment. Now at this point," Dostoevsky concludes, "it is possible even to calculate without error."[12]

We may call attention at this point to a consistent pattern or schema—beginning with "The Landlady"—in Dostoevsky's thinking on the creative process: first, the primary stage, the "first ecstasy" or inspiration in which artistic thoughts flash through the mind; second, the stage of mental embodiment, the formation in creative consciousness of the "idea of the image," of a "complete image," the "image in relief"; finally, the stage of "artistic fulfillment," the concrete shaping of the image, its material embodiment.

But what is the actual relation between the second and third stages of creation? Is the stage of "artistic fulfillment" merely a mechanical giving birth to an already completed form? The most striking example of this conviction may be found in Dostoevsky's letter to Maikov in May, 1869. Here he sets forth in detail his idea—previously communicated to Maikov—for a series of folk ballads on Russian history. These ballads, Dostoevsky hopes, will constitute a great national book and will serve to rejuvenate the self-consciousness of Russian man; they will embody "our view" and represent a "new word." The ballads will end up with fantastic pictures of the future. "I would not hold back here *from any kind of fantasy.*" "And therefore," Dostoevsky sums up with characteristic fervor, "this is not simply a poem and a literary preoccupation —this is science, this is preachment, this is an exploit."[13]

Dostoevsky's idea, it hardly need be noted, is heavy with "tendency." Further, he is proposing that another writer, Maikov, carry out this exploit! (The private Dostoevsky forms here a revealing contrast with the public Dostoevsky—the critic of Dobrolyubov.) Now it is unquestionably the unusual nature of his idea and the unorthodox character of his request to Maikov that explain his somewhat nervous "digression" at the beginning of his letter. Here he distinguishes between two stages of the creative process. The essence and length of the verses, Dostoevsky writes, depend upon the soul of the poet and appear suddenly, completely ready-made in his soul, even independent of himself.

> I shall make an important digression: a poem, in my opinion, is like a natural precious stone, a diamond in the soul of the poet, quite ready-made in all its essence, and just this is the first work of the poet, as a *maker and creator,* the first part of creation. If you wish it, not he is the creator but life, the mighty essence of life, the living and essential god putting its strength in places throughout the whole work, but most of all in the great heart and in the strong poet, so that if the poet himself is not creator—(and one must agree with this, particularly you as a connoisseur and poet yourself, because really a creative work suddenly comes out of the soul of the poet quite whole, finished, and ready)—if it is not he himself who is creator, then at least his soul is that very mine which gives birth to the diamond and without which they would be found nowhere. At this point there follows the *second* task of

the poet, no longer so profound and mysterious, but only that of the artist: this is, on receiving the diamond, to refine and polish it. Here the poet is just about like a jeweller.[14]

How different the emphasis is here from Dostoevsky's letter to his brother in 1856, in which he placed such stress upon Pushkin's endless pastings and scorings, in which he warned his brother not to confuse inspiration with work! Dostoevsky's explanations, here, it is true, do not radically contradict his two- or three-stage theory of creation; yet there is a romantic extravagance in his concept of the "mystery" of creation; and this reduction of the artist (as opposed to the poet-creator) to the matter-of-fact status of a jeweller is unexpected from him. We have already suggested the reasons for the unusual emphases in these comments on the creative process. Dostoevsky unquestionably realized the artificial character of his proposal to Maikov. Understandably he must have wished to allay precisely any impression that he regarded the poet as somebody who can be called upon to fulfill an order from the outside— hence his special emphasis upon the organic character of creation; hence also, his emphasis upon the fact that both he and Maikov have a common spiritual nexus. He stresses at the outset that the idea for the ballads was "born in me precisely . . . *for you,* or to put it better, is inseparable from the image of you *as a poet.*" Dostoevsky is delighted to learn—and quite understandably—that "you yourself are *inspiring yourself with the very same idea and finding it necessary* to write it."[15]

The tendency to underplay the role of artist-craftsman is not characteristic of Dostoevsky; in this respect his letter to Maikov conveys a somewhat false impression. One must bear in mind, too, that in his letter to Maikov Dostoevsky is concerned, specifically, with the genre of poetry, the birth of a *poem.* The experience of many poets certainly supports Dostoevsky's theory of poetic creation. It is noteworthy, however, that he transferred his theory of poetic creation (as set forth in this letter) to the sphere of the novel. "The poem is ready and has been created beforehand, as must always be the case with the novelist," Dostoevsky wrote in his *Diary of a Writer* in 1876, in connection with a "future novel."[16] Here, however, Dostoevsky has in mind the poetic core, the conception or idea of the novel; the novel is certainly not formed within him in any literal sense. "In order to write a novel,"

Dostoevsky soberly observes in his notebook, "one must store up, first of all, one or several strong impressions, really experienced in the heart of the author. Herein is the task of the poet. From this impression there develops a theme, plans, and a harmonious whole. Here, now, is the task of the artist, although the artist and poet help one another in both areas—in both instances."[17] We are certainly closer here to Dostoevsky's considered view of the roles of "poet" and "artist" in artistic creation than we are in his letter to Maikov in May, 1869. What Dostoevsky had in mind when he suggests the interaction of poet and artist seems best illustrated by some remarks on his own creative process in his previously cited letter to his brother Mikhail in 1858. Inspiration must not be confused with work; on the other hand, inspiration must always be present. "I, for example, immediately write down a scene just as it comes to me at first, and I am happy with it. But then for whole months, years, I rework it, inspire myself with it *several times,* and not once (because I love this scene), and several times I add to it or take away something, as has already happened with me, and believe me—it came out far better."[18] A novel, it follows, cannot be rushed, "because inspiration depends in much upon time."[19]

Dostoevsky's work on *The Devils* excellently illustrates the extraordinary complexity of his creative process. "They say the tone and manner of an artist's story must be born by itself," Dostoevsky wrote the critic Strakhov apropos of his work on his novel. "This is true, but sometimes you get entangled in them and you seek them." Nothing, according to Dostoevsky, had given him as much trouble as this novel. "At first, i.e. even at the end of last year, I looked upon this thing as something that had been painfully hammered out, composed; I looked upon it from above. Then real inspiration visited me and I suddenly fell in love with the thing, seized it with both hands—and I had to throw out what I had written."[20]

The process of artistic creation, then, as Dostoevsky both experienced and understood it, in the final analysis defies any schematic ordering. We can speak only of a movement toward form, of a creative and continuous interaction of elements and resources in the creator, ranging from the subconscious action of imagination to the formulation of poetic idea and image through the conscious and laborious casting and recasting of the image in the heat of constant reinspiration. Dostoevsky's tendency, however, to structure the problem of the creative process in terms of the interacting roles of "poet" and "artist" points to his own intensive struggle to attain a harmony between these two functions, to master form. The poet for Dostoevsky is primary creator; but primary creation is ecstatic, inspirational, centrifugal in action. "The idea is too good," he writes in connection with *The Idiot,* and he fears that the "execution" of the novel may be inadequate, especially since he is working in haste and abroad.[21] "This is a real poem," he writes S. A. Ivanova in 1869 apropos of his plan for a work on the theme of atheism. His "goal and hope," he writes a little later, lies in "achieving a complete synthesis of my artistic and poetic idea, i.e. in the desire to express myself as fully as possible before I die."[22] "There is much that is hastily written in my novel, much that is drawn out and unsuccessful, but here and there I have succeeded," he writes about *The Idiot.* "It is not my novel but my idea that I vouch for."[23] "As for artistic quality, I don't know, it seems as though it ought to be successful," he writes later in connection with *The Devils.* "The idea is bold and big. The point is that I always take themes beyond my strength. The poet in me always puts a strain on the artist, and this is really bad."[24]

The problem of mastering the surge of images and ideas, of controlling the excited energy of creative consciousness—a problem first raised in the portrayal of Ordynov—was certainly a central one for Dostoevsky. Strakhov called Dostoevsky's attention to this problem. "You clutter up your works, make them too complicated," he wrote to Dostoevsky in 1871. "If the texture of your stories was simpler, the effect would be stronger."[25] Dostoevsky responded to this criticism:

> You have pointed out with frightful precision my chief shortcoming. Yes, I have suffered with this and I do suffer; to this day I absolutely have never been able (never learned) to master my means. A multiplicity of separate novels and tales simultaneously are squeezed by me into one, so that there is neither measure nor harmony . . . not coping with my means and being carried away by [my] poetic outburst, I undertake to express an artistic idea that is beyond my strength. (N.B. Similarly the force of poetic outburst in V. Hugo is stronger than the means of execution. Even in Pushkin one finds traces of this duality. And in this way I am ruining myself.)[26]

Dostoevsky, of course, did not clutter up his novels, nor are they too complicated; rather, they are the direct fulfillment of the creative tasks he set out to resolve, the precise shaping of the material of life he observed in his mind's eye. Strakhov himself recognized that Dostoevsky's "shortcoming" was linked with the "merits" of his art; he understood that in the final analysis he was proposing "absurd advice: to cease being yourself, to cease being Dostoevsky." But if Strakhov erred in characterizing Dostoevsky's novels as too complicated, he quite correctly recognized that Dostoevsky's most serious creative problem centered on the mastery of his ample means. It is significant that Dostoevsky posits "measure and harmony" as his principle ideal. One recalls his evaluation of the completed manuscript, *Poor Folk,* in 1845. "This is a severe, harmonious piece" ("eto veshch' strogaja i strojnaja")—words which seem to echo Pushkin's famous paean to classical St. Petersburg: "I love thee, creation of Peter, I love thy severe, harmonious aspect." Harmony and measure, of course, are to be found in Dostoevsky's works; but it is not the Olympian, rational, contained, essentially optimistic balances or values of classical art, or of a Pushkin, or even a Tolstoy, but the tense measure and harmony that comes from the clash and ultimate, yet always precarious, reconciliation of turbulent and contradictory elements.

But if Dostoevsky is positing classical "measure and harmony" as his ideal, then he is proposing absurd advice to himself. He is asking, in effect, for a vision of life and for a formal aesthetic embodiment of that life, which is free of those unresolved and potentially destructive tensions and antitheses which we find in much of his work, in particular, for example, in *Notes from the Underground.* This is his dream. "What a horror—the soul of man!" O. Pochinkovskaya remarked to Dostoevsky in 1873 after reading *Notes from the Underground.* "But also what a terrible truth!" Dostoevsky, Pochinkovskaya reports, smiled broadly and answered: "Kraevsky told me at that time that this is my real *chef d'oeuvre* and that I ought always to write in this vein, but I don't agree with him. It is really too gloomy. *Es ist schon ein überwundener Standpunkt.* I am *able* now to write in a more cheerful, conciliatory vein."[27] Motifs of Christian reconciliation indeed are heard increasingly in the last decade of Dostoevsky's life and work; more and more he felt in Christianity a foundation firm enough to resist the *perpetuum mobile* of rational scepticism and despair. But it is

questionable whether these developments are reflected aesthetically in his novels in any major movement toward his classical
ideal of measure and harmony. Strakhov observed in his reminiscences that death prevented Dostoevsky from making new advances in his art, "kept us from seeing, perhaps, far more harmonious and lucid works." He may have been correct. But in the void
of speculation one may wonder whether a harmonious and lucid
Dostoevsky novel is not (as Strakhov himself seems to have
sensed) a contradiction in terms.

Dostoevsky's ideal of harmony and measure, nonetheless, attests
to his pervasive quest for form, for control of the primary creative
forces in himself. Belinsky defined *"classical* art" as "the full and
harmonious balancing of idea with form, while the *romantic* is the
preponderance of idea over form."[28] Dostoevsky's creative dynamic, in this sense, might be viewed schematically as consisting of
a tension between two impulses: that of the "poet," the romantic
and centrifugal outburst ever threatening to overwhelm form, and
that of the "artist," the striving for unity, form, equilibrium. I. I.
Lapshin suggests the emphasis or direction in this tension of impulses; starting out with the notion of the "striving for form" and
the "striving for expression" as the two basic tendencies in art, he
writes apropos of Dostoevsky: "Not a scorn [for artistic form] but
a *fateful* preponderance of the striving for expressiveness over the
feeling for form." Yet this strong movement toward expressiveness,
though negatively revealed in some of Dostoevsky's secondary
works, did not prevent him, Lapshin notes, from attaining a "striking feeling for form" in his great works. The striving for expressiveness is itself fruitful in giving birth to new artistic forms.[29] Here
one may observe, however, that the new artistic forms are not so
much the result of a striving for expressiveness, as the result of an
objective need to give expression to a "new reality" and a new vision of that reality. It is precisely here that Dostoevsky's "shortcoming"—his penchant for a dense and complex novelistic texture
—ceases to be a shortcoming and must be recognized as a central
aesthetic merit.

Financial needs, Dostoevsky remarked in a letter he drafted to
M. N. Katkov in 1865, were bearing down heavily upon him; at
the same time he had to work intensively on *Crime and Punishment.* "I am constantly being torn from work, I am losing golden

time, and with a distraught spirit . . . must sit down to what is above all a poetic piece, one which demands both tranquility of spirit and a definite mood."[30] Dostoevsky strikes no new note here. His constant complaint, from the beginning of his literary career, is that he is compelled to write for money, to meet a deadline, and therefore to spoil things. "My work won't tolerate compulsion," he wrote in 1845.[31] "From poverty I am *compelled* to make haste and to write for money, consequently *inevitably to spoil things*," he writes to his brother Mikhail in 1859.[32] And again in 1880: "I cannot write off the cuff, I must write artistically, I am obliged to that god, poetry."[33] Yet all his life, with the exception of the last few years, Dostoevsky wrote under one or another form of compulsion: the need for money or the necessity of meeting a deadline.[34] In addition to financial and journalistic pressures, he suffered from a variety of physical ailments throughout his life, among them, as is well known, epilepsy. Much of the evidence of Dostoevsky's letters suggests that "tranquility of spirit" was the exception rather than the rule in his periods of intense creativity. Writing as a whole appeared to have placed great strains upon him. "In general I work nervously, with anguish and worry," he wrote in 1880. "When I work intensely I am sick, even physically."[35] But he could work with combined "pleasure and agitation," as we note in a letter of 1867.[36] Dostoevsky naturally desired surcease from the various pressures under which he wrote. Yet we are probably not too far from the truth in suggesting that his creative muse responded favorably to pressures. We may cite, in this connection, a revealing remark which appears in a letter written by Dostoevsky at the time of his incarceration in the Petropavlovsk Fortress in 1849. He complains of painful hemorrhoids, pains in the chest, a heightened impressionability at night, monstrous dreams, the rocking of floors; he continues: "When such a nervous period came upon me in the past, I made use of it in order to write—one always writes best and most in such a state." And he adds a moment later (and his words define his life): "intensive work *con amore*—here is real happiness. Work, write—what is better?"[37]

One may note here, as a matter of related interest, that Dostoevsky views the dream world (including that of the nightmare) as a sphere of creativity analogous to, if not identifiable with, creative imagination. In *Crime and Punishment* he calls attention to the extraordinarily vivid sense of reality which is so often obtained in a nightmare. The dreamer encounters subtle and unexpected artistic details of a kind that he could not invent in real life "even if he were such an artist as Pushkin or Turgenev." The devil in Ivan Karamazov's nightmare expresses substantially the same thoughts. Even Leo Tolstoy, he insists, could not invent such "a complex and real reality." "And yet such dreams are seen sometimes not by writers at all, but by the most ordinary people, officials, feuilletonists, priests. . . . All this is really a complete enigma: a government official once even confessed to me himself that all his best ideas came to him when he was sleeping."

Dostoevsky was fully aware of the reality of subconscious creation. The "dreamer" type in his early stories functions almost entirely on this level of consciousness. "I create whole novels in my dreams," the hero of "White Nights" observes. At the end of his life Dostoevsky summed up his theory of subconscious creation —a theory which first found expression, as we have seen, in "The Landlady." He observed to his young friend, E. N. Opochinin: "The poet (by poet I understand any writer) always must be as it were filled up—work is always going on in him, imperceptible to him himself. That which it is creating wants to emerge. Poetic work, however prolonged it is, does not depend upon will: an *invisible force* moves it."[38] In his reminiscences of Dostoevsky, Strakhov points to unconscious creation as a special feature of Dostoevsky's own creative process. According to Strakhov, he would always postpone his work to the last minute and would then take it up only when he had just enough time to get it done. Strakhov calls this kind of procrastination "writer's laziness."

> The point is that inner work constantly was going on within him, a constant growth and movement of ideas was taking place, and it was always difficult for him to break off from this work in order to write. While remaining, to all appearances, idle, he, in fact, was working indefatigably. . . . "By the way"—he himself says on the first page of *The Insulted and Injured*, where he brought himself out onto the stage—"it always was more pleasant for me to ponder over my works and to dream about how I would write them than in fact to write them, and really, this was not from laziness. Now why is this?"

And Strakhov answers that this was because writing for Dostoevsky was "almost always an interruption of inner labor, an exposition of something that might have been developed still further to the point of a full perfection of imagery." In contrast to the majority of writers who subject their work to endless revisions and gradually arrive at a clear image, Dostoevsky "often dreamed of what splendid things he might work out if he had the leisure; however, as he would say himself, the best pages of his works were created at once, without revisions—of course, as the consequence of an already *matured* thought."[39]

Strakhov here closely parallels Dostoevsky's own theory of the creative process, one which places such strong emphasis upon the maturing of a "complete image" within the writer. Dostoevsky's dream of creating splendid things at leisure clearly was not organic to his restless creative ethos or to the anxious content of his art. He envied Turgenev, Tolstoy, and Goncharov because they had *time* to write; he appeared to stress leisure as a key to artistry; but it was a key only to a particular kind of artistry, a particular kind of form and style which was not his own. No other Russian writer, Dostoevsky once wrote, ever worked under such difficult conditions as he constantly worked under. "Turgenev would die from the very thought."[40] Quite possibly, but then Turgenev was an entirely different kind of artist; the attributes of "moderation and beauty," which Merezhkovsky rightly considered central to Turgenev's art and outlook, were rooted in an aesthetic temperament and an artistic interest entirely different from those of Dostoevsky. The young aristocrat who could spend hours watching the slightest movements of an insect on a leaf was not destined to write *Notes from the Underground;* nor was the plebeian Dostoevsky ever to write anything resembling "Bezhin Meadow."

The idea of writing as a means of obtaining emotional relief or catharsis is expressed in one form or another by many of Dostoevsky's characters; it is associated most often with the theme of confession in his work. "I began to describe all this to you in part to unburden my heart," Dostoevsky's first hero, Makar Devushkin, writes to Varvara. Often there is a compulsive need to write. "Perhaps I will really get some relief from writing these notes," the man from the "underground" observes. He has a particular recollection which oppresses him and of which he feels he must rid himself. "For some reason I believe that if I write it down, I will be free of it." Stavrogin's confession, his "document"—observes the narrator in the originally suppressed chapter of *The Devils*—is like the casting about of a sick man; he wishes to find a position in which "if only for a moment he can find relief. Not even to find relief, but merely to replace if only for a moment the former suffering with another. . . . The author [Stavrogin] declares that he could not but write, that he was 'compelled to.' " Stavrogin is driven to self-expression by a tormenting need for punishment. "I want everybody to look at me," he writes at the conclusion of his confession. "Whether this will relieve me—I don't know."[41]

The "notes" of the man from the "underground" or of Arkady Dolgoruky in *The Raw Youth,* the confession of Stavrogin, the ruminations of the hero of "A Gentle One" are not conscious efforts at artistic creation. But we have here nonetheless a primary effort, through some sort of expression, through form, to attain at least a measure of order and harmony in internal being. The expression of one's thoughts is a *forming,* a clarification. The internal monologue of the hero of "A Gentle One" is an instructive example. "He justifies himself," Dostoevsky writes, "now accuses her, and goes in for evasive explanations: here is both crudeness of thought and heart; here also is profound feeling. Little by little he really *clarifies* the whole thing to himself and gathers his 'thoughts to a point.' A series of memories which he evokes inexorably leads him, finally, to *truth;* the truth inexorably elevates his mind and heart." Clarity and truth, here, are not the result of a logical exposition of thoughts, the controlled application of reason; indeed reason (which has become irrational here) threatens complete chaos in the hero. Clarity and truth, to the extent to which they finally emerge, are a function of expression which finally brings itself "to a point," into a focus, into some sort of rudimentary order and form. Self-expression is not art, but insofar as it strives toward form it is primary aesthetic experience.

The writer Ivan Petrovich in *The Insulted and Injured* points directly to the aesthetic character of catharsis through writing. Like many of Dostoevsky's heroes, he, too, is tortured by memories from the past. He explains to the reader why he proposes to set down in writing his impressions of the past. "When put down in writing they will acquire a more tranquil, more harmonious character; they will resemble less a delirium, a nightmare. . . . The mechanics of writing alone are worth something; it will calm me, cool me off, set into motion in me former habits of the author, turn my memories and sick dreams into work, into an occupation" (Pt. I, Ch. 2).

We may find here and there in Dostoevsky's critical writings as well as in his letters reflections of this notion of art as performing a cathartic function for the artist, of art as a means of coming to grips with the internal "nightmare." Dostoevsky's analysis of the creative dynamic of Nekrasov's poetry—with its powerful motif of love and compassion for the people—is dominated by a psychological view of the creative process. Nekrasov the poet, Dostoevsky insists, cannot be understood apart from Nekrasov the man, the citizen. Why did Nekrasov so love the people, why did he go to them? "Because . . . love for the people for Nekrasov was *a way out of his own sorrow for himself*. . . . Serving the people with his heart and talent he found all his purification before himself."[42] Art in Dostoevsky's view became for Nekrasov one of the polarities of his self-division; the lofty image of the people, the ideal of beauty and truth which he found in its suffering and which he embodied in his verse served to transform his self-division into a creative dialectic of opposing parts; in the people he found a point of striving outside himself. Dostoevsky writes objectively of Nekrasov, but it seems, too, that in some respects he is speaking of himself out of his own experience.

Dostoevsky comments on art as a means of coping with self-division and suffering in two letters written in the last year of his life. A young painter, E. F. Junge, had complained to him of her "duality," her spiritual distress and unhappiness. "I feel very close to you," he wrote in reply, "because this *duality* in you is precisely what I have in me, and what I have had in me all my life. This is a great torment, but at the same time it is a great pleasure: It is a strong consciousness, the necessity for a self-accounting and for the presence in your nature of a need for a moral duty toward yourself and humanity. That is what this duality means."[43] Dostoevsky offers Junge heartfelt advice: "Do not abandon art and give yourself over to it more than ever before. I know . . . that you are not very happy. But by living in solitude and lacerating your soul with recollections you can make your life too gloomy. The one refuge, the one medicine is—art and creative work."[44] Dostoevsky's view of human existence as a tension between earthly suffering and a striving for a lofty ideal is reflected in the practical advice he gives to Junge. Art will not resolve the devastating duality in man, but it provides a refuge from self-annihilating solitude. For Dostoevsky, quite clearly, art became a sphere both for self-accounting and expression of that sense of moral duty toward self and humanity.

"Can an abnormal state of affairs, an abnormal and difficult relationship between good people stretch out endlessly, for whole years, to death itself without any resolution?" M. A. Polivanova asked Dostoevsky in a letter in 1880. "Is it possible that this resolution depends only upon personalities? Can man be eternally divided and not desire, not make an effort to get out of such a situation?"[45] The question raised is a universal one, Dostoevsky wrote in reply. "Man, of course, can be eternally *divided* but naturally he will suffer from this." If there is no hope of "a good all-reconciling solution," then one must seek a way out "in some other outside activity which can give food for the spirit, quench its thirst." At this point in his letter Dostoevsky remarks that he considers that he is "less capable" and has "less right" than anyone to answer the questions posed by his correspondent.

> This is because my position as a writer is too special in respect to such questions. I always have ready and on hand my writer's work, to which I give myself over avidly, in which I place all my strivings, all my joys and hopes, and I give them release through this activity, so that whenever just such a question presents itself to me *personally,* I always find spiritual activity which at once removes me from the burdensome reality to another world. Having such a way out when confronted by the difficult questions of life, I am of course bribed, because I am secure, and I can even make judgments with partiality, subjectively.[46]

Artistic activity is viewed here as an area for full self-expression; it provides not so much a refuge from the questions of life, as a means of dealing with them on a higher plane. Artistic activity is an area for sublimation and objectification of the difficult questions of life; art provides security, aesthetic distance, the detachment that makes it possible to deal firmly, perhaps even one-sidedly, with the very questions with which the individual, outside of art and on his mundane and involved plane of living, might be at a loss or even loathe to answer.

Literature is a primary source for the study of reality. "I can study characters from writers," Dostoevsky wrote in 1839 in connection with his goal of finding out " 'what . . . man and life mean.' "[47] Life in its turn reveals the reality of the world of literature. "To study the life of people is primary with me—both as a goal and amusement," Dostoevsky wrote in 1844, "so that now I am completely convinced, for example, of the existence of Famusov, Chichikov, and Falstaff."[48] His discovery of the reality of Gogol's Akaky Akakievich and Pushkin's Samson Vyrin is reflected, of course, in the literary adventures of Makar Devushkin in *Poor Folk*. Literature and life merge in the imagination of Dostoevsky.

In his early feuilletons in 1847 and in his stories about the "dreamer" Dostoevsky describes a psychological state in which imagination triumphs over reality. At the same time, he describes the primary workings of creative imagination and observation. The dreamer in "White Nights" describes his walks through the streets of St. Petersburg, his encounters with people. "They, of course, do not know me, but I know them. I know them intimately; I have almost made a study of their faces and am delighted when they are gay, and downcast when they are under a cloud."[49] In his description of the dreamer type, the hero of "White Nights" discloses a subconscious plane of observation. The dreamer moves through the streets, steeped in himself and in his fantasy, unaware of what goes on about him, unconscious of passersby. "But the very same fantasy has caught up in its playful flight the old woman and the curious passersby and the laughing girl and the peasants . . . and capriciously has woven all and everything into its canvas like a fly in a spider web." The conscious mind is closed; but the subconscious mind is actively open, filtering reality in, artistically organizing it.

The dreamer, living a life of the imagination, shrinks on contact with the real world; yet at the same time the contrast between the world of the imagination and the real, prosaic world stimulates the artist-dreamer. The young adolescent girl, Netochka Nezvanova, breaking out of the magic circle of a purely imaginative world, speaks of her enjoyment of the bustle of town life as she walked to her music lessons. "I liked so much this background for the beginning of my artistic life, the contrast between this petty everyday life, these trivial but living cares, and art which awaited me but two steps from this life, on the third story of a huge house, packed top to bottom with residents who, it seemed to me, had nothing to do whatever with any art."

Dostoevsky describes in "Petersburg Visions in Verse and Prose" (1861) his emergence from the romantic world of the dreamer, how he came to recognize the real world of "quite prosaic figures" about him, and how this new world of reality was drawn into the sphere of his artistic observation and imagination. But he insists that he is still a "mystic" and a "fantasist." "Now I dream, I dare say, although in the same way, yet of other persons; but old acquaintances sometimes knock at my door." He relates how he recently read in a newspaper about a certain Soloviev, "a new Plyushkin," "a new Harpagon," who had died in terrible poverty, though in possession of much gold. He tells how he meditated on this case; and then, once when walking, "there suddenly appeared before me in the crowd a kind of figure, not a real one, but a fantastic one. Really, I can in no way renounce the fantastic mood." In his brief encounter he "immediately guessed that this was the same Harpagon who had died with half a million in his rags. . . . And there and then (I have a quick imagination) there suddenly was limned an image, very similar to Pushkin's miserly knight. It suddenly seemed to me that my Soloviev was a colossal figure." But then, Dostoevsky writes, he realized that he was plagiarizing Pushkin—"and matters turned out in quite a different way." And he proceeds to recount his new imaginative reconstruction of Soloviev. "Six years ago Soloviev probably lived somewhere; he was young," and so on.[50] What is striking in Dostoevsky's creative process—as it is revealed in his discussion of Soloviev—is the interplay of various elements: a fact from a newspaper, a "real" street encounter, literary images (the misers of Pushkin, Gogol, Molière); through it all is felt the excited action of a creative imagination shaping and reshaping the materials of reality.

The raw material of Russian life is imaginatively re-formed in Dostoevsky's creative consciousness; it is humanized, purified. In his sketch "Milieu" (*Diary of a Writer,* 1873), Dostoevsky briefly recounts the newspaper story of a woman who, as the result of long years of beatings administered by her husband, finally hangs herself. "For a long time I kept dreaming about the whole situation, and I am dreaming even now," Dostoevsky writes. "I kept picturing to myself [the husband's] figure." And he proceeds to reconstruct for the reader his imaginative account of how the husband tortured his wife. "Have you ever seen how a peasant whips his wife? I have. He begins with a rope or a strap. The peasant's life is devoid of aesthetic pleasures—music, theaters, newspapers; naturally something must fill it. After binding his wife or thrusting her legs into the opening of a floor board, our little peasant would begin, probably, methodically, coldbloodedly, even sleepily with measured blows, not listening to cries and entreaties." He listens with delight but gradually grows wild with pleasure. This is the kind of sadistic scene Dostoevsky describes in *Notes from the House of the Dead;* there, too, he stresses the delight in disfiguration. Dostoevsky's imagination wanders further. He remarks to the reader that "in other circumstances" the peasant woman might have been a Juliet or Beatrice from Shakespeare or a Gretchen from *Faust,* might have had in embryo something not inferior to what one finds in the noble class: "a loving, even a lofty heart, a character full of the most original beauty." "And this very Beatrice or Gretchen is being whipped, whipped like a cat!" Dostoevsky observes. The animal shrieks of the suffering peasant woman go to the husband's head. The stage has been set: as far as Dostoevsky and the reader are concerned, the husband is beating a lofty embodiment of the feminine ideal. " 'I will wash your feet and drink the water,' cries Beatrice in an inhuman voice." Drawing to the end of his description of this awful scene, Dostoevsky remarks, almost laconically: "She hanged herself in May, early in the morning, probably on a bright spring day." The court recommended clemency for the husband. "Clemency to whom, for what?" Dostoevsky exclaims. "One feels as though in some kind of a whirlwind; you are seized and whirled and whirled."[51] The reader, too, is caught in a whirlwind, but it is created by more than the knowledge of the court decision. The whirlwind here is the shock of encounter with the disfiguration, the moral *bezobrazie* of human nature. With the magical names of Beatrice and Gretchen, however, Dostoevsky points—as though in a draft conception of a story—to the transfiguration of his anonymous peasant martyr into a symbol of disfigured humanity, an embodiment of a lofty moral-aesthetic ideal.

One cannot, of course, speak of a real aesthetic transfiguration of the peasant woman in the sketch. Dostoevsky declares that he has actually "seen" a peasant beating his wife; his description of the beating has all the marks of that obsessive, hypnotic self-involvement which we find in Myshkin's description of an execution. Here, perhaps, is the pulsating realism of the nightmare—typical of Raskolnikov's description (in *his* nightmare) of a peasant beating a horse. The nightmare of disfiguration is all but triumphant in Dostoevsky's journalistic sketch; in his novels, however, the form of beauty, the moral and spiritual attributes of the Russian Gretchen constitute an antithetical dream, a dream of purified humanity.

Many pitfalls, Dostoevsky recognized, threaten the creative success and integrity of the artist: an inability to master, artistically, the surge of imagery and ideas; uncritical subordination to "tendency," or, on the other hand, a severing of all links with reality; a kind of intoxication with one's talent, which can lead the most sober man astray. Apropos of this last pitfall, Dostoevsky believed that "a certain almost ignoble, excessive 'responsiveness' " is inherent in all men of talent. "Belinsky, in a conversation with me, compared this 'responsiveness' with 'prostitution of talent' and greatly despised it, regarding, of course, as its antithesis, a certain fortitude of soul which would always be able to master this responsiveness, even in the presence of a most ardent poetic mood."[52]

One of the most serious dangers, Dostoevsky suggests again, may lie in a fear or uncertainty over one's own talent and a corresponding excess of vanity which conceals this fear and thus immobilizes self-criticism. The condition is exacerbated by the fact that the sensitive individual necessarily must counterpose his ego to a public that is frequently crude and uncomprehending. Dostoevsky writes in a letter in 1847:

God, how many disgusting, vile and limited greybearded wise heads, connoisseurs, pharisees of life there are, *priding them-*

selves on their experience, i.e. their characterlessness . . . good-for-nothings who eternally preach satisfaction with fate, faith in something, limitation in life, and satisfaction with one's place, without looking into the essence of these words . . . with inexhaustible petty malice condemning the strong, passionate soul who cannot bear their vile, day-to-day routine and calendar-like existence. Scoundrels they are with their vaudeville, material existence. They are scoundrels![53]

But the proud stance of the artist may be pierced by a painful sensitivity to the moods and evaluations of the public he scorns. In the same letter Dostoevsky remarks that "you will soon read *Netochka Nezvanova.* This will be a confession, like *Golyadkin,* although in another tone and style." "My pride is frayed," he comments in connection with unfavorable reactions to "The Double." "But brother! How pleasant it is to be understood!"[54] From the heights of exaltation over the high acclaim accorded to *Poor Folk,* Dostoevsky fell into moods of depression over the reception given to "The Double" and "Mr. Proharchin." "I have a most brilliant future, brother!" Dostoevsky had written a year before;[55] now he speaks of the "dissolution of my fame."[56]

In the section of *Netochka Nezvanova* devoted to the violinist Efimov, we find an echo of Dostoevsky's own trials as a young writer, his sensitivity before the critical public.[57] Here there is protest against that public, but here also is a sharp critique of what might be called the negative romantic ego in the artist. The musician "B" chides Efimov over his despondency.

What torments you? poverty, privation? But poverty and privation form the artist. They are inseparable with the beginning. Nobody needs you now, nobody even wants to know you; that's the way of the world. Wait, it will be different when they learn that there is a gift in you. Envy, petty vileness, and most of all, stupidity, will weigh upon you even more heavily than privation. Talent needs sympathy, it wants to be understood, and you will see what kind of people will surround you when you attain ever so little of your aim. They will set at nought and will look with scorn at what you have achieved through strenuous labor, privations, hunger, sleepless nights. They will not encourage or console you, your future comrades; they will not point out to you what is good and true in you, but with malicious joy will single out every mistake you make.

The musician "B" is not trying to build up a defensive conceit in Efimov. Rather he warns him against pride, against scorning humble labor. "You are too impatient, you are sick with impatience, you are not simple enough, you are too subtle, you think too much, give too much work to your brain." The artist, then, must free himself subjectively from dependence upon the public, upon its moods and evaluations; at the same time he must not fall into the fatal net of vain and romantic self-exaltation (in Efimov's case the obverse side of a profound insecurity). The ruinous focus of Efimov's instability is his dream of becoming a famous man. He thirsts for fame. "And if such a feeling becomes the chief and single motive of the artist," observes "B," "then this artist is no longer an artist, because he has already lost the chief artistic instinct, that is, love for art simply because it is art, and not something else, not fame." The integrity of the artist is inseparable, therefore, from his commitment to his art; but this is not a commitment devoid of pride or ambition. In a letter to the actress A. I. Shubert in 1860, Dostoevsky remarks that she is very engaging when she at times "laughs over everything prosaic, ridiculous, presumptuous, stupid." Then, as though picking up the thread of an unexpressed thought, he continues: "Pride is a good thing; but in my opinion it is necessary to have it only for central goals, for that which you yourself have posited as the goal and purpose of your whole life. All the rest is rubbish."[58]

Art and man, we have seen, are historically inseparable for Dostoevsky: man finds his highest strivings embodied in the ideals of form created by the past. Likewise in the sphere of artistic creation man's striving toward a higher ideal, a striving ultimately for self-transfiguration, finds direct and organic expression in the creative process. The commitment to art is a total commitment: all the energies, all the resources, all the moral and spiritual strivings of self—on subconscious and conscious levels—are mobilized in the quest for form. Form for Dostoevsky is life; the destruction of form is death. The creative striving *to live* is preeminently an aesthetic striving for Dostoevsky, a striving for form. On the other hand, the creation of form in art, the very functioning of the creative process, involves an ordering and shaping of self. The artist is not transfigured (like Myshkin in his moment of "beauty and prayer"); but the work of art is the self's ideal experience of form; even more, it is the full realization of human potential and striving. But the path or process leading to that final experience of form—the birth of the work of art itself—is *struggle,* an immense and unending task of mastery of self in reality and reality in self.

11   Correspondences

"I AM WEAK IN PHILOSOPHY (but not in my love for it; in love for it I am strong)," Dostoevsky wrote his friend Strakhov in 1870.[1] In a certain sense this self-characterization is quite apt. Dostoevsky was an artist who did not learn philosophy or know it in any strict professional sense; but he constantly philosophized and did his most ardent thinking in imagery. Strakhov gave the following account of the workings of Dostoevsky's mind in philosophical realms:

> The most general and abstract thoughts frequently acted upon him with great force; and he would draw tremendous inspiration from them. He was, in general, to the highest degree an ecstatic and impressionable person. A simple idea, sometimes an old and well-known one, suddenly would fire him, would appear to him in all its meaning. One might say that in an unusual way he *felt thoughts*. At such times he would give expression [to a thought] in its various aspects, would express it sometimes in a very sharp image, although he would not elucidate upon it in a logical manner, would not develop its content. Above all he was always the artist, thought in images, and was guided by feelings.[2]

It would have been interesting, of course, if Strakhov had recorded some of his philosophical discussions with Dostoevsky.[3] But it is unlikely that we would find in them any systematic exposition on Dostoevsky's part of his ideas or even any clear and precise information on the genesis of his ideas. Strakhov recalls in the reminiscences we have cited how it used to amuse Dostoevsky when, in the course of conversations on abstract questions, he would identify Dostoevsky's ideas with this or that philosophical point of view. "It seemed that it was difficult to think up anything new, and he, jokingly, would console himself with the fact that he coincided in his thoughts with this or that great thinker."[4] Strakhov, elsewhere in his reminiscences, calls Dostoevsky an "unconscious Slavophile." Often when Strakhov would note that this or that idea was expressed by the Slavophiles, Dostoevsky would frankly confess: "I didn't know that."[5] One might say that Dostoevsky was a natural, as opposed to professional, philosopher—unconscious or uninterested for the most part in where, when, or how he absorbed his ideas or to whom he was beholden. Like the dreamer-flâneur in his wanderings through the streets of St. Petersburg in "White Nights," Dostoevsky moved through life weaving all and everything of philosophy into the canvas of his artistic consciousness.

Dostoevsky, as his letters alone attest, read widely. Yet precise data on if and when he read this or that work in philosophy or aesthetics is meager. It is almost certain that he read Schiller's aesthetic and philosophical essays at an early date; he was involved with his brother Mikhail on a project of translating the works of Schiller.[6] He evinced a strong interest in one letter in Chateaubriand's *Le Génie du Christianisme* in 1838, but we do not know for certain if he read this work at that time.[7] It has often been pointed out that Dostoevsky, on release from Omsk prison in 1854, asked his brother to send him, among other books, "Kant's *Critique de raison,* and if at all possible . . . Hegel's *History of Philosophy.* My whole future is linked with this!"[8] His future may indeed have been linked with Hegel's ideas but not with this particular volume of Hegel. Strakhov wrote later that the "history of philosophy of Hegel in the original," which Dostoevsky had asked his brother to send him, "remained unread, and he presented it to me as a gift shortly after our first meeting."[9] Dostoevsky, according to Strakhov, had studied German but had let it lapse completely and at the end of his life read only French among foreign languages.

In the final analysis, of course, it is almost meaningless to ask *where* and *from whom* did Dostoevsky get such and such a philosophical idea? The period of the 1840s, in which Dostoevsky matured as a creative artist and thinker, was saturated with the philosophical ideas of German and French thinkers. The critic Belinsky, even if his knowledge of German were limited, was full of the ideas, for example, of Schelling. Yet as D. I. Chizhevsky has noted, the ideas of Schelling were so widespread and frequent in the literature of the period that it is difficult to determine how

Belinsky mastered them.[10] The same may be said of the ideas of
Schiller, Hegel, and others. One did not have to read these authors
in the original or even in translation to be imbued with their ideas.
Dostoevsky clearly was a thinker who drew freely and unsystem-
atically from all sources; he was capable, as Strakhov noted, of
sympathizing with and understanding different and contradictory
views. His aesthetic ideas must be evaluated finally in their natural
environment, in the artistic matrix of his novels. Here one perceives
their contradictory unity, their raison d'être. Dostoevsky's philosophical ideas, when examined outside their natural environment,
tend to lose both their vitality and unity, tend to disintegrate, as it
were, into fragments of Schiller, Hegel, and others. Nonetheless it
is important to attempt to focus, if only briefly, Dostoevsky's aesthetic thought against the background of European aesthetic
thought. The quest here, of course, is not for "influences," for the
direct or devious paths of acquaintance with European philosophers, but for correspondences.

We are at liberty, in one sense, to seek correspondences between
Dostoevsky's aesthetic thought and almost every phase of aesthetic
thought up to and including the period of German romantic philosophy. In many respects the history of aesthetic thought, at least
until the critical age of Kant, is a history of redevelopment of certain basic formulas elaborated in the protean age of Plato. Dostoevsky's aesthetic thought, or, more precisely, his higher aesthetic,
has distinct affinities with the aesthetics of antiquity, the Christian
aesthetic of the Middle Ages and Renaissance, as well as with early
nineteenth-century German romantic thought (which was more
Platonist, perhaps, than it cared to admit). If it is the roots of Dostoevsky's higher aesthetic that one seeks, one can point to Plato:
his vision, in the *Symposium* and elsewhere, of absolute beauty, of
a beauty-in-itself, apart from the material world, toward which
man ascends in his search for total harmony; the triadic unity of
the good, the true, and the beautiful; the concept of archetypal
beauty, of eternal models for the fine arts; the understanding of
beauty in terms of certain formal principles of perfection, and so
forth. We noted earlier the Platonist character of Dostoevsky's
central pronouncement on beauty and art in "Mr. —bov and the
Question of Art."

But the Christian content of Dostoevsky's aesthetic thought is pronounced; it grows more and more dogmatic toward the end of his life. The aesthetic outlook embodied in the preachments of Zosima in *The Brothers Karamazov,* for example, might have emerged directly from medieval Christian aesthetic with its preoccupation with the theological "image," its passion for symbolism and allegory, its projection of morality into aesthetics, its aesthetic optimism, its deification of art. Medieval symbolism, as Edgar De Bruyne observes in his *L'Esthétique du Moyen Age,* in its theological and philosophical interest loves the image.[11] God has created all things in his image, and it is natural for us to discover in forms the "vestiges" of beauty, wisdom, divine art. It is through the sensuous images of his invisible beauty that God recalls to us the pure beauty of his truth. "Omnis visibilis pulchritudo invisibilis pulchritudinis imago est." All beauty is a theophany, a symbol of the inexpressible, of the Beauty immanent in all that is beautiful. "Here we are at the threshold of mysticism," De Bruyne remarks at the conclusion of his discussion of medieval aesthetic symbolism.[12] There is no question that Dostoevsky stands at this threshold in *The Brothers Karamazov.* In any case, his aesthetic is deeply imbued with symbolic and allegorical interpretations of beauty as well as moralistic theories of art.

Immanuel Kant is the gateway to modern aesthetics. In considering Dostoevsky's aesthetic thought in the light of Kant's *Critique of Judgement* one must cut back through the great movement of German romantic thought which followed upon Kant's thought—a movement which, as René Wellek has noted, "rather tended to weaken the distinctness of the realm of aesthetics and more and more made art a short cut to the absolute, a popular version of philosophy. Art was exalted but at the price of being lost in the Platonic triad of the beautiful, the good, and the true."[13] Dostoevsky, in respect to his higher aesthetic, is a child of German romantic philosophy. As an artist and thinker he was totally alien to the precise logical mode of thinking of Kant; the subtle formal distinctions, the fine divisions and subdivisions that are characteristic of Kant's thought find no parallel in Dostoevsky's critical writings. Yet substantively one may juxtapose their aesthetic ideas.

Dostoevsky wrote in a letter in 1876 that he had always wanted and still wanted "to write about literature, and about something about which nothing has been written since as far back as the 30s: *'About Pure Beauty.'* "[14] How did he understand "pure beauty"? Is this the pure, free beauty of Kant? There is no evidence that Dostoevsky subscribed to anything resembling the Kantian notion of a pure, free beauty, a notion which, as Israel Knox noted, excludes from the realm of pure, free beauty "almost everything that is truly significant, that possesses the least vestige of meaning (human and animal beauty, portraits, sculpture, architecture, the sublime)."[15] But what Kant excludes from the realm of pure, free beauty, he brings back in the category of dependent or adherent beauty. Thus, he admits of an ideal of beauty, but an ideal to be sought only in the human figure. "Here the ideal consists in the expression of the *moral*"; here there is a union of the pure ideas of reason with great imaginative power. An estimate of such beauty, Kant insists, can never be purely aesthetic.[16]

Pure beauty, in Dostoevsky's understanding, is linked with the good and the true; and the aesthetic experience of higher beauty (in nature and art) is always broadening out into moral and spiritual sentiment and perception. Emotion, imagination, and intellect are continually defining and qualifying the aesthetic experience of higher beauty. But higher beauty liberates; it raises man above the petty and egoistic. "So, at times," the narrator writes in *Netochka Nezvanova,* "one looks up into the blue heavens and one feels that one is ready to spend whole hours in sweet contemplation and that the soul becomes freer, more tranquil in these moments." But the "sweet contemplation" here is far from Kant's pure, disinterested, concept-free kind of aesthetic judgment. A concept or norm of beauty is very clearly in the background. Thus, the lines we have just cited come in the middle of a description of the beautiful face of Alexandra Mikhailovna. The features of her face—Dostoevsky's ideal of figural beauty emerges here—were "regular, and the thinness and paleness, it seemed, even more exalted the severe charm of her beauty." The narrator expounds ecstatically upon her glance—light as day, full of a calm goodness, "clarity, serenity of spirit, reconciliation, and love." The passage we have cited above then follows. The narrator concludes by saying that an artist would give half a lifetime to capture those moments when Alexandra Mikhailovna shifted from a quiet timid mood to a lofty spiritual exaltation, to a pure, strict enthusiasm which combined with a childish simplicity and faith. The experience of natural beauty, in this example, the "sweet contemplation," is in fact psychologically and aesthetically subordinated to an ideal of beauty, to an adherent (in the Kantian sense) type of beauty. The experience of nature is called upon only to confirm the moral-aesthetic experience of the human ideal of beauty. Dostoevsky's own reactions to the beauty of nature, painting, and music would seem to confirm Kant's view that "the feeling of pleasure or displeasure [in the judgment of taste] denotes nothing in the object, but is a feeling which the subject has of itself and of the manner in which it is affected by the representation."[17] The painter Alexandre Calame— and, we might add, Myshkin as well—was steeped in a kind of sad contemplation, as he looked off into the mountains, the clear sky, the misty distance. He "put his soul" into the painting, did not photograph nature, "but only took it as a means to imbue the spectator with his own tender, peaceful, sweetly contemplative disposition of spirit."[18] Whether Dostoevsky would follow Kant in concluding that the feeling of pleasure or displeasure in the judgment of taste "denotes nothing in the object" is another question. Nature lies unconsciously before us, Dostoevsky acknowledged, but the form of beauty in art, the image, and, above all, the ideal human image, is embodied value and meaning.

But the initial experience of beauty, in Dostoevsky's understanding, is a free experience, a liberating one; it simply brings pleasure. A humble and hungry clerk is on his way to his office. He passes a house, a fine example of architecture, "but having accidentally raised his head, he encounters the house, and his heart quickens. Architecture produces its effect because art is irresistible. He feels pleasure and with a new zeal he hurries to work."[19] Here the aesthetic experience, in the Kantian sense, is indeed "disinterested" and not at all confused with moral or religious categories of experience. Dostoevsky, like Schiller before him, recognized that art is not directly "tendentious." The aesthetic experience is without any constraint; man yields freely to the apparently purposeless pleasure of beauty, art (the Kantian notion of "purposeless purposiveness"). But out of this encounter comes a purposeful sense of being, a renewed sense of life and form which transfigures man from within.

The aesthetic experience, then, must first of all be one of pleasure. In the preparation of reading materials for the people (in educational programs) Dostoevsky insists that everything must be sacrificed to the element of "entertainment"; reading should "act on the imagination of the ordinary folk." He recalls his reading to soldiers and observes: "I by no means wanted to educate my audience, but only to give pleasure to it, and I wanted this because I myself got an enormous pleasure from [reading to them]."[20] Art is conceived here almost as play. But in the play and pleasure there is idea. Apropos of a story by Uspensky, Dostoevsky remarks that the reader will laugh throughout his reading of the story "and if so, then the idea of the writer has already acted upon you."[21] His concern for the entertaining quality of his art was so great that he wrote in 1870: "At least it [*The Devils*] will be entertaining (and I have reached the point at which I place the element of entertainment above artistry). As for the artistic element, I don't know, I think it ought to have a success."[22] This uncertain attitude toward the purely artistic level of his own work was, as we have noted earlier, typical of Dostoevsky. But as he himself notes in his *Diary of a Writer,* to "compose with talent means to compose entertainingly, because the best book, whatever it may be and whatever it treats, is entertaining." Dostoevsky's own works, of course, are a striking illustration of his own notion.

The notion of the "beautiful and the sublime" is on the lips of Dostoevsky's heroes—usually with irony—and Dostoevsky himself, as we noted at the outset of this study, projects this phrase as a kind of defining slogan of the 1840s. There is no evidence, however, that Dostoevsky clearly (if at all) distinguished between the categories of the beautiful and the sublime. Nonetheless, it is probably correct to say that *a* notion of the sublime (not necessarily Kantian) is acknowledged by Dostoevsky, indeed, arouses his aesthetic-religious consciousness. The feeling of the sublime in both Kant and Dostoevsky involves a subjectively experienced disjunction between man and nature. But in Kant the grandeur of the sublime gives birth in man to a sense of the grandeur of his moral worth, to a sense of destination. It is the category of the sublime in Kant, more than anything else, which serves to unite aesthetic with moral experience. In Dostoevsky's universe, the experience of the sublime in nature or in art evokes a permanent and poignant sense of spiritual disjunction between man and nature, a sense of alienation from nature and anguish for a lost ideal. Such is the character of Myshkin's experience before the Lake of Four Cantons or of Versilov's dream of the "Golden Age" inspired by Claude Lorrain's painting "Acis and Galatea" (in *The Raw Youth*). Such is man's paradoxical "enthusiasm" before the "ideals of beauty created by the past," an anguish for the ideal toward which man reaches out in pain, according to Dostoevsky. That which gives rise, in Kant's words, to "a feeling of the beauty and the dignity of human nature,"[23] is experienced by Dostoevsky negatively, subjectively, as a measure of some deep inadequacy, as an anguish for a *lost*—or future, but in any case inaccessible—beauty, a nostalgia for the infinite. Chateaubriand in *Le Génie du Christianisme,* apropos of the eternal yearning of the soul before the infinite, speaks of (and indeed illustrates in his own effusive feeling for beauty and the sublime in nature) that "instinctive melancholy" in man which makes him harmonize with scenes of nature and which puts him in spiritual contact with another higher reality. Chateaubriand here gives expression to the medieval romantic feeling for beauty. The corollary of the desire for absolute beauty, De Bruyne writes in his study of medieval aesthetics, is "melancholy before the fugitive character of all that charms us here below." In defining the dynamic character of the medieval feeling for beauty, De Bruyne cites the twelfth-century philosopher and theologian, Hugh of St. Victor: "Lorsque nous admirons la beauté des choses visibles nous jouissons, certes, mais nous éprouvons en même temps un vide immense. Les formes excitent notre désir et ne le remplissent pas. . . . Aussi ne permettent-elles pas de nous arrêter à elles, elles nous excitent à toujours vouloir plus et mieux, elles nous pressent de passer de l'image à la réalité."[24] This feeling before beauty, with its poignant sense of the void and at the same time its concealed moral and metaphysical imperatives, is deeply characteristic of the dynamic of the feeling for higher beauty, the feeling for the sublime, in Dostoevsky.

In his definition of the aesthetic experience Kant draws a sharp line between sensation and feeling. In opposition to those who stressed the primacy of sense qualities in aesthetic experience, Kant affirms that the judgment of taste consists in an entirely disinterested satisfaction; it is contemplative and indifferent to the existence of the object. Pleasure and pain, in the meaning of sense, are extruded from the aesthetic judgment by Kant, along with emotion and experience in general. Kant, then, sharply delimits the realm of aesthetic experience; on the other hand, this realm, as we encounter it in the Dostoevsky novel, is boundless.

In *The Critique of Judgement* Kant comments on those people who consider an interest in beauty to be a mark of good moral character; these people, he writes, have been "contradicted by others who appeal to the fact of experience, that virtuosi in matters of taste, being not alone often, but one might say as a general rule vain, capricious, and addicted to injurious passions, could perhaps more rarely than others lay claim to any preeminent attachment to moral principles."[25] The example, of course, refers to virtuosi of taste who *also* are addicted to injurious passions; it does not raise the question—very central to Dostoevsky—of a coincidence of taste and injurious passions. Kant's ground rules eliminate any consideration of this question: the Totskys, Stavrogins, Dmitry and Fyodor Karamazovs would certainly be barred admittance to the Kantian realm of authentic aesthetic experience. Dostoevsky, as a public critic and philosopher of aesthetics, would also bar admittance to these men; but in his larger capacity as novelist and poser of problems, he takes his point of departure—to use Kant's words—from the "fact of experience"; he is very much concerned with the aesthetics of evil—aesthetic delight experienced in sexual debauchery, violence, humiliation of others, and self-humiliation. The last and, perhaps, most vividly real of Dostoevsky's "underground" heroes, Fyodor Karamazov, confesses that all his life he "found pleasure in being offended, would take offense for the sake of aesthetics [*dlja estetiki obizhalsja*] because it is not only pleasant but sometimes also beautiful [*krasivo*] to be offended; that's what you forgot, great elder: the beautiful! This I'm going to note down in a little book!" We do not know whether Dostoevsky considered Fyodor's discovery to be worthy of putting down in a book, whether the problem raised by Fyodor's experience would have found its way into Dostoevsky's desired study "About Pure Beauty." In his critical writings the notion of the higher ideal, of authentic lofty beauty, is preserved in all its purity;

it keeps a respectful distance from "another ideal," a base ideal; but in his novels the two ideals (like Lyamshin's musical intermingling of "La Marseillaise" and "Ach, du lieber Augustin" in *The Devils*) are in constant interaction. The empirical evidence of human experience in Dostoevsky's novelistic universe—viewed in its raw, unexplained state—seems to demolish the Kantian limits of aesthetic experience. The breakdown of these barriers is already quite explicit in *Notes from the Underground*. Here the man from the "underground" affirms (and through his own personal experience—demonstrates) that man can find pleasure in humiliation and self-humiliation, debauchery, and (as far as mankind is concerned) all kinds of violence and bloodshed. Here in "consciousness," as K. Mochulsky expressed it, "the ethical plane is replaced by the aesthetic plane."[26] The connection between the good and the beautiful is sundered. But as we know, it is impossible definitively to identify Dostoevsky with this position. To the question: is aesthetic experience linked with the ethical good? Dostoevsky answers by posing another question: which *kind* of aesthetic experience? The experience of higher beauty or the experience of lower beauty—"beauty in Sodom"? For *man* (the Dmitry Karamazovs) in his blindness, these experiences merge into the single notion of "beauty"; for Dostoevsky, the artist-teacher and philosopher, these experiences cannot and must not be confused. Here there is a real ambivalence of view within Dostoevsky. Yet it is the essence of his whole being and world view that he insists upon living with this contradiction. Here is an example of his "reflexion": he has animatedly given himself over to the idea of a complex, two-faced beauty, yet he has preserved within his consciousness an unyielding point from which he examines, judges, and censures his own ideas.[27]

In his concept of the ugly in the fine arts Dostoevsky in his public pronouncements adheres to positions outlined by Kant and, later, Schiller. It is difficult, he observes, in connection with Klodt's "The Last Spring," "to present the repulsive in a beautiful way."[28] "Beauty of art," Kant observes, "is *a beautiful representation* of a thing."[29] The superiority of the fine arts consists "in the beautiful descriptions it gives of things that in nature would be ugly or displeasing."[30] Ugliness (disease, devastations of war, and the like) can be very beautifully described and even represented in pictures. But Kant makes an important qualification. "One kind of ugliness alone is incapable of being represented conformably to nature without destroying all aesthetic delight and consequently artistic beauty, namely, that which excites *disgust*."[31] Schiller, in his "Reflections on the Use of the Vulgar and Low Elements in Art," follows in the path of Kant's thought when he observes that "a great mind and a noble spirit . . . will itself know how to ennoble the vulgar, and precisely by superadding to it something spiritual and by discovering in it some great element [*eine grosse Seite*]." But Schiller, like Dostoevsky, is most admiring in the fine arts of the Italians and still more of the ancient Greeks who rejected the vulgar, common subject. "These always went to the ideal."[32]

Dostoevsky's belles lettres of course are notable for their depiction of the "low," ugly, and disfigured. But why is the writer or poet permitted to represent the "low" and the painter called upon to depict the lofty? Schiller provides an answer to this question. The artist, he writes, must not fear to show us his heroes under a contemptible exterior as soon as he is sure that he can give expression to their inner worth. "But what can be allowed the poet is not always permitted to the painter. The former merely brings his object before the imagination; the latter, on the contrary, brings his object before the senses. Therefore not only is the impression of the painting more lively than the poem, but the painter, if he only employs his natural signs, cannot make the interior spirit [*das Innere*] so visible as the poet through his arbitrary signs, and thus only the interior spirit [*das Innere*] can reconcile us with the exterior."[33]

Dostoevsky expresses a somewhat analogous view to Schiller's in his discussion of a painting by F. A. Bronnikov depicting a dying gladiator (based on a Lermontov poem) at the 1860–61 Academy of Arts exhibition. "In the painting the gladiator is literally dying, but since, as in the poem, he recalls the motherland as he dies—this recollection is repeated by Bronnikov over the gladiator in the clouds, rather mistily." Dostoevsky discusses some other paintings which take as their point of departure themes from Ja. P. Polonsky, Pushkin, and Goethe. He observes that it is "hardly likely that such things can ever be successful. In a literary work there is set forth the whole history of a feeling, while in painting—only one moment." Painting, then, lacks a perspective in depth, according to Dostoevsky; it is less capable than poetry of conveying *das Innere*. He suggests that the painter either compose five or six vestal virgins, giving expression to various shades of feeling, "or not take up an impossible task."[34] What is essential to Dostoevsky's thinking here is, clearly, that a work of art in one genre cannot be communicated to, or translated into, another genre. "Pictures are too difficult to be expressed in words," Dostoevsky wrote in 1873 in his *Diary of a Writer*.[35] And these sentiments are echoed by the hero of "The Dream of a Ridiculous Man" who complains about the difficulty of conveying the beauty and harmony of his dream in "our weak words." Dostoevsky, it is interesting to note, was highly sceptical over the possibility of successfully staging his novels. He granted permission at one time to a request to put *Crime and Punishment* on the stage, but he observed that "such attempts almost always do not succeed, at least entirely. There is a kind of mystery of art according to which the epic form never finds its correspondence in the dramatic. I even believe that for various forms of art there exist categories of poetic thoughts corresponding to them, so that one thought can never be expressed in another form which does not correspond to it." He adds, however, that it is quite another matter if one reworks and changes a novel, preserving an episode or two, in order to make it into a drama, or if one takes the original idea and completely changes the subject.[36]

The insistence on the unity of poetic thought and form (genre) is at the basis of several critical observations in "The Exhibition in the Academy of Arts: 1860–1861." Here Dostoevsky insists that "stage naturalness is not the same as naturalness. Therefore, even the beautiful on the stage is not the same as the beautiful in nature and in other arts, for example, literature. . . . One theatrical play may be very good on stage, but not in reading, and precisely the same in reverse. But in particular the pictorial quality of the stage is never good in painting." As an example, Dostoevsky points to the representation of stages from ballets and operas in illustrated journals printed abroad.[37]

In his defense of the autonomy of art in "Mr. —bov and the Question of Art" and in other essays, Dostoevsky essentially stands on positions elaborated by Kant and Schiller. He is far from the epicurean and egoistic "art for art's sake" aesthetics of Théophile Gautier. He seeks not to free art from service to man and society, but to affirm its natural independence in this service. Art for Dostoevsky is an "organic whole" with its "own, integral, organic life." Yet at the same time art, beauty, gives organic expression to man's life and to his deeper spiritual needs. Art is inseparable from man. The purposiveness of art, therefore, lies not *outside,* but in art itself and in its specificum: beauty. Art discovers its function by being itself; beauty is useful because it is beauty. Dostoevsky's position is summed up in Kant's notion of "purposeless purposiveness." Here Kant's analogy of the organism of nature with art is fundamental to the notion of the essential autonomy of art. There is no reason to assume, Kant affirms in his introduction to the "Critique of Teleological Judgement," that "things of nature serve one another as means to ends."[38] For Kant, the thing is itself an end, the parts of the thing combining of themselves into "the unity of a whole by being reciprocally cause and effect of their form."[39] Purposiveness in an object of nature is the harmonious interaction and unity of parts, independent of any outside purpose or causality; it is a self-fulfillment.

The Kantian analogy of art and the organism found subsequent expression, in one form or another, in German philosophical thought in the nineteenth century—in Goethe, Schelling, the Schlegel brothers, and others. Echoes of it, indeed, are evident in Dostoevsky's own "organic" view of art; here, however, Dostoevsky is probably giving expression to the more immediate impact of the "organic view" of literature of his literary associate, Apollon Grigoriev, and to some of the philosophical writings of Strakhov. The thinker must learn from life in its organic manifestation, Grigoriev insisted.[40] Life is an organic unity and the striving for "organic unity with life in its deepest roots" is the basis of all art. Art fulfills its destiny by being alive and national and by giving expression to the higher concepts of life.[41]

"Everything goes past like a river and the changing taste and various shapes of men make the whole game uncertain and delusive," Kant wrote by hand in his own printed copy of his *Observations on the Feeling of the Beautiful and Sublime.* "Where do I find fixed points in nature, which cannot be moved by man, and where can I indicate the markers by the shore to which he ought to adhere?" The question which Kant poses—not in despair, but in profound longing, as one commentator observes[42]—is in many respects the question which tormented Dostoevsky. For Kant, however, the question takes the form of a pure philosophical problem to be worked out in the controlled sphere of logical thought; for Dostoevsky the problem of finding markers in a sea of relativism is the consuming quest of his life and art. The sense of profound crisis that underlies Dostoevsky's own quest is evidenced in the anguished words of the man from the "underground": "Where are my primary causes on which I can rest, where are the foundations? Where can I find them? I exercise myself in thought and, consequently, with me every primary cause immediately drags after it another still more primary one, and so on into infinity. Such precisely is the essence of all consciousness and thought." The quest here is Kantian, but the total atmosphere of disorientation and the confession and affirmation of the complete impotence of consciousness and thought in this quest belong to the crisis of culture of the late nineteenth and twentieth centuries.

What separates Dostoevsky from Kant, in the final analysis, is his sense of the bankruptcy of all rationalistic philosophy;[43] what links them, however, at the source of their quest is unquestionably the central place occupied by aesthetics in the philosophical outlook of each writer. For Kant the aesthetic experience effects a synthesis between the realm of necessity and freedom, between the natural and the moral order; for Dostoevsky, as for Schiller, the aesthetic awakening of man presages his moral transfiguration. "Knowledge does not regenerate man," Dostoevsky wrote in 1861, "it only changes him, but it changes him not into one general, stereotyped form, but in accordance with the nature of this man."[44] Dostoevsky believed that only the "ideal of beauty," instilled in the soul of man, can lead to the resolution of the moral and social problems afflicting man. He, of course, found this ideal of beauty in its highest embodiment in the image and word of Christ.

It is unquestionably Friedrich Schiller, himself deeply preoccupied with Kant's antithesis between the natural and the moral order, who contributed much toward the shaping of Dostoevsky's aesthetic humanism. Schiller, like Kant, seeks a synthesis between these antitheses. Man ought to be neither one nor the other. "Nature ought not to rule him exclusively, nor reason conditionally. The two legislations ought to be completely independent of one another and yet completely united."[45] The ideal of a beautiful humanity, Schiller believed, can only emerge from a union of both of these elements.

"I have always believed in the force of the humane, aesthetically expressed impression," Dostoevsky wrote apropos of art and aesthetic education. He echoes the central theme of Schiller's philosophical letters *On the Aesthetic Education of Man:* the aesthetic education of humanity through the refinement of aesthetic sensibility. Aesthetic culture, the aesthetic condition, will not reform man; it will bring him only to the condition where he can make of himself what he will; it will bring him the freedom to "remodel the work of need into the work of his own free choice, to elevate physical to a moral necessity."[46] Out of the antitheses of man's "natural character," which is selfish and violent, and his "moral character, which . . . first must be formed" will emerge a "third character," which might serve as a pledge to a still unseen morality.[47] Dostoevsky's whole conception of Dmitry Karamazov is in many respects a realization and, at the same time, paradoxically, a sober realistic testing of Schiller's ideal perspective for man— the "child of nature."

Schiller, then, steps forth and proclaims art as the daughter of freedom. Yet at the same time he recognizes that "utility is the great idol of the time" and that "in these crude scales the spiritual service of art has no weight."[48] But it is precisely beauty of art—and specifically the fine arts—which for Schiller points the way toward the salvation of humanity, points out to man "the direction toward the good."[49] Beauty for him unites the ideals of the good and the true, all that is sacred to man; it is ideal form, and in seeking its model, Schiller, thoroughly imbued with Winckelmann-Hellenism, appeals to ancient Greece, the nation with the most highly developed "feeling for beauty."[50] The quest for form, the emphasis upon form as the realization of freedom, is central with Schiller as it is with Dostoevsky.

In the middle of one of his speeches defending Dmitry Karamazov, the defense attorney Fetyukovich remarks, apropos of the arguments of the prosecutor, that there are things which are even worse than a most malicious and unfair attitude toward the case. "Such as, precisely, when we are, for example, swept up by a kind of artistic game, the need for artistic creation, the making of a novel, so to speak." Fetyukovich himself, of course, is carried away by his own extraordinary talent, by the game (rather than the moral substance) of his case. The problem of aesthetic lying is raised by Dostoevsky in the introduction to a discussion of a legal case in which the noted lawyer V. D. Spasovich was involved. (Significantly, Dostoevsky parodied Spasovich in the figure of Fetyukovich in *The Brothers Karamazov*.) "What is talent?" Dostoevsky asks. "Literary talent . . . is the ability to say or express well what a talentless person will say and express badly." In this connection, he notes, there arises an "insoluble question: does talent possess a man or the man—his talent?" And Dostoevsky adds that on the basis of his observation of past and present talents, "man with extreme rareness is capable of mastering his gift . . . talent almost always enslaves its owner, so to speak, grabbing him by the scruff of the neck . . . carrying him far, far away from the right road." Thus, he observes, a certain liar in Gogol began to tell a story and might have told the truth " 'but of their own accord such details appeared' " that it was impossible to tell the truth; or a worldly liar and jokester of Thackeray's always likes to leave behind him a burst of laughter, reserving the cleverest witticism for the end. "Do you know: I think it is very difficult to remain and, so to speak, preserve oneself as an honest man, if one is so concerned with saving the wittiest word for the end." All this Dostoevsky relates to a certain "ignoble, excessive 'responsiveness,' " which he considers inherent in all men of talent and capable of leading the most sober man astray.[51]

Dostoevsky is principally concerned here with nailing down what he considered the lying artistry of Spasovich's legal talents; at the same time, it is evident that, in general, he is linking artistic instinct (talent) with pure play, with the game. On the social stage such play may be morally reprehensible, may represent a "game" with values, conscious or unconscious deception; but on the stage of art, we infer, aesthetic lying is the essence of the artistic impulse; it is telling a story, creating a novel. The virtuosity of Ivan Ilych in court, the pleasure he finds in playing with the victim-defendant—in Tolstoy's *The Death of Ivan Ilyich*—is, objectively, almost criminal; the vicarious enjoyment of the actor on the stage, however, his intoxication with his own role, is art. The notion of art as a game is encountered in *The Brothers Karamazov*. Kolya Krassotkin at one point insists to Alyosha that the rumor that he played robbers with the other boys for his own pleasure, to amuse the boys, is slander. Alyosha replies:

> But think of it this way: adults go to the theater, for exam-
> ple, and presented there are the adventures of all sorts of
> heroes, sometimes there are robbers and wars, too—now isn't
> that really just the same thing, in its own form, of course?
> And the game of war or robbers which young people play in
> their recreation: this really is also burgeoning art, the need for
> art being born in a young soul, and these games sometimes
> are formally better composed than in the performances in the
> theater; the only difference is that people go to the theater to
> look at actors, while here the young people themselves are
> acting. (Pt. IV, Bk. 10, Ch. iv)

Play, the game, the artistic instinct, art, is for Dostoevsky in-separable from man. Here in Alyosha's remark is doubtless an additional explanation of what Dostoevsky meant in "Mr. —bov and the Question of Art" when he said that art was "born with man," that it gave expression to a basic "need." The need for beauty, for unity, form, the full expression of one's nature, is ex-pressed first of all in the primitive "play" instinct.

Dostoevsky's thinking in this area moves along channels pre-pared by Kant and Schiller. Schiller's conception of beauty is based on his view of man. Man for him is neither exclusively matter nor exclusively spirit. "Beauty as the consummation of his humanity, therefore, can be neither exclusively mere life . . . nor can it be exclusively mere form [*Gestalt*] . . . it is the common object of both impulses, that is, the Play-impulse."[52] Schiller conceives of two basic impulses—the Material-impulse [*der Stofftrieb*] and the Form-impulse [*der Formtrieb*]. The action of both is directed toward truth and perfection. Beauty, finally, is the object of the Play-impulse. There is no degradation of beauty here, for it is only in play that man displays his twofold nature. And man plays only with beauty. "Through beauty sensuous man is led to form and thought; through beauty spiritual man is brought back to matter and the world of sense restored."[53] In beauty, then, man finds the unity of all aspects of his nature, integration, full identity. Here, too, in beauty, society finds its highest development. "Only the communication of the beautiful unites society, because it relates to what is common to all. . . . Beauty alone makes all the world happy, and every being forgets its limitations as long as it experiences her enchantment."[54] It follows from all this that one of the most "important tasks of culture is to subject man to form even in his purely physical life and . . . to make him aesthetic, since the moral condition can be developed only from the aesthetic, but not from the physical condition."[55] "In a word: beauty must be exhibited as a necessary condition of humanity."[56]

In Schiller's writings the highest type of man is the aesthetic type. Yet in the final analysis, as D. I. Chizhevsky observed, the ideal man for Dostoevsky is not *homo aestheticus* but *homo religiosus,* an Alyosha Karamazov.[57] In Dostoevsky's thought, especially in the last decade or more of his life, we are struck by the emphatic Christian religious synthesis of the aesthetic and moral categories. "There is no virtue if there is no immortality," Ivan Karamazov declares. And the strands of religion and morality are closely interwoven in man's "aesthetic strivings." The young Dostoevsky considered Schiller a "Christian poet," although in this respect (the *Christian* element) he placed him far below Victor Hugo.[58] It would be difficult, however, to speak of Schiller's aesthetics as Christian in the sense that we may speak of Dostoevsky's. If we sought a thinker who resembled Dostoevsky in the Christian religious emphasis of his aesthetics, it would not be Schiller but François-René de Chateaubriand. Chateaubriand has been mentioned as a possible early influence on Dostoevsky, but little has been said of their affinities as thinkers.[59] Both writers, despite their differences in background and cultural orientation, were deeply preoccupied with religion and with the eighteenth-century rationalist and materialist negation of religion; both passed through phases of doubt and Voltairian scepticism in their youth; and both reaffirmed their religious faith through an essentially aesthetic apprehension of Christianity. "Vous n'ignorez pas que ma folie est de voir Jésus-Christ partout, comme Mme. de Staël la perfecti-

bilité," Chateaubriand writes in his *Lettre à M. de Fontanes.* "J'ai
malheur de croire, avec Pascal, que la religion chrétienne a seule
expliqué le problème de l'homme."[60] God for Chateaubriand is
"beauté par excellence," la "souveraine beauté," la "beauté divine"; the "artiste" is he who shapes the body of man between his
fingers, the "grand peintre."[61]

The aesthetic justification of Christianity, the representation of
Christianity not only as truth but as beauty, is Chateaubriand's
central purpose and idea in *Le Génie du Christianisme,* a work
which first had been titled, significantly, *De la Religion chrétienne
par rapport à la Morale et aux Beaux Arts.* The author described
himself as "celui qui a voulu faire aimer le christianisme par la
beauté de son culte."[62] Like Dostoevsky, it is in its aesthetic and
moral dimensions that Chateaubriand finds the ultimate proof
and justification of Christianity.

There are many points of correspondence in aesthetic thought
between Dostoevsky and Chateaubriand: the central place accorded to the aesthetic element in the development of man (an
idea linked directly with Christianity by Chateaubriand); the synthesis of a classical conception of form with a Christian aesthetic
symbolism; the theory of the *beau idéal,* especially as applied to the
fine arts (beauty is regular, symmetrical, classical beauty; we must
paint beautiful nature, not imitate monsters); the romantic (and
medieval) nostalgia for the infinite; the concept of the "perfect
hero" as the embodiment of the "beautiful ideal" (Chateaubriand's
Christian *chevalier*); above all, the close intertwining of morality
and religion and of these and taste. "Morality is the foundation
of society . . . morality is born of religion."[63] But religion and virtue
are inseparable from beauty. "Quiconque est insensible à la beauté
pourrait bien méconnaître la vertue." The fine arts are not in themselves an end; ils "conduisent par la religion à la pratique des ver-
tus." On the other hand, "celui qui aime la laideur n'est pas fort
loin d'aimer le vice."[64] The source of bad taste and vice—both, for
Chateaubriand, go hand in hand—is atheism. But good morals depend upon good taste. Of one thing Chateaubriand, like Dostoevsky, is certain: if all is matter, if there is no immortality, then there
can be no virtue or vice and consequently no morality. When men
lose the idea of God, Chateaubriand declares, they rush into crimes
in spite of laws and executioners. "Il n'y a point de morale, s'il n'y
a point d'autre vie."[65]

These ideas, of course, are not peculiar to Chateaubriand; he is as much a child of his age as Schiller. His uniqueness consists, in part, in his poetic synthesis of religion and aesthetics, his justification of faith in terms of aesthetic sensibility, his tendency, as Victor Giraud expressed it, to conceive of everything *sub specie pulchritudinis*[66] and, finally, his passionate mobilization of an aesthetic Christianity in a crusade against Voltairian scepticism and irreligion. "Il faut une religion ou la société périt," he wrote in one of his early essays.[67] This idea underlies *Le Génie du Christianisme*. It is only in Dostoevsky that we find a similarly massive and dramatic mobilization of aesthetics and religion in an effort to stem the dissolving currents of rationalism and scientific scepticism.

Schiller's "aesthetic man," it has been noted, was far from satisfying the romantic aspirations toward totality.[68] In Schelling's thought aesthetics breaks through to the infinite. "Science, in the philosophy of Schelling," Hegel wrote, "attained its absolute standpoint; and although art had already begun to assert its peculiar rights and dignity in their relation to the highest interests of man, it was only now that the *notion* itself and the scientific position of art were discovered."[69]

Art, the artist, the act of artistic creation achieve their highest moment of exaltation in the philosophy of Schelling. Philosophy, he allows, attains the highest, but it brings to that point only a fraction of man. "Art brings *the whole man* as he is . . . to the cognition of the highest," Schelling writes in his *System of Transcendental Idealism,* "and herein consists the eternal difference and wonder of art."[70] The idea of beauty "unites all other ideas." "I am convinced that the highest act of reason is the aesthetic act, embracing all ideas, and that truth and goodness are made kindred only in beauty. . . . Poetry . . . assumes a new dignity; it becomes what it was in the beginning—the teacher of mankind."[71] Art for Schelling is vision, and the vision is of the absolute, a moment in which the infinite is expressed in finite form. The infinite "represented in finite form is beauty. The basic character of every work of art . . . is therefore beauty, and without beauty there is no work of art."[72]

Dostoevsky's veneration of art and beauty as lofty embodiments of the good and the true, his notion of the lofty mission of art and of the artist as seer, his whole view of reality as a vast realm lying beyond the ordinary vision of man, unquestionably bear the imprint of the transcendental idealism of Schelling. "What we call nature," writes Schelling in his *System of Transcendental Idealism,* "is a poem that lies enclosed in a secret marvellous cipher." Through the world of senses the "land of imagination toward which we strive" appears, as in a mist. The images and places of the world of the imagination, which only incompletely glimmer through the cover of the real world, emerge when the wall between the real and the ideal worlds is lifted. Nature for the artist is "only the incomplete reflection of a world which exists not outside of him, but in him."[73] So also toward the end of his life, Dostoevsky defined the task of realism as that of seeking "man in man." The real and the ideal merged in his artistic consciousness.

Certainly Dostoevsky shares with the German romantic philosophers in general, and with Schelling in particular, something that we can define only as *monumentalism.* One is struck by this quality in Schelling's introduction to his *Philosophy of Art;* here he proposes to construct "not art as art, as this *particular object.*" Rather, he writes, "I construct the universe in the form of art, and the philosophy of art is the science of totality in the form or power of art."[74] This is ecstasy, Napoleonism sublimated in philosophical strivings and in the striving for the Absolute. Dostoevsky was already deeply imbued with this grandiose ethos when, as a young man, he noted that poetry divines God and thus fulfills the task of philosophy. "Poetic ecstasy is the ecstasy of philosophy"; this is profoundly true of Dostoevsky's own ethos as an artist. His most extraordinary heroes, Myshkin and Ivan, are both poet-philosophers, dangerous quasi-seers. An almost unchecked, all-embracing passion of poetry inspires Dostoevsky's sense of man and human destiny; and a permanent philosophical craving for the Absolute (as exhibited, for example, in Ivan Karamazov's monumental rebellion) finds its irrefutable justification in poetry. Ivan is all but destroyed, morally and intellectually, in *The Brothers Karamazov,* but Ivan the poet is ascendant over all.

"It may be said that while we prefer Hegel to Schelling," wrote Bernard Bosanquet, "this is partly because Schelling is best represented in Hegel."[75] Hegel is unquestionably the great watershed of aesthetics in the nineteenth century; his monumental lectures on aesthetics, published in 1835 after his death, are an astonishing summary and development of aesthetic thought from Kant to Schelling. When Dostoevsky wrote in 1876 that he had long wished to write "About Pure Poetry"—"something about which nothing has been written since as far back as the 30s"—he may very well have been referring to Hegel's lectures on aesthetics published in 1835 (and adapted into French by Bénard in 1840–51). In any case, Dostoevsky, along with his contemporaries, grew up in an atmosphere of Hegelianism as one grows up breathing air.

The highest destination of art is what it has in common with religion and philosophy, Hegel affirms in the introduction to his lectures on aesthetics. Art brings to consciousness the highest interests of spirit (mind). But philosophy, not art, is the highest form, the last phase in the evolution of absolute spirit. The purest form of knowledge is conscious thought. In art, thought is alienated from itself. But the spirit apprehends itself not only in the form most intimate to it, which is thought, but also in its alienated state in art. That is why, in Hegel's view, art only receives its true consecration in philosophical science.

Hegel's general concern with the rationalization of the concept of beauty and his relegation of art to philosophical science, of course, is not characteristic of Dostoevsky's mature interest in, and understanding of, art. Nothing is higher than art for Dostoevsky —if we understand art and the specificum of art, beauty, as the symbol and embodiment of goodness and truth. Hegel and Dostoevsky differ, it may be further noted, not in their evaluation of the past function of art, but in their view of its contemporary function. Hegel insists that modern society is "beyond the stage of reverence for works of art as divine objects deserving our worship." "Art is no longer able to discover that satisfaction of spiritual wants, which previous epochs and nations have sought for in it and exclusively found in it, a satisfaction which, at least on the religious side, was associated with art in the most intimate way."[76] Hegel arrives at the striking conclusion that "art is and remains for us, on the side of its highest possibilities, a thing of the past."[77] The golden age of Greek art, as well as that of the later Middle Ages, is over, according to Hegel. He posits the alienation of the artist in a reflective culture and, on the plane of cultural utility, he envisages art as ceding first place to the science of art.

Almost the entire body of Dostoevsky's critical and creative work attests to his recognition that modern society and modern man have lost touch with the beauty and ideals of the art of antiquity and the Renaissance. But what is accepted by Hegel as progress or as an inevitable stage in historical development is viewed by Dostoevsky as a crisis of culture. This sense of crisis is exactly conveyed by Dostoevsky's notion that "the aesthetic idea in the new humanity is beclouded," that a society attempting to base itself on positivism is "confused in desires and in ideals." In contrast to Hegel, Dostoevsky continues to view the fine art of the past, the ideals of the past, the antique notion of beauty itself, as a symbolic key to the resolution of man's moral and spiritual dilemma. He continues to view fine art (and literature as well)—in Hegel's words—"on the side of its highest possibilities," and he finds, for example, in the poetry of Alexander Pushkin, an embodiment of the ideals of goodness, truth, and beauty of which he is so enamored. Hegel insists that in modern society "we are invited by art to contemplate it reflectively, not, that is to say, with the object of re-creating such art [*Kunst wieder hervorzurufen*], but in order to ascertain scientifically its nature." But Dostoevsky looks to art precisely *Kunst wieder hervorzurufen;* he seeks in art, beauty, an aesthetic awakening, a reshaping of man and his reality according to the aesthetic-religious ideal. As to the question of the universal *need* for art, however, Dostoevsky is quite close to Hegel's view that man realizes himself externally in art, rediscovers himself through art, satisfies the demands of his spiritual freedom "by making explicit to his inner life all that exists."[78]

Dostoevsky's affinity with Hegel is very great in fundamental areas of aesthetic thought: the problem of the nature of artistic representation of reality and the theory of type. His view—expressed in his discussion of genre painting in 1873—that *reality as is* is nonexistent, his view that man apprehends nature in his "idea," his whole concept of the "ideal" (in the sense of type) and of type itself, lead us back directly to Hegel's treatment of the "idea" and the "ideal" in his lectures on aesthetics. Art, Hegel affirms, issues from the absolute idea itself; its end is the sensuous representation of the Absolute. But the "idea, viewed as the beautiful in art, is not the idea in the strict sense. . . . It is rather the idea as carried into concrete form. . . . The idea as fine art . . . is the idea with the more specific property of being essentially individual reality. . . . The idea as so conceived, a reality, that is to say, moulded in conformity with the notional concept of the idea, is the ideal."[79] Beauty, then, is the "idea of the beautiful," but "the idea in a determinate shape, as ideal."[80]

It is in the Hegelian context that we must understand Dostoevsky's appeal to modern genre painters, in "Apropos of the Exhibition," to "give more leeway to the idea and not to fear the ideal," his view that the poet-portrait painter trusts "his idea (ideal)," not the "projecting reality." Dostoevsky's critique of genre painting strikingly recalls Hegel's own argument. Art in its purification, Hegel believes, reveals the ideal. This is true, he observes, even in portrait painting, where the painter disregards many external details of form, texture, and color in an effort to apprehend and deliver the subject "selected in its universal character and permanent spiritual individuality." It is one thing to imitate the purely superficial outlines of a physiognomy; it is another "to detect and delineate the particular features which reveal the fundamental soul-life or character of the sitter."[81] The nature of the ideal, Hegel points out, consists just in this reference of "all points of external existence to their spiritual significance." The ideal, then, is "the reality selected out of the mass of chance particulars, insofar as the inner core in this external totality thus raised in opposition to universality is itself manifested as living individuality."[82]

Hegel's conception of the artistic representation of reality, his idealism, might in fact be viewed as a symbolic realism. Thus, he insists that the forms borrowed from immediate nature "to determine an ideal content must be assumed to be thus taken symbolically in the usual sense of the term, namely, that they are not thus immediately significant in themselves, but only as the external embodiment of that which is inward and spiritual, the content, in fact, they express."[83] We are very close here, indeed, to the substance of Dostoevsky's own defense of his so-called "fantastic" realism, to his view that his "idealism" is more real than his critics' shallow "realism."

The creation of the ideal in art is for Hegel, as for Dostoevsky, a question of poetry. "Is art to be prose or poetry?" Hegel asks. And he replies that "what is truly poetic in art is just that which we have called the ideal."[84] The ideality of a work of art, according to Hegel, exalts objects otherwise unimportant, transmutes the prosaic into the poetic. Dostoevsky's use of the term "ideal" in his discussion of Russian genre painters, as we noted earlier, reflected his preoccupation with the fine arts; but it also emphasized his deep concern with the fine arts as a medium for the expression of man's higher spiritual reality. Though he appreciates some of the genre paintings on exhibit, he clearly seeks better artistry, deeper spiritual content. The appeal for the "ideal" in Russian painting is an appeal for a deeper truth about Russian life, an appeal for more poetry. Indeed, artistic representation of reality, the penetration to the idea (ideal) of reality, both in the concrete sense of type and the abstract sense of universal truth, is always *poetic* representation. In his defense of the reality (typicality) of the Russian family in Pushkin's *Eugene Onegin,* Dostoevsky, it will be remembered, in the final analysis asks for "a little understanding of *poetry.*" "What about poetic truth?" Dostoevsky remarks apropos of the reality of Pushkin's monk Pimen. Leskov's creation of a new positive type, Savely Tuberosov, issues from a union of "poetic inspiration" with "a careful study of Russian life." A writer may select material from reality that strikes the reader as exceptional or fantastic in its occurrence in ordinary life. But "for the poet . . . there are the general, universal, and, I think, eternally inexhaustible depths of spirit and human character." Similarly Hegel insists that "it is the task of the artist to grasp the object in its universal relations and, in the envisagement it presents, to let fall everything which stands in a wholly external or indifferent relation to content."[85] Hegel goes on to define the correct orientation of the artist to surrounding reality. In a few words he presents what may be considered an archetype for all criticism of naturalism, including Dostoevsky's own critique of photographic realism.

> An artist . . . will refuse to accept all forms and means of expression offered him by the external world, on the mere ground that he finds them there. His main effort will be, if at least his aim be a real poetical creation, to secure that which will appropriately work in with his own imaginative conception; and, if he looks to Nature for assistance in supplying him with details, or, generally, as material to translate into his work, he will utilize such, not because he finds them so in

Nature, but because they fall in their *right* place as a part of his composition and are rightly made for him. This "right" of the artist is a higher one than the mere right of immediate fact.[86]

In a certain sense Hegel has provided a theoretical basis for understanding not only the painting of earlier ages, but much of the imaginative art of the twentieth century which vigorously has affirmed its right to depict the "idea" of reality in other than merely representational forms. The modern painter, in his imaginative depiction of a new reality, has exercised his freedom to select such data as illumine his idea of reality; he has denied in his search for new forms what the German philosophical idealist denied in his search for the Absolute: a "recognizable" reality with its imperative to represent reality "as is"; he has created his own symbolism to convey his imaginative concept of reality.

The breakdown of the concept of form—recognizable form—in the fine arts in the twentieth century would hardly have been welcomed by Dostoevsky. Yet paradoxically his own writing seems to stand somewhere on the threshold of that modern revolution in form. L. P. Grossman observes in one of his studies on Dostoevsky that the basic problem Dostoevsky faced in respect to composition was to "smash the prejudice about the organic unity of material as the basic condition of the artistically beautiful. He profoundly believes that the sweep and power of the whirlwind movement of persons and events around a single conception can overcome the stark incompatibility between these hostile elements."[87] Not only in general areas of composition and structure of his novels, but also in style and language, Dostoevsky's art invokes new notions of the "artistically beautiful." Grossman observes in another study that the "hostility of Dostoevsky to revolutionary-democratic ideas directed him also toward anti-social tendencies in art. It drew him by 1864 to the development of the theme of the spiritual underground. Thus was revealed a portent of that 'decadence' which noticeably colors the works of the aging novelist." The pathological experiences of Dostoevsky's heroes, all their disorder, irrationality, and loss of logical thought and speech were "carefully given embodiment by the creator of *The Devils* and *The Brothers Karamazov*. One of the most characteristic expressions of such a sick, overrefined, and decadent art is unquestionably 'Stavrogin's Confession.' "[88] Grossman is certainly correct in pointing out that Dostoevsky in his various characterizations sought out and utilized forms of speech which corresponded to the disorder represented. But whether this phenomenon is an expression of a "decadent art" —whether, indeed, Dostoevsky's interest in the "spiritual underground" takes its provenance from his political conservatism and can be termed "anti-social"—is very questionable. Grossman points to "Stavrogin's Confession" as an example in which the breakdown in the hero's moral and spiritual consciousness is accompanied by a breakdown in his whole style of speech. Certainly Stavrogin's language may be considered unformed and ugly—and precisely in terms of Dostoevsky's own norms of higher beauty—but Stavrogin is not Dostoevsky, and "Stavrogin's Confession" remains a work of art. It has its own form; most important, it was intended to function within a larger artistic structure. One must, of course, define the term "decadent." Grossman speaks of "Stavrogin's Confession" as the "first typical model of a 'decadent' style," but he does not elaborate.[89] It is fairly clear, however, that he uses the term in a pejorative sense. We should confine ourselves merely to saying that in his characterizations of certain types, as in his techniques of the novel, Dostoevsky sought out *artistic* forms to convey what he termed the "new reality," both as it manifested itself in a "disintegrating" social reality and in the "spiritual underground" of man. This entire reality may be termed, if one wishes, "decadent"; but the art is not decadent, either morally or aesthetically. Here, as Dostoevsky himself remarked in connection with the improvisation in Pushkin's "Egyptian Nights," everything depends upon the author's "point of view." And the "point of view" which provides the moral-aesthetic norm in "Stavrogin's Confession" is Tikhon.

Dostoevsky, Strakhov wrote, depicts "miraculous idylls amidst the greatest filth; generosity, tenderness, magnanimity in the most vulgar circumstances. . . . Dostoevsky went very far on this path: it was terrible to see how Dostoevsky would go down deeper and deeper into the spiritual abysses, into the frightful abysses of moral and physical corruption (this is his own word). But he comes out of them unharmed, that is, without losing the measure of good and evil, beauty and monstrosity [*bezobrazie*]."[90] He discovered flashes of beauty under the disfigured and repulsive exterior of man,

Strakhov wrote again, and for this he forgave people and loved them. "This tender and lofty humanity can be called his muse, and just this gave him the measure of good and evil with which he descended into the most terrible spiritual abysses. He firmly believed in himself and in man, and that is why he was so sincere, so easily took his own subjectivity for complete realism. By muse I understand that idealized character, that formation of mind and heart which a man takes when he begins to write and create."[91]

Strakhov grasps the whole tragic content of Dostoevsky's art and philosophy—and points to a concealed thought in himself—in the phrase: "so easily took his own subjectivity for complete realism." Dostoevsky's subjectivity—his muse, his idealized character—was shaped by the powerful aesthetic humanism of a whole generation of European and Russian thinkers and writers; and this subjectivity retained throughout Dostoevsky's life the imprint of naïveté, of utopia, of the idyll of a happy and good humanity. Schiller wrote in his essay "On Simple and Sentimental Poetry" that the idea of a condition of innocent and happy humanity (*die Idylle*) "and the belief in the possible reality of the same is the only thing that can reconcile man to all the evils to which he is subjected on the path to culture." It is the task of the man concerned with culture to show that this idea, this "possible reality" is real and can be realized in the sensuous world. But since "real experience, far from nourishing this belief, much the contrary continually contradicts it, so here it is the task of poetry to come to the aid of reason in order to bring this idea to view and to realize it in a single case."[92]

The idealistic ethos here is infinitely noble, but it is also latent with tragic implications. We have come full circle here to the "strange contradiction" which Belinsky had noted in Schiller: the great distance separating his ideal from his sense of the real. As a poet, Schiller did not suffer from this strange contradiction; his flight is ever sustained. It remained for Dostoevsky to suffer through this contradiction in his life and art. It was his lot simultaneously to feel the utmost evil in the world, to despair over it, and to feel the highest good; even more, it was his destiny to believe that *only* faith in an absolute beauty, perfection, and goodness could reconcile man to the terrible evil in his own nature. The contradiction posed by "The Legend of the Grand Inquisitor" is archetypal for Dostoevsky: the Grand Inquisitor is the embodiment of all earthly truths, the rational bearer of the "proof" of man's spiritual weaknesses and moral turpitude. Yet it is man's faith in a higher beauty, in Christ, in moral-aesthetic perfection (a really *tragic* faith here) which renders this truth incomplete and makes viable man's tragic actuality.

Strakhov, then, was right: Dostoevsky took—or *mistook*—his own subjectivity for complete realism. He did not believe in what he believed—and yet he believed! This permanent contradiction, spiritually exhausting him and continually renewing him, was his personal tragedy. Yet the artistic embodiment and resolution of this tragedy in his art remains his greatest glory, for in his art and through his art, he transfigured the spiritual underground. In art and only in art did he fully believe. Art provided him, in the final analysis, with the unity he lacked in his life; art and the ideal of beauty, both as a medium and as an abstract ideal for human achievement, was the bridge that for him linked freedom and necessity, the real and the ideal, the finite and infinite—all that German philosophy dreamed of from Kant to Schelling. But Dostoevsky's art does not vanish into the Absolute: his most poetic dreams are pervaded by a poignant realism, and his starkest realism is mitigated by a poignant dream. "Prove true, imagination, O, prove true!" Viola cries out in *Twelfth-Night*. Such is the final distillation of Dostoevsky's philosophy of art.

Appendix   Dostoevsky and the Fine Arts

DOSTOEVSKY maintained a deep interest throughout his life in painting, sculpture, and architecture. A certain formal aptitude in the arts may have been indirectly stimulated through his studies in drawing and draughtsmanship as a student in the Engineering School.[1] Throughout his life, in any case, he retained an amateur interest in sketching, to which his drawings in his notebooks attest. V. S. Nechaeva, in her article "Illustrators of Dostoevsky," divides his drawings into three groups: first, the drawing of details of an ornamental character (often with careful shading); second, drawing of an architectural character, chiefly elements of Gothic architecture (the detail of a Gothic window repeatedly appears, for example, in the notebook to *The Devils*); finally, the drawing of heads (more rarely, figures). Among the latter are some portraits, several self-portraits, and a number of attempts to depict characters about whom he writes in his notebook.[2] I. I. Lapshin claims to have seen a drawing of Fyodor Karamazov done by Dostoevsky himself. "More than a quarter of a century ago," Lapshin writes in 1923, "I saw in the home of the unforgettable Ja. P. Polonsky a portrait of Fyodor Pavlovich Karamazov, sketched in pencil by F. M. Dostoevsky. The drawing fully corresponded to the iconographic characterization of Fyodor Pavlovich which is given in the novel and was executed, I thought, rather skillfully."[3]

During his visits to Europe, especially during his four-year residence abroad (1867–71), Dostoevsky was a regular visitor to the great European art museums. "I saw all the pictures of Rembrandt, Rubens, the genre pictures of David Teniers," Dostoevsky's wife notes in her diary, June 2, 1867, after a visit to the famous Dresden Gallery. "At half-past four Fedya arrived and we went around the gallery once again. Fedya pointed out the best works and talked about art."[4] "Farewell, gallery, I thank you for those happy hours which you gave us," Madame Dostoevsky later writes in her diary in connection with the Dresden Gallery. "Fedya speaks as though he is saying good-by forever to the gallery; he says sadly that he will probably never once come here again."⁵ "Florence is nice . . . roses are flowering in the Boboli gardens in the open air," Dostoevsky writes Apollon Maikov, December 11, 1868. "But what treasures in the galleries! Lord, I looked at [Raphael's] 'Madonna della Sedia' in 1863; I looked at it for a week and only now have I seen it. But even apart from it how much there is that is divine."⁶

The diary and reminiscences of Madame Dostoevsky provide important documentation of Dostoevsky's mature taste in painting. According to Madame Dostoevsky, he ranked the works of Raphael above everyone in painting and regarded the Sistine Madonna as his greatest work, "the most lofty manifestation of human genius"; he could stand for hours before the striking beauty of this picture.⁷ "Fedya led me to the Sistine Madonna," Madame Dostoevsky writes in her diary, April 18, 1867, describing the deep impression made upon her by the painting. "Fedya finds sorrow in the smile of the Madonna. . . . I didn't like the infant in the hands of the Mother of God. Fedya is right in saying that he doesn't have a child's face at all."⁸ Svidrigailov in *Crime and Punishment* may be expressing Dostoevsky's view when he remarks that the Sistine Madonna has "a fantastic face, the face of a sorrowful God-afflicted woman." Dostoevsky was "ecstatic" over Raphael's "S. Giovan Battista nel Deserto" in the Uffizi Gallery in Florence.⁹

The name of Raphael, frequently encountered in the letters and works of Dostoevsky, first appears in a letter of 1845, in which Dostoevsky notes that Raphael "painted for years, polished, revised, and the result was a miracle, gods were created under his hand." He contrasts Raphael with the French painter Horace Vernet who "paints a picture in a month . . . but the work isn't worth a penny. Decorators they are!"¹⁰ "Do you know how strong *'one man'* can be: Raphael, Shakespeare, Plato, (or) Columbus, or Galileo?" we read in the notebook to *The Devils*. "He will remain for a thousand years and regenerate the world—he will not die."¹¹ A copy of the Sistine Madonna hung in Dostoevsky's workroom. Gravures of the "great Italian masters of the past centuries" hang on the walls of Father Zosima's cell in *The Brothers Karamazov*.

The cult of the Madonna is clearly felt throughout Dostoevsky's works. The Italian Madonnas, it seems, represented an ideal of facial and figural beauty to Dostoevsky, even in the 1840s. The adolescent hero of "A Little Hero," a work published in 1857 but written in 1849, notes something special in the beauty of Madame M. which sets her apart from the crowd of beautiful women. He speaks of her "quiet, gentle features, recalling the luminous faces of the Italian Madonnas . . . the irreproachable beauty of pure, regular lines"; this was a pale, thin face stamped with the "somber severity of an obscure, concealed anguish," through which, nonetheless, shined "a primordial, childlike, clear face— the image of still recent years of confidence and, perhaps, naïve happiness." The portraits of Madame M. and Alexandra Mikhailovna in *Netochka Nezvanova* provide rich material for the formulation of Dostoevsky's early ideal of feminine beauty.

Dostoevsky—his wife recalls—"valued the talent of Titian extremely highly, especially his famous painting 'Der Zinsgroschen,' and would stand for a long time without taking his eyes off that genius-inspired depiction of the Savior."[12] "This magnificent painting, as Fedya put it, can stand alongside Raphael's [Sistine] Madonna."[13] Other paintings which gave Dostoevsky

> lofty joy and which he invariably went to see on every visit [to the Dresden Gallery], ignoring other treasures, were Murillo's "Maria mit dem Kind," Correggio's "Die heilige Nacht," Annibale Carracci's "Christus," P. Battoni's "Die büssende Magdalena," Ruisdael's "Die Jagd," Claude Lorrain's "Küstenlandschaft (Morgen und Abend)" (these land-escapes my husband called the "golden age" and speaks of them in *The Diary of a Writer*), Rembrandt van Rijn's "Rembrandt und seine Frau," Anthony Van Dyck's "König Karl I von England"; among the watercolor and pastel works he very much valued Jean Liotard's "Das Schokoladenmädchen."[14]

In her diary Madame Dostoevsky recalls that she and her husband looked several times at the Holbein Madonna in the Dresden collection. Myshkin in *The Idiot* admires Alexandra Ivanovna's "beautiful" and "sweet" face but discovers in it a "secret sadness." "You have a kind of special touch in your face such as in Holbein's Madonna in Dresden." Dostoevsky, as we have noted earlier in this study, was deeply impressed by Holbein's "Christ in the Tomb," in the museum of Basel.[15] He was not impressed, however, by a photograph of Holbein's "Dance of Death," where death is represented as surrounded by various people.[16] Dostoevsky did not like the work of the nineteenth-century German artist Wilhelm von Kaulbach. He went to the Berlin Museum specifically to see Kaulbach's works but found in them, as he wrote in one letter, "only cold allegory and nothing more." But he liked the other pictures in the museum, especially the old masters, and he regretted that on his first visit to Berlin he had not visited the museum.[17]

Claude Lorrain's paintings, "Morning" and "Evening," mentioned by Madame Dostoevsky as among her husband's favorite paintings, are not in the Dresden art collection but in the Hermitage in Leningrad. It is Lorrain's "Acis and Galatea"—in the Dresden collection—that Dostoevsky called the "golden age"; but "Morning" and "Evening," it has been noted, are imbued with the same movingly idyllic mood.[18] "Fedya took me to look at the paintings of Claude Lorrain dealing with mythological subjects," Madame Dostoevsky notes in her diary.[19] Dostoevsky's interpretation of Lorrain's "Acis and Galatea" is, of course, his own. The meeting of Acis and Galatea, based on Ovid's *Metamorphoses* (Book XIII), against the background of the rays of a setting sun, are emotionally perceived by Dostoevsky as man's "golden age," his primeval paradise. Lorrain's painting, in Dostoevsky's special interpretation, is the basis for Versilov's story about the first days of European humanity; it is represented indirectly in "The Dream of a Ridiculous Man," as well as in Stavrogin's dream (in "Stavrogin's Confession").

Dostoevsky, like Schiller, gave expression in his writings to what Lionello Venturi has termed the "myth of the unique and unreachable perfection of Greek art"—a myth which found its chief proponent in the art historian Winckelmann.[20] Dostoevsky is impressed with the "divine beauty" of the Venus of Milo and the Venus of Medici. When he sees the statue of the Venus of Medici in Florence, he calls it a "work of genius."[21] A young man looks once at the Apollo of Belvedere, Dostoevsky writes in "Mr. —bov and the Question of Art," "and god is indelibly imprinted in his soul in his grand and endlessly beautiful image." " 'This marble after all is god' and you, however much you spit at it, will never take away its divinity."[22] He speaks of the "past ideals" of beauty and cites Fet's poem "Diana" with its sculptured image of a classical goddess. Dostoevsky shares the Greek "reverence for beauty; and, of course, nothing in the world is more beautiful than a beautiful body."[23] The ideal of figural beauty is of course the Greek ideal.

Apropos of Dostoevsky's ideal of figural beauty, one might note that something of the classical sculptural ideal is felt in his physical and moral-aesthetic conception of Alyosha. This "angel" or "cherubim" is "shapely," "very handsome, evenly proportioned, of middle height . . . with a regular, though somewhat elongated oval of a face . . . broadly placed eyes, extremely thoughtful and obviously extremely tranquil." Temperamentally, he is characterized neither by gloominess nor by cheerfulness; "he was even-tempered and serene." On the moral plane, he has that chastity of image which Dostoevsky associates with the correct aesthetic impression of higher beauty. Of Grushenka, also, Dostoevsky writes significantly: "Her body, perhaps, suggested the form of the Venus of Milo." Alyosha, it may be recalled, is not sensually aroused by Dostoevsky's Russian Venus of Milo. In this respect he wholly confirms Dostoevsky's view—expressed, coincidentally, in connection with the statues of the Venus of Milo and Venus of Medici—that "one must be morally rather highly purified to look on this divine beauty without confusion."[24]

Among the articles attributed to Dostoevsky, "The Exhibition in the Academy of Arts: 1860–1861" is of the greatest interest from the standpoint of Dostoevsky's approach to painting. His evaluation of the paintings of Jacoby, Klodt, and various other artists already have been discussed in different parts of this study. The article, in its main emphasis, is an appeal for painting which breaks through surface realism to an apprehension of deeper spiritual realities. Dostoevsky sharply attacks the Academy of Arts for the "utilitarian character" of its teaching, for its emphasis upon educating specialists. Thus, "history is taught from the standpoint of costumes . . . architecture, perspective without descriptive geometry (i.e. the rule of perspective—*by feel*), the theory of the fine arts without general philosophical preparation, anatomy from the point of view of bones, muscles, and clothes, without a natural history of man, etc." Without general education and especially without education in the universities, "we will never break out of more or less successful daguerreotyping or out of impassible pseudo-classicism." Apropos of some paintings on the theme of Charon, ferrying souls across the river Styx, Dostoevsky remarks that such a task is offered to pupils of the Academy on the grounds "that here one can draw the body, that without the body there can be no academic pictures." Emphasis upon anatomy, he observes, is understandable, "but this is only a means, and not a goal."[25]

> Pseudoclassicism in painting, or better, academism, is not concerned that Charon is a feeble old man and not concerned that he is transporting souls and not bags of flour, and therefore his boat is not heavy . . . academism is not concerned that Charon is not angry, that he only got angry upon seeing a living man, Dante, amidst the shadows, and then his anger disappeared. . . . What need has academism for all these considerations which might occur when contemplating the given theme!

If it's a ferryman, let him be a muscular ferryman! But the viewer may reconcile himself with these paintings depicting Charon if he remembers that they are students' work and that therefore the painters only sought nature in them, strove for faithfulness in drawing and shading, "and from this standpoint the pictures are very satisfactory."[26]

The problem of the depiction of the unusual or exceptional is raised in the review of the exhibition in connection with a painting by I. K. Ayvazovsky. The painting depicts a herd of white sheep, brightly illuminated by the sun, rushing into a churning sea. Exaggerated nature exists, but "it is still not art." Dostoevsky remarks that "all this is possible; there is natural truth here, but there is no artistic truth." The hunter's tall tale may be physically possible, but no painter would want to paint it, and the writer S. T. Aksakov would not include it in his stories. The sun, Dostoevsky remarks, creates miracles with its light and shade. But these miracles must be given their real place in art; they must be rare in the measure that they are rare in the course of the day, month, year. "Do not forget to transmit to us the ordinary, daily, humdrum movements of the sun." Dostoevsky vigorously defends, later on, the appearance of the exceptional and seemingly fantastic fact in his own writing. But the exceptional fact or occurrence, as it appears in his own art, is for Dostoevsky revelatory or symbolic of a deeper social and human reality; what he is criticizing in Ayvazovsky is sense-less, capricious fantasy. In general, he compares Ayvazovsky's talent with that of Alexandre Dumas-père. Both artists scorn the ordinary and strive for effects which border on caricature. All this, Dostoevsky allows, is entertaining, but it is not art. "Dumas is not an artist for the very reason that he cannot restrain himself in his unbridled fantasy from exaggerated effects." He lacks a sense of measure. "True artists have an amazing sense of measure, feel it with extraordinary precision."[27]

In his review, "Apropos of the Exhibition," in *Diary of a Writer* in 1873, Dostoevsky discusses the paintings of five prominent painters, V. G. Perov, A. I. Kuindji, V. E. Makovsky, N. N. Gué, and I. E. Repin. He opens his review with the question: "Is it pos-sible over there [in Europe] to understand our artists and from what point of view will they be evaluated there?"[28] And Dostoevsky replies, a little further on, that in his opinion "everything char-acteristic, everything that is ours, preeminently national (and, therefore, everything that is truly artistic) is . . . unknowable to Europe." Gogol, Turgenev, and Pushkin, he insists, will be unintel-ligible translated into any European language. All Russia's great talents, he believes, are destined to remain unknown in Europe for a long time. On the other hand, he notes, "we understand Dickens in Russian. . . . And yet how typical, original, and national is Dickens!" All this Dostoevsky attributes to the Russians' "special gift" for understanding foreign nationalities (a gift which he found most highly developed in Pushkin).[29] Turning to painting, he ob-serves that in Europe Russian landscape painters will not be under-stood: not the painters of the Crimea, Caucasus, or even the steppe, but the painters of "our Russian, preeminently national landscape, i.e. of the northern and central regions of our European Russia . . . this 'gaunt nature,' whose entire typicality consists, so to speak, in its lack of character." And Dostoevsky cites at this point A. I. Kuindji's "A Glimpse of Valaam"; the scene is quite lovely, but there is nothing "special" or "characteristic" about it. What will Europeans comprehend of Russian genre painting? Do-stoevsky thinks little of Russian achievement in historical paint-ing, but of Russian genre painting "we have something to be proud

of and something to show."[30] He points to V. E. Makovsky's painting, "Amateurs of Nightingale Singing," and gives a detailed description of what is happening in the painting. Here, as in his other
analyses of paintings, Dostoevsky focuses upon the thematic element in the painting and its broad social, moral, or ideological import as a picture of Russian life: one of the men sitting at a table
has his back to us, "but you know that he is 'suffering' no less than
his comrade."[31] Although Dostoevsky is acutely conscious and
critical—and precisely in "Apropos of the Exhibition"—of art
which tendentiously shouts its message to you; although he is concerned with the deeper spiritual—and for him, therefore, artistic
—values of painting, his focus is nevertheless upon the painting's
message. He is little concerned—at least in his public discussion of
painting—with the *means* whereby the artist conveys his message,
with the structure, materials, use of space, color, and the like.
Dostoevsky is particularly attracted to I. E. Repin's painting, "The
Volga Haulers." When he heard about this painting, he was immediately "frightened." "Among us it is somehow accepted that the
haulers are particularly fit to depict a certain social thought about
the unpaid duty of the upper classes to the people." But much
to Dostoevsky's joy, all his fears turned out to be unfounded. These
were "real haulers and nothing more," and they were not shouting
out to the people about their unhappiness. Dostoevsky insists, finally, that a deeper social purpose is in fact fulfilled here, but in
an untendentious, naïve way.[32] But why is Repin's "The Volga
Haulers" a good painting? Dostoevsky does not answer this question, or, at least, he does not answer it in aesthetic terms relevant
to the medium. Does Repin's painting stand above other paintings simply because of what Dostoevsky terms its "humble innocence of thought"? And is Repin's painting innocent in this sense?

An intuitive aesthetic judgment is unquestionably implicit in
Dostoevsky's liking for Repin's painting (as it is, unquestionably,
in his dislike of Jacoby's painting), but his awareness of the aesthetic value of the painting is linked exclusively with his evaluation of its idea. At least this would seem to be the case where the
theme of the painting is particularly close to Dostoevsky. Gué's
painting of Christ and the disciples, discussed earlier in this study,
is an excellent example of a painting rejected by Dostoevsky chiefly
because the painter's idea of Christ did not correspond to Dostoevsky's notion of the ideal of Christ.

A concern with color values in painting is evident, to some extent, in "The Exhibition in the Academy of Arts: 1860–1861." Dostoevsky notes the influence of Flaxman on the paintings devoted to the theme of Charon, but "only that of his drawing; . . . his artistic essence is not reflected either in composition or in color."[33] Apropos of the work of the Swedish painter M. Larsson, Dostoevsky notes that his thirty paintings are distinguished by their tremendous size, tremendous prices, and their brownish-yellow color. "Brownish-yellow waves strike against brownish-yellow stones under a brownish-yellow sky. Physiology says that there are people who have an abnormal vision in respect to colors and pigments. But in ordinary people this is not so noticeable as in the painter. If the painter does not distinguish yellow from blue, then there occur such sad phenomena as the works of Mr. Larsson." One of his pictures, depicting a shipwreck under a setting sun, would have been good, Dostoevsky notes, "if the water, sky, and cliffs had their natural color."[34] Dostoevsky may well have been correct in his low evaluation of the Larsson paintings, but his reasoning suggests that he had not passed beyond popular standards of realism with respect to use of colors.

One must turn to Dostoevsky's novels, in the end, to determine the special character of his feeling for the fine arts. His imagined paintings (the execution scene in *The Idiot* and the suicide of a child in *The Raw Youth*) reveal his strong sense of the relation between the emotional content of a painting (its idea) and its structure. In his *Diary of a Writer* in March, 1877, Dostoevsky sets forth his idea for a painting which would have a "moral center." The setting for the painting is the birth of a child in the "impossible" poverty of a poor Jewish shanty. "Here much humor could even be expressed and terribly to the point: humor after all is wit of a profound feeling, and I like this definition very much." The "illumination," Dostoevsky adds further on, "could be made extremely interesting: on a warped table a greasy, guttered candle is burning out, and through the only window, icy and covered with frost, breaks the dawn of another day, a difficult day for poor people." In the middle of his description Dostoevsky remarks that "there is such misery, gentlemen, I swear to you there is, the purest realism—realism, so to speak, reaching the fantastic."[35] L. P. Grossman, in his discussion of this idea for a painting, notes that here are to be found "all the special features of [Dostoevsky's] artistic system."[36] Here, in a sense, is Dostoevsky's *Poor Folk* in painting. All details relate to the moral center or idea of the painting. The "fantastic" character of the poverty and misery is conveyed, aesthetically, in the fantastic illumination. "The Rembrandtian illumination" here, Grossman observes, "astonishingly corresponds to the character of descriptions by Dostoevsky himself."[37] Grossman cites the many "pictures" in Dostoevsky's novels which are illuminated by the last flickerings of candles: the gathering around the mattress of Mr. Prokharchin, Efimov (in *Netochka Nezvanova*) playing the violin for the last time, Raskolnikov and Sonya reading the bible, Verkhovensky awaiting the suicide of Kirilov, a match in the hand of the man from the "underground" lighting up the face of Liza, and so on.

Dostoevsky's tragic vision of reality is indeed a "vision" that finds graphic representation in his verbal art, in his passing descriptions of the world, natural and man-made, inhabited by his heroes. "His house made a deep impression on me," remarks Ippolit Terentiev in *The Idiot* apropos of Rogozhin's house. "It was like a graveyard, but, it seems, he likes it, which, of course, is understandable: such a full, direct life as he lives is too full in itself to be in need of any background." The same thought may, in a sense, be directed to Dostoevsky's novels and to the life therein limned: it is too full, the point of illumination too vivid, to require any background; but that background, as it makes its presence felt, more often than not is somber in character and Rembrandtian in illumination. The light is in a consuming darkness. Old Ikhmenev in *The Insulted and Injured,* after learning of the death of B., bitterly comments:

> Indeed, how can one not die! And we live well and . . . it's a nice place, look! And with a rapid, involuntary gesture of the hand he pointed out to me the foggy perspective of the street, illuminated feebly by lamps flickering in the damp mist, the filthy houses, the wet and shiny slabs of the sidewalks, the somber, angry, and drenched figures of the passersby—this whole picture which was enclosed by the black dome of the Petersburg sky, as though filled in with India ink. We came out finally onto the square; before us in the blackness rose up

the monument, illuminated from below by gas jets, and still further off loomed up the dark, huge mass of St. Isaac's, dully setting itself off from the gloomy color of the sky. (Pt. I, Ch. 11)

The vision of a consuming darkness embraces the natural landscape. Thus, Varvara Petrovna, in Dostoevsky's first novel, *Poor Folk*, trapped in St. Petersburg, recalls her "golden childhood" in the village, her love of autumn, the late autumn landscape when winter was approaching. "At that time everything becomes more somber, the sky frowns with its clouds, the yellow leaves strew the paths along the edges of the bare woods, and the woods become blue, blacken—particularly in the evening when the damp fog lowers and the trees flicker out of the fog, like giants, like shapeless, fearful visions." Varvara Petrovna, now ill, is convinced that she will die in autumn. So also, on the night of the murder of Shatov in *The Devils*—a murder in lantern light—the huge, century-old pines in the Stavrogin park loom up as "vague and somber blots" in the darkness.

Such is the "landscape" of Dostoevsky's novels—reflecting an interior, spiritual landscape, defining the entire mood of uncertainty, anxiety, nightmare, and death that prevails in the inner life of man. The image of the setting sun recurs throughout his novels as a poignant symbol of vanishing life and beauty. The shadows, as in Claude Lorrain's "Acis and Galatea," are falling. Maria Timofeevna (in *The Devils*) goes to the edge of the lake:

On one side was our monastery, and on the other—our mountain with its pointed top, that's what they call it, peaked mountain. I would go up this mountain, I would turn with my face to the east, I would fall to the earth, weeping, weeping, and I would not remember how long I was weeping, and I didn't remember anything then and I don't remember anything now. I would then get up, I would go back, and the sun was setting, oh so large, so gloriously, so spendidly—do you like to look at the sun, Shatushka? It is good, yet it is sad. I would turn again to the east, and then this shadow, this shadow from our mountain far across our lake was racing like an arrow, narrow, long-long, almost for a mile, right to the island on the lake, and it would cut that island right in two, and as it cut it in two, at this moment the sun would set altogether, and everything would suddenly be extinguished in darkness.

This extraordinary scene is a painting, almost an abstraction in which forms are recognized as reality, and recognizable reality dissolves into abstract forms, into mythopoetic design, a primeval play of dark and light. This is fantastic realism in graphic art.

When we attempt visually to realize the landscape of reality in Dostoevsky's novels we come to the conclusion that his latent talent in the fine arts was not as a colorist (we are not concerned here with his symbolic use of color), but as a graphic artist or as a master of the fine pen and ink drawing. Such a drawing comes at the conclusion of *The Devils* at the moment when Stepan Verkhovensky sets out across the countryside on his "last pilgrimage." A fine rain kept falling, stopping, and falling. Stepan Verkhovensky "suddenly stopped and looked around. An old black road, rutted by wheels, lined with willows, stretched out before him like an endless thread; to the right—a bare stretch, the stubble of a harvest long past; to the left—bushes, and beyond them, a wood. And in the distance—in the distance a barely perceptible line of the railroad going off slantwise, and on it the smoke of some train; but the sounds were no longer audible." The poignant poetry of this sketch is anticipated a few lines earlier in a striking phrase: "The highway: this is something long-long, whose end is not visible, like a man's life, like a man's dream." The poetry of space, of distance, of eternity, of a lost dream often infuses Dostoevsky's dramatic visions of nature and urban landscape (Raskolnikov's vision across the Neva and, later, across the Siberian steppe, Myshkin's moments of poignant contemplation before the natural splendors of Switzerland, the distant perspective of the lost paradise in "The Dream of a Ridiculous Man").

" 'Ghosts,' " Dostoevsky wrote Turgenev in 1863, "is like music. And by the way: how do you view music? As pleasure or as a positive necessity? In my opinion it is also language, but expresses that which consciousness has not *yet* mastered (not reason, but all of consciousness), and therefore is of *positive* use."[38] Dostoevsky, though not a student or connoisseur of music, greatly enjoyed it. As a youth, in the 1840s, he regularly attended operas and concerts. His friend and doctor, S. D. Janovsky, recalls that Dostoevsky had a particular preference for Rossini's *Guillaume Tell,* enjoyed listening to Mozart's *Don Giovanni,* and was ecstatic over Vincenzo Bellini's *Norma.* When Meyerbeer's *Les Huguenots* was performed in St. Petersburg "Fyodor Mikhailovich positively went into ecstasies over it." Janovsky notes also that Dostoevsky at that time liked to watch dancers, but also enjoyed dancing himself. "Fyodor Mikhailovich liked dancing as an expression of spiritual satisfaction and as a true sign of health." "Ballet he knew about only through hearsay, but never, at that time, attended one."[39]

It is interesting to note that on at least one occasion Dostoevsky conceived of the structure of his work in musical terms. While working on *Notes from the Underground,* he wrote to his brother Mikhail: "You understand what a *transition* is in music. Just so here. In the first chapter there is obviously chatter; but suddenly this chatter in the last two chapters is resolved by a sudden catastrophe."[40] Dostoevsky introduced music and musicians into his novels, for example, the violinists Efimov and "B," the concert of the virtuoso S. in *Netochka Nezvanova,* the bizarre piano improvisation of Lyamshin in *The Devils,* the passionate singing of Velchaninov in *The Eternal Husband.* "To sing this short but extraordinary piece [by M. I. Glinka]," remarks the narrator, "it was essential—really essential to have real inspiration, real passion, or a full poetic mastery of it." Passion and poetry in literature, in painting, in music: this is the heart of art as Dostoevsky understood it. The Russian composer Glinka was a favorite of his. Madame Dostoevsky remarks, in connection with Velchaninov's singing, that Dostoevsky told her several times how impressed he was in his youth by Glinka's rendition of this song.[41] Among Russian composers Dostoevsky also liked A. N. Serov, especially his opera *Rogneda.*[42]

"My husband was very fond of the music of Mozart, Beethoven's *Fidelio,*" Madame Dostoevsky remarks, beginning her list of Dostoevsky's musical preferences among European composers.[43] On the basis of his own comments, as well as the observations of those who knew him, it is clear that Mozart and Beethoven were his favorites. "He ranked the music of Mozart and Beethoven far above everyone," an acquaintance of Dostoevsky, N. Fon-Fokht, noted.[44] "Today they played the works of Mozart," Madame Dostoevsky notes in her diary, June 5, 1867. "Fedya was wholly carried away by it."[45] S. V. Kovalevskaya recalls Dostoevsky as saying that "of all musical works he loves Beethoven's *Pathétique* sonata best of all, and that this sonata steeps him in a whole world of forgotten sensations."[46] He was particularly fond of Beethoven's overture to *Fidelio*. "My angel," he writes to his wife from Ems in 1876, "today in the morning I listened to Beethoven's overture to *Fidelio*. Nothing more lofty than this has been created! This is in a light, graceful style, but with passion; in Beethoven, passion and love are everywhere. He is the poet of love, of happiness, and of love's anguish."[47] Other favorite pieces of his, according to Madame Dostoevsky, were Mendelssohn's *Hochzeitsmarsch* and Rossini's *Stabat Mater*.[48]

Dostoevsky apparently did not especially like Chopin's music, once calling it "tubercular."[49] His wife states that he "distinctly did not like the works of Richard Wagner."[50] And this testimony is supported by Dostoevsky in a letter to her from Ems in 1879. Although the music is good here, he writes, "Mozart and Beethoven are a rarity, but Wagner continually (the most boring German canaille in spite of his fame), and all kinds of rubbish."[51] But in an editorial note in *Grazhdanin* in 1873, Dostoevsky remarks of Wagner, apropos of a communication from Germany: "Such phenomena as . . . the music of Wagner, which is full of profound tasks, shows at least that German artistic creation is still alive, still inspired by the most lofty strivings."[52] This comment, however, seems more a judgment of the head than the heart. We gather from a comment in a letter to his wife from Ems in 1875 that Dostoevsky did not think much of Offenbach or Strauss (which of the Strauss composers is not indicated).[53]

Dostoevsky's tastes in music do not lend themselves to classification. A. S. Dolinin, however, essentially regarding Dostoevsky as a romantic, insists that "Beethoven must have been particularly comprehensible and close to Dostoevsky as the most lofty expression of romanticism."[54] But this attempt to objectify Dostoevsky's (actually quite complex) literary affiliations in his subjective tastes seems rather arbitrary in view of the diversity of his tastes. Why was Wagner or Chopin not close to Dostoevsky? What kind

of romanticism did Dostoevsky find in Mozart? The unity of Dostoevsky's tastes in music, as in painting, is to be sought not in
any objective notion or classification which unites the various
works he enjoyed, but in his own subjective disposition. "What
does romanticism ask if its lofty ideas are not developed in [Cor-
neille's] *Le Cid?*" the young Dostoevsky exclaims in 1840. There
is no evidence that the mature Dostoevsky subsumed Beethoven,
Mozart, Racine, Claude Lorrain, or Raphael under the heading of
romantics, but there is some basis for saying, perhaps, that these
artists struck identical chords in his subjective consciousness. Here,
however, we are in danger of passing into a realm of critical im-
pressionism—of identifying the reverie that the *Pathétique* sonata
evoked in Dostoevsky with the poetic mood evoked by Claude
Lorrain's painting, or of affirming that the "lofty harmony of
sounds" which Dostoevsky found in Mozart and Beethoven were
for him aesthetically and emotionally of the same character as
those evoked by the paintings of Raphael. Certainly Dostoevsky
is united subjectively in his tastes. Whether these tastes in the various arts can really be closely correlated and whether, finally, they
can be classified without doing violence to him is another question.

Dostoevsky's interest in architecture, in forms and masses, in
spatial relationships, was undoubtedly stimulated, at least in its
purely technical aspects, by his early training as a military engi-
neer. But his interest in architecture extended beyond technique.
His friend and doctor, S. D. Janofsky, recalls how in the 1840s Dostoevsky would set off sometimes to the other end of St. Petersburg
to admire "some building or an entire group of houses." "He himself told me that he did this not out of love for art, but for nature,
that he admired not so much the technical features of the building
as the charm of its illumination, for example, in the setting sun."[55]
Here, of course, what appears to have intrigued Dostoevsky was
the abstract, geometrical forms created by the interplay of structure, light, and shadow. But architecture, as Dostoevsky noted,
"produces its effect because art is irresistible." And Dostoevsky's
interest in architecture can by no means be divorced from his general aesthetic sensibility, his sensitivity to art in nature and nature
in art.

Architecture is embodied culture. Dostoevsky recognized that
the houses in which men live reflect the way of life, the ethos of

the people who build and inhabit them. The world of the Rogozhin merchants (in *The Idiot*) is revealed in the architectural lines of their ancestral home.

> This was a large, gloomy, three-storied house, without any architecture, of a dirty green color. Some, though very few houses of this kind, built at the end of the last century, have been preserved almost without change precisely in these streets of St. Petersburg. . . . They are built solidly with thick walls and very few windows; on the ground floor the windows sometimes have iron bars. The ground floor is usually occupied by a money changer's shop. A member of the sect of castrates who runs the store usually rents a flat upstairs. Both outside and inside one senses something inhospitable and dry; everything is somehow hidden away, concealed; but why one gets this impression from the exterior impression of the house alone—this would be difficult to explain. The architectural disposition of lines has, of course, its secret. Such houses are inhabited almost exclusively by merchants. (Pt. II, Ch. 3)

The Rogozhin house is "without any architecture." It is in all essential respects a formal embodiment of formlessness; it partakes of the personality of its owner and of a whole era.

St. Petersburg for Dostoevsky is history, whether seen from the vantage point of the 1840s, when he evaluated the history of Petersburg in a positive way and rejected the view that Petersburg architecture was "characterless" and lacking in nationality;[56] or from the vantage point of the 1870s when he found the originality of St. Petersburg architecture precisely to be its "lack of character and impersonality" (the "whole characterlessness of the idea, the entire negative essence of the Petersburg period" is in its architecture).[57]

Dostoevsky was deeply impressed by architecture in Europe. He remarked to his brother Nicholas in a letter from Paris in 1863 that "this time I liked Paris' exterior, i.e. its architecture. The Louvre is an impressive piece, and this whole embankment, right up to Notre Dame, is an amazing thing. It is a pity, Kolya, that you, preparing to be an architect, have not gone abroad. An architect cannot be a person who has not been abroad. No drawing will convey a true impression."[58] Dostoevsky wrote a very short while later, in *Winter Notes on Summer Impressions,* that as a youth, studying architecture, he used to sketch the Cologne Cathedral. His first impression of it in Europe was "only lace, lace and only lace," but when he returned to the Cathedral a second time "I felt like 'begging its forgiveness on my knees' for not having perceived its beauty the first time."[59] Dostoevsky's slight irony here does not conceal the impact of the impression. Of the Milan Cathedral he writes: "huge, marble, Gothic, all completely carved and fantastic, like a dream. The interior is extraordinarily fine."[60] St. Mark's in Venice is an "amazing, incomparable piece."[61]

A Note on Sources

THE PRIMARY SOURCES used in this study of the aesthetics of Dostoevsky are his own works: his critical essays, feuilletons, and reviews, his letters, notebooks, and belles lettres. The memoirs of his wife, A. G. Dostoevsky, of his friend and literary associate, N. N. Strakhov, and of various other people who knew him have also been utilized.

Apart from four feuilletons written in 1847 and a short introduction to an almanac in 1845, Dostoevsky contributed numerous articles to the journals *Vremja* and *Epokha* which he edited in 1861–64; in 1873 he edited the paper *Grazhdanin* and contributed a weekly piece under the title of *Dnevnik pisatelja* (*Diary of a Writer*). He revived this column in *Grazhdanin* in 1876–77, then dropped it in order to work on *The Brothers Karamazov,* and finally issued a few more numbers of this column in 1880–81 shortly before his death. With a number of exceptions, Dostoevsky's critical and journalistic writings may be found in Volumes 11, 12, and 13 of the thirteen-volume edition of his works edited by B. Tomashevsky and K. Khalabaev in 1926–30.

Much material of literary interest may be found in the *Diary of a Writer* (Volumes 11, 12). Of particular interest from a literary standpoint are the various critical and polemical essays which Dostoevsky wrote—frequently anonymously—for his journals *Vremja* and *Epokha* (Volume 13). N. N. Strakhov is a source for the identification of many of these writings. Two very valuable articles, "Vystavka v akademii khudozhestv za 1860–1861" ("The Exhibition in the Academy of Arts: 1860–1861") and "Rasskazy N. V. Uspenskogo," ("Stories of N. V. Uspensky"), published respectively in *Vremja* in October and December 1861, were attributed to Dostoevsky by L. P. Grossman and included in the twenty-second volume of the "Prosveshchenie" Russian edition of Dostoevsky's works (1911–19). Grossman's reasons for attributing these articles to Dostoevsky may be found in his preface to these articles in *Polnoe sobranie sochinenij F. M. Dostoevskogo 22,*

(Petrograd, 1918), 101–07, 142–44. The editors of the thirteen-volume Russian edition of Dostoevsky's complete works (1926–30), on the other hand, raise some doubts as to Dostoevsky's authorship of "The Exhibition in the Academy of Arts: 1860–1861"; they consider it "probable," though not "absolutely certain" that Dostoevsky wrote "Stories of N. V. Uspensky." Cf. F. M. Dostoevskij, *Stat'i za 1845–1878 gody, 13,* (Moscow-Leningrad, 1930), 607–08. Both articles are included by the editors in a section entitled, "Articles Attributed to Dostoevsky," in Volume 13. More recently the Dostoevsky scholar G. M. Fridlender offers the view that Dostoevsky's authorship of "Stories of N. V. Uspensky" is "almost unquestioned." Cf. his article, "Dostoevskij-kritik," in *Istorija russkoj kritiki, 2,* (Moscow-Leningrad, 1958), 274. V. V. Vinogradov in his recent study *Problema avtorstva i teorija stilej* cites from both of the articles under question but only observes that they are attributed to Dostoevsky. There is no question in my mind as to Dostoevsky's authorship of "Stories of N. V. Uspensky." As to "The Exhibition in the Academy of Arts: 1860–1861," certain parallels between this article and "Mr. —bov and the Question of Art" (for example, the view of certain writers divorced from reality as "mad"—cf. pp. 90–91 and p. 532 in Volume 13), as well as with other writings of Dostoevsky, suggest that Dostoevsky—if he did not write the entire article—certainly directly participated in its preparation as the editor and guiding spirit of the journal in which it appeared. The aesthetic questions raised in the criticisms of M. P. Klodt's "The Last Spring," A. Calame's "The Lake of Four Cantons," and Diday's painting of the Reichenbach waterfalls in Switzerland, as well as the scenes themselves, appear—as I have indicated in my study—to have entered into the fabric of *The Idiot*. In general, the aesthetic positions maintained in "The Exhibition in the Academy of Arts: 1860–1861" are identical with those advanced elsewhere by Dostoevsky; in utilizing material from this essay I have been particularly concerned with bringing out this identity.

Notes

All citations to Dostoevsky's criticism and belles lettres, unless otherwise indicated, refer to the thirteen-volume edition of his works edited by V. Tomashevsky and K. Khalabaev in 1926–30. Volume 13, a collection of Dostoevsky's critical and journalistic essays, is referred to as *Stat'i*. Dostoevsky's *Diary of a Writer* is referred to as *Dnevnik pisatelja*. All citations to Dostoevsky's letters refer to the four-volume Russian edition edited by A. S. Dolinin in 1928–59. The edition is referred to simply as *Pis'ma*.

Introduction

1. N. N. Strakhov, *Biografija, pis'ma i zametki iz zapisnoj knizhki F. M. Dostoevskogo* (St. Petersburg, 1883), p. 359.

2. Quoted by A. S. Dolinin in *V tvorcheskoj laboratorii Dostoevskogo* (Moscow, 1947), p. 137.

3. *Pis'ma, 1* (No. 27), 75.

4. Friedrich Schiller, *Über die ästhetische Erziehung des Menschen,* in Schillers Werke, ed. L. Bellermann, *8* (Leipzig und Wien, 1895–97), 197 (Ninth Letter).

5. *Pis'ma, 2* (No. 269), 10.

6. Ibid., *1* (No. 116), 246.

7. "G. —bov i vopros ob iskusstve," *Stat'i, 13,* 60.

8. *Pis'ma, 2* (No. 357), 291.

9. "Russkaja satira," *Dnevnik pisatelja, 12,* 28.

10. "*Anna Karenina,* kak fakt osobogo znachenija," *Dnevnik pisatelja, 12,* 208.

11. N. Lossky remarks (apropos of Dostoevsky's love of ideal beauty in Raphael and others) that there *is* an "exalted beauty" in Dostoevsky's works. "But most often this beauty is embodied in a living content, so moving in its drama, that the reader cannot concentrate on the aesthetic side of Dostoevsky's creative work. . . . One must read over and experience the works of Dostoevsky many times in order to attain that tranquility and breadth of contemplation which are necessary for the vision of their beauty." N. Losskij, *Dostoevskij i ego khristianskoe miroponimanie* (New York, 1953), pp. 207–08. Certainly in his works Dostoevsky attains mastery of form; certainly, also, there is "exalted beauty" in his spiritual vision. But the distinction between the beauty of a Raphael Madonna and the beauty of a Dostoevsky short story or novel remains a vital one. The beauty Lossky seems to have in mind—a beauty remembered in tranquility—is an impressionistic, disembodied beauty; it is not the complex beauty of a Dostoevsky work, a beauty which always contains, even as it masters, the chaos from which it emerged.

1: A Strange Contradiction

1. "Rossijskoe obshchestvo pokrovitel'stva zhivotnym," *Dnevnik pisatelja, 11,* 168–69.

2. Ibid., p. 170.

3. Ibid., p. 167.

4. The "decade of the 1840s": the reference here is to the peak period of romantic-philosophic ferment in the first half of the nineteenth century in Russia. As D. I. Chizhevsky points out, the notion of the "1840s" is a purely arbitrary designation. Chizhevsky fixes the "remarkable decade"—a term used by a memoirist of the period—between, approximately, the years 1835 and 1847. Cf. D. I. Chizhevskij, *Gegel' v Rossii* (Paris, 1939), p. 32.

5. V. G. Belinskij, "Literaturnye mechtanija," *Sobranie sochinenij v trekh tomakh,* 1 (Moscow, 1948), 11, 16, 21.

6. Belinskij, "Rech' o kritike," ibid., *2,* 349.

7. Ibid., p. 344.

8. Belinskij, "Stikhotvorenija M. Lermontova," ibid., *1,* 668.

9. "Russkaja satira," *Dnevnik pisatelja, 12,* 32.

10. "Smert' Zhorzh-Zanda," *Dnevnik pisatelja, 11,* 308–09.

11. "Knizhnost' i gramotnost'," *Stat'i, 13,* 107.

12. Belinskij, "Literaturnye mechtanija," *Sobranie sochinenij, 1,* 19.

13. Belinskij, "Sochinenija Aleksandra Pushkina: Stat'ja vtoraja," ibid., *3,* 236–37.

14. The view of man expressed here is similar, of course, to the Grand Inquisitor's pessimistic evaluation of man in *The Brothers Karamazov.* The "diplomat" who turns up in one scene in *The Insulted and Injured* (Pt. III, Ch. 9) anticipates the Grand Inquisitor; his "repulsive idea" is that the spirit of reform will soon bring people to their senses, they will soon see their mistake and return to the old. "Without *us* they cannot get along" ("Bez *nas* nel'zja"). The diplomat's motto is: "Pire ça va, mieux ça est!"

2: The Romantic Image of the Poet

1. *Pis'ma, 2* (No. 1), 550.

2. E. N. Konshina, ed., *Zapisnye tetradi F. M. Dostoevskogo* (Moscow-Leningrad, 1935), p. 179.

3. Strakhov, *Biografija, pis'ma i zametki,* p. 373. The full observation reads: "With a total realism to seek man in man. This is chiefly a Russian feature, and in this sense I am, of course, national (because my tendency flows from the depths of the Christian folk spirit)—although it is unknown to the Russian people today but will be known to future [Russians]. They call me a psychologist: untrue, I am only a realist in the higher sense, that is, I depict all the depths of the human soul."

4. *Pis'ma, 1* (No. 12), 50.

5. Ibid.

6. *Pis'ma, 2* (No. 1), 551.

7. Ibid., *1* (No. 12), 51.

8. Ibid., (No. 10), p. 46.

9. Belinskij, "Gamlet, drama Shekspira," *Sobranie sochinenij, 1,* 303, 337.

10. *Pis'ma, 1* (No. 16), 56.
11. Ibid. (No. 12), p. 51.
12. M. P. Alekseev, *Rannij drug F. M. Dostoevskogo* (Odessa, 1921), pp. 17–18.
13. *Pis'ma, 1* (No. 16), 56.
14. Ibid., p. 57.
15. Ibid., pp. 57–59.
16. Ibid. (No. 10), p. 47.
17. Ibid. (No. 16), p. 58.
18. Ibid. (No. 12), p. 51.

3: Into the Vortex

1. *Pis'ma, 1* (No. 27), 76.
2. Dostoevsky mentions, or briefly comments upon, in this letter: Homer, Seneca, Shakespeare, Ronsard, Jodelle, Malherbe, Corneille, Racine, Pushkin, Byron, Schiller, Hoffmann, Hugo, and Goethe. Ibid. (No. 16), pp. 54–59. An earlier letter of August 9, 1838, also contains indications of the young Dostoevsky's readings: Shakespeare, Balzac, Chateaubriand, Goethe, and others. Ibid. (No. 10), pp. 45–47.
3. Cf. Strakhov, *Biografija, pis'ma i zametki,* pp. 41, 49. Themes that appear in Dostoevsky's later writings, Leonid Grossman notes, may be found in Pushkin's "Boris Godunov" and Schiller's "Maria Stuart," for example, the right of the strong individual to transgress through blood in the name of the general good, the possibility of building the happiness of the masses on the suffering of a tormented child; the rivalry of two heroines. Cf. Leonid Grossman, *Dostoevskij* (Moscow, 1962), p. 36.
4. *Pis'ma, 1* (No. 18), 63.
5. Ibid. (No. 22), p. 69.
6. Ibid. (No. 26), p. 73. Work on *Poor Folk* apparently convinced Dostoevsky that his vocation was not drama. "Write dramas—well, brother. For this years of work are necessary, and tranquility, at least for me. . . . Drama today has turned into melodrama. Shakespeare is paling in the twilight . . . seems like a god, a manifestation of the spirit of Brocken or Harz." Ibid. (No. 27), p. 76.
7. Cf. "Peterburgskie snovidenija v stikhakh i proze," *Stat'i, 13,* 154–72. The first part of "Petersburg Visions" is a poetic retrospective of Dostoevsky's early literary evolution.
8. Ibid., p. 157.
9. Ibid., pp. 156–57.
10. Ibid., pp. 158–59.
11. "Rjad statej o russkoj literatury: Vvedenie," ibid., *13,* 50.
12. This is one of the most frequently cited statements (or alleged statements) of Dostoevsky. It does not, however, appear in any of his writings.
13. "Rjad statej o russkoj literatury: Vvedenie," *Stat'i, 13,* 49.
14. "Russkaja satira," *Dnevnik pisatelja, 12,* 30.
15. Belinskij, "Peterburgskij sbornik," *Sobranie sochinenij, 3,* 72, 82, and, in general, 68–86.
16. *Pis'ma, 1* (No. 30), 82.
17. Ibid. (No. 31), p. 85.
18. Ibid. (No. 32), pp. 86–87.

19. Belinskij, "Russkaja literatura v 1843 godu," *Sobranie sochinenij, 2,* 615–16.

20. *Pis'ma, 1* (No. 32), 86.

21. Cf. Belinsky's letter to K. D. Kavelin, December 7, 1847, in E. A. Ljatskij, ed., *Belinskij pis'ma* (St. Petersburg, 1914), *3,* 312.

22. The humanism of Gogol and of "The Overcoat" is not in question here; Devushkin does not perceive it any more than he is conscious of the fact that he apprehends "The Station Master" in the sentimental vein of the parable of the prodigal son—a parable which Pushkin parodies in its moralistic (though not its broadly humanistic) aspect. To suggest that Dostoevsky humanizes the little man is not to imply that "The Overcoat" is devoid of humanism or that its hero is a mere clod. Akaky Akakievich quivers with humanity. By humanization here we understand only man's coming to consciousness, his realization of his own humanity, his recognition of his true image. Gogol makes us realize his hero's humanity, but at the same time he makes of his hero a strange tragicomic grotesque. The broader implications, then, of "The Overcoat" are inaccessible to Devushkin. But his rejection of "The Overcoat" hints at an intolerable truth in that tale—a truth which Belinsky alluded to in the last days of his life when he wrote K. D. Kavelin, October 22, 1847: "Individuality [*lichnost'*] is only just beginning to make its appearance among us, and therefore the Gogolian types are at present the truest Russian types." Ibid., p. 300.

23. See Chapter 7 of this study, pp. 106–08.

24. Belinskij, "Rech' o kritike," *Sobranie sochinenij, 2,* 345. This is a favorite notion of Belinsky. In an article in 1839 we find almost the identical sentence. Cf. Belinskij, "Gore ot uma," ibid., *1,* 465.

25. "Peterburgskaja letopis'," *Stat'i, 13,* 20–26.

26. *Pis'ma, 1* (No. 44), 106.

27. "Peterburgskaja letopis'," *Stat'i, 13,* 29.

28. "Starye ljudi," *Dnevnik pisatelja, 11,* 8.

29. Ibid., p. 10.

30. Ibid., p. 9. Belinsky, Dostoevsky writes, as a socialist necessarily had to demolish Christ's teaching, call it false and ignorant philanthropy. "But all the same there remained the beatific image of the God-man, his moral inaccessibility, his wonderful and miraculous beauty." Ibid., pp. 8–9.

31. Belinskij, "Mentsel', kritik Gete," *Sobranie sochinenij, 1,* 430–31.

32. Ibid., p. 437.

33. Belinskij, "Rech' o kritike," *Sobranie sochinenij, 2,* 363.

34. Belinskij, "Sochinenija Aleksandra Pushkina: Stat'ja sed'maja," *Sobranie sochinenij, 3,* 454.

35. Ljatskij, ed., *Belinskij pis'ma, 3,* 324.

36. Cf. N. F. Bel'chikov, *Dostoevskij v protsesse petrashevtsev* (Moscow-Leningrad, 1936), p. 85.

37. Ibid., p. 86.

38. Ibid., pp. 124–25.

39. Ibid., p. 125.

40. Ibid., p. 197.

41. Ibid., pp. 81, 82.

42. Ibid., pp. 82, 83.

43. Ibid., p. 83.

44. "Knizhnost' i gramotnost': Stat'ja pervaja," *Stat'i, 13,* 104.

45. Bel'chikov, p. 84.

4: Rebirth of Conviction

1. A. S. Dolinin, ed., *F. M. Dostoevskij, stat'i i materialy*, 2 (Leningrad, 1925), 540.
2. *Pis'ma, 1* (No. 75), 166.
3. Ibid., p. 165.
4. "Odna iz sovremennykh fal'shej," *Dnevnik pisatelja, 11*, 139.
5. *Pis'ma, 1* (No. 79), 183–84.
6. Ibid. (No. 61), p. 142.
7. Konshina, ed., *Zapisnye tetradi*, p. 155.
8. *Pis'ma, 1* (No. 79), 184.
9. M. N. Katkov, "Vstuplenie k razboru Pushkina," *Russkij vestnik, 1* (1856), 155–73, 306–25.
10. A. S. Dolinin makes this point in his notes to *Pis'ma, 1*, 532.
11. Katkov, p. 312.
12. Ibid., pp. 165, 166.
13. *Pis'ma, 2* (No. 7), 570.
14. Ibid. (No. 16), 593.
15. "Ob'javlenija o podpiske na zhurnal 'Vremja,' " *Stat'i, 13*, 503.
16. Cf. V. Vysheslavtsev, "Dostoevskij o ljubvi i bezsmertie (Novyj fragment)," *Sovremennyja zapiski, 50* (Paris, 1932), 293.

5: Two Kinds of Beauty

1. P. N. Sakulin and N. F. Bel'chikov, ed., *Iz arkhiva F. M. Dostoevskogo, Idiot* (Moscow-Leningrad, 1931), p. 102.
2. Konshina, ed., *Zapisnye tetradi*, p. 222.
3. *Pis'ma, 2* (No. 387), 363. "I love beauty," the nihilist Peter Verkhovensky exclaims in *The Devils*. "I am a nihilist, but I love beauty."
4. "G. —bov," *Stat'i, 13*, 86–87.
5. Cf. Vysheslavtsev, "Dostoevskij o ljubvi i bezsmertie (Novyj fragment)," p. 297.
6. Friedrich Schelling in the last chapter of his *System des transzendentalen Idealismus* repeatedly emphasizes that art is born in *contradiction*. "Every aesthetic work emerges from a feeling of endless contradiction." But this contradiction is resolved in beauty. Cf. F. W. J. Schelling, *Werke*, ed. Otto Weiss, 2, (Leipzig, 1907), pp. 293–98. I. I. Lapshin noted this parallel in his *Èstetika Dostoevskogo* (Berlin, 1923), pp. 47–48.
7. "Otvet russkomu vestniku," *Stat'i, 13*, 216–17. The phenomenon of a sensualism that invades and corrupts the realm of beauty is an issue in two early works of Dostoevsky—"The Landlady" and *Netochka Nezvanova*. In the latter work Netochka comments on the dazzling beauty of her childhood friend Katya: "Perhaps for the first time the aesthetic sense was aroused in me, the sense of the artistic awakened by the beautiful was revealed for the first time and—that was the source from which my love [for Katya] arose." Yet both the "element of the beautiful" in Katya and the feeling it evokes in Netochka are torn with conflict. The beautiful in Katya was enveloped in a "false form" of pride which distorts and perverts it; and the sensual feelings that it gave rise to in Netochka are correctly characterized as "abnormal." In this strange and feverish episode of the relationship between Netochka and Katya, Dostoevsky explores the phe-

nomenon of "beauty in Sodom," as he expressed it in *The Brothers Karamazov*. The beauty of Katya is corrupt; evil is a part of her nature. Dostoevsky is far from sharing the Rousseauesque view expressed by Netochka: "Everything about her was beautiful; not a single of her vices was born in her—all were engrafted and all were in a state of conflict. Everywhere was visible a beautiful element which had taken for a time a false form." It is not accidental that the name of Jean Jacques Rousseau and the theme of education are parodied by Dostoevsky in the figure of Madame Leotard in *Netochka Nezvanova*.

8. "Peterburgskaja letopis'," *Stat'i, 13,* 31.

9. Strakhov, *Biografija, pis'ma i zametki,* p. 372.

10. "Otvet russkomu vestniku," *Stat'i, 13,* 215.

11. Ibid.

12. "Neskol'ko slov o Zhorzh-Zande," *Dnevnik pisatelja, 11,* 315.

13. "Art helps human development in a strong and mighty way, acting upon man plastically and through the image [*plastichno i obrazno*]. But criticism is just as natural and has quite as legitimate a role in the work of human development as does art. It consciously analyzes what art presents to us only in image." "Rasskazy N. V. Uspenskogo," *Stat'i, 13,* 551.

14. "We, publicists and critics," Belinsky declared according to Dostoevsky, "only deliberate, we try in words to explain this, but you, an artist, in a stroke, at once in an image, present the very essence, so that one might almost feel it with one's hand, so that everything suddenly becomes comprehensible to the least reasoning reader! This is the secret of artistry, here is truth in art!" ("Starye vospominanija," *Dnevnik pisatelja, 13,* 32.) "The poet thinks in images; he does not *argue* [*dokazyvaet*] truth, but *shows* it [*pokazyvaet*]." Belinskij, "Gore ot uma," *Sobranie sochinenij, 1,* 464.

15. The notion of the "image" as ultimately real embodied form is very strong in Dostoevsky. It is very characteristic that he recalls Belinsky as saying that "one might almost feel it [the verbal image] with one's hand."

16. "G. —bov," *Stat'i, 13,* 82.

17. "Rasskazy N. V. Uspenskogo," ibid., p. 553.

18. "G. —bov," ibid., p. 89. Mankind, Dostoevsky believed, had "already defined in part its eternal ideals (so that all this already has become world history and is connected by humanity with the present and with the future, indissolubly and forever)." Ibid., p. 88.

19. Ibid., p. 70.

20. "Obraztsy chistoserdechija," ibid., p. 184; see also, "Otvet russkomu vestniku," ibid., p. 215.

21. "Vystavka v akademii khudozhestv za 1860–1861 god," ibid., p. 535. See "A Note on Sources," pp. 231–32.

22. Ibid.

23. Cf. "Po povodu vystavki," *Dnevnik pisatelja, 11,* 77–79.

24. Konshina, ed., *Zapisnye tetradi,* p. 221. The Russian word *obozhanie* has been translated here as "worship"; the notion of "deification" is more literally exact. Hence Dostoevsky's further remark: "And for there to be worship, God is necessary." The notion that man has an innate need to bow down to something is recurrent in Dostoevsky's writings. Makar Ivanovich, for example, in *The Raw Youth* expresses Dostoevsky's idea: "It is impossible to be a man and not to worship something [chtoby ne preklonit'sja]; such a man could not bear himself, nor could there be such a man. And if a man should reject God, then he will bow down before an idol—before a wooden one, or a gold one, or one made of

thought. They are all idolaters and not infidels" (Pt. III, Ch. 2, Sec. iii). In "Mr. —bov and the Question of Art" the object of man's worship is art, beauty, "the image of beauty"; the religious character of this worship is clearly hinted at, though not explicitly stated.

25. Lydie Krestovsky, in her interesting study on ugliness in art, makes this point in the course of a consideration of the three notions *forme, figure,* and *image* in the French language. "L'image, dans la langue russe, est l'axe de la Beauté. La laideur, la difformité est litteralement traduit par sans *image*—(besobrazié) ce qui correspond en quelque sorte au mot français informe—sans forme." L. Krestovsky, *La laideur dans l'art à travers les âges* (Paris, 1947), p. 36.

26. *Pis'ma, 2* (No. 318), 154. In a conversation with E. Opochinin, Dostoevsky speaks with great warmth and sympathy of the cult of the icon among the Russian people. "One must believe, strive toward the invisible God, but also worship Him on earth through a simple native custom. They can tell me that such faith is blind and naïve, but I answer that such faith must be. After all, not everybody can become a theologian." Cf. E. N. Opochinin, "Besedy s Dostoevskim," in *Zven'ja,* ed. L. P. Grossman, 6 (1936), 468. In this connection see also A. Dolinin's lengthy discussion of Dostoevsky's reference to "the words of Khomjakov on the Miraculous Icon" (in the letter to Maikov just cited), in his notes to *Pis'ma, 2,* 439–41.

27. Aglaya's words "obraz chistoj krasoty" appear in quotation marks in the text of *The Idiot.* Is she deliberately or unconsciously misquoting the lines "genij chistoj krasoty" from Pushkin's poem "K A. P. Kern" (the suggestion of my colleague Richard Gustafson) just as she misquotes Pushkin's poem "Zhil na svete rytsar' bednyj" by substituting the initials N. F. B. (Nastasja Fillippovna Barashkova) for A. M. D.? (*Genij,* of course, in one of its meanings is "perfection, or, the highest embodiment of something," that which, in fact, is symbolized by the notion of *obraz.*) If this is the case there would appear to be a general merging of images of perfection—the Platonic, medieval-Christian, and Pushkin ideals—in Aglaya's mind.

28. Kant also finds in the admiration for beauty something akin to moral and religious feeling, something before which man bows. In his "Critique of Teleological Judgement" he expresses the thought that the final end of our true being may be delineated to our minds quite freely by a reverence for the moral law. In this case "we accept into our moral perspective a cause harmonizing with that end and with its accomplishment, and accept it with deepest veneration . . . and we willingly bow down before it." At this point Kant observes in a footnote: "Both the admiration for beauty and the emotion excited by the profuse variety of ends of nature . . . have something about them akin to a *religious* feeling. Hence they seem primarily to act upon the moral feeling (of gratitude and veneration toward the unknown cause) by means of a mode of critical judgment analogous to the moral mode, and therefore to affect the mind by exciting moral ideas. It is then that they inspire that admiration which is fraught with far more interest than mere theoretical observation can produce." Immanuel Kant, *The Critique of Judgement,* trans. J. D. Meredith (Oxford, 1961), p. 159.

29. Fet's poem is a representative example of the so-called anthology poetry in the 1840s and 1850s—a genre preoccupied with images and themes of antiquity and noted for its classical and "plastic" style. No other poem of Fet, B. Ja. Bukhshtab has noted, evoked such an ecstatic response among writers and general public as the anthological "Diana" "with its plastic expressiveness, its measured,

precise epithets, and mathematically strict intonations of Alexandrine verse."
See Bukhshtab's introductory essay, "A. A. Fet," in A. A. Fet, *Polnoe sobranie
stikhotvorenij,* ed. B. Ja. Bukhshtab (Leningrad, 1959), p. 31.

30. See Plato's *Symposium,* in The Works of Plato, ed. Irwin Edman (New
York, 1928), p. 373.

31. "G. —bov," *Stat'i, 13,* 89.

32. Ibid., p. 90.

33. Dostoevsky, as is well known, was an epileptic himself. He described
to his friend and literary associate, N. N. Strakhov, the moments preceding an
epileptic attack. "For several moments I experience a happiness such as is impossible in one's ordinary condition and of which other people have no conception.
I feel a complete harmony in myself and in the whole world, and this feeling is
so strong and sweet that for several seconds of such bliss one might give up ten
years of life, maybe one's whole life." Strakhov, *Biografija, pis'ma i zametki,*
p. 214.

34. "Pushkin (ocherk)," *Dnevnik pisatelja, 13,* 385.

35. *Pis'ma, 2* (No. 279), 31.

36. Ibid. (No. 294), p. 71.

37. See Dostoevsky's letter to his brother Mikhail, March 26, 1864. Ibid., *1*
(No. 193), 353.

38. "Idealisty-tsiniki," *Dnevnik pisatelja, 11,* 342.

39. The man from the "underground," however, confronts human and metaphysical reality with a philosophy which, paradoxically, in certain fundamentals
is close to the philosophy of life which Dostoevsky advances in "Mr. —bov and
the Question of Art." Man in health, Dostoevsky believed, lives most of all when
he is in struggle, in discord, and striving for an ideal. We find in the philosophy
of life of the man from the "underground" an atheistic version—or conversion—
of Dostoevsky's religious-aesthetic outlook. When workmen have finished their
work, remarks the man from the "underground," they can go to the tavern. "But
where can man go?" "Who knows . . . perhaps the whole goal on earth to which
mankind is striving lies only in this incessant process of attaining, in other words,
in life itself, and not really in the goal which, it goes without saying, must always
be nothing other than twice two makes four, i.e. a formula." In the life of the
man from the "underground" Dostoevsky makes crystal clear that this outlook—
expressed, figuratively, in man beating his head unremittingly against the wall—
is catastrophe, tragedy, the philosophical *cul de sac* of man without faith.
(Dostoevsky—unlike Camus—does not idealize the tragic posture of "underground" man before the wall.) But the common denominator in the philosophy
of the man from the "underground" and in the aesthetic philosophy of "Mr.
—bov and the Question of Art" is the emphasis upon struggle and striving as
the condition of creative (for the "underground" man, *livable*) life. Both philosophies are directed against inertia, stasis.

40. "G. —bov," *Stat'i, 13,* 95.

41. *Pis'ma, 2* (No. 550), 212.

42. Konshina, ed., *Zapisnye tetradi,* p. 287. The interdependence of the moral
and aesthetic categories, on the one hand, and the direct dependence of both upon
the religious, on the other, is strongly emphasized in the notebooks to *The Devils.*
See, for example, the "speech of Sh." at a public gathering on p. 312 of the notebooks just cited. "Society is created by morality and religion. The moral elements
stem from religion. The aesthetic strivings must be affirmed, the conception of
good and evil."

43. Ibid., p. 292.
44. Ibid., p. 207.
45. Ibid., p. 221.
46. Ibid., p. 155
47. Ibid., p. 222.
48. Ibid., p. 296.
49. "Otvet russkomu vestniku," *Stat'i, 13,* 218.
50. "Obraztsy chistoserdechija," ibid., 184.
51. "Otvet russkomu vestniku," ibid., 215. Dostoevsky is particularly concerned here with a defense of Pushkin's "Egyptian Nights" with its "'ultimate expression of passion'" in the figure of the debauched Cleopatra. Dostoevsky insists that a reading of "Egyptian Nights" can produce "a pure artistic impression." He rejects any identification of it with the works of the Marquis de Sade. "This *ultimate expression* about which you are talking so often," Dostoevsky writes in his polemical piece, "for you may be really seductive; for us, however, there is presented in it only a distortion of human nature which has reached such frightful proportions—and is presented *from such a point of view* by the poet (and point of view is the main thing)—that it produces not at all an erotic, but a crushing impression." Ibid., p. 216. Pushkin, then, has maintained his aesthetic distance from his subject; such distance provides perspective and therefore an artistic representation which structures the corruption of Cleopatra as a deviation from a norm. Thus, Dostoevsky seems to suggest, we do not lasciviously enjoy—but are repelled by—the sight of Pushkin's Cleopatra. Art, here, cancels lust. All this assumes, however, a certain "development" of the spirit. For example, Dostoevsky allows that "Egyptian Nights" might have a "dangerous" effect upon an adolescent. In adolescence a person "is not formed either physically or morally." "Obraztsy chistoserdechija," ibid., p. 184. It should be noted here that Dostoevsky's portrayal, or interpretation, of Cleopatra's savage sensuality is an extremely subjective evocation of Pushkin's image, one which is as revealing of Dostoevsky himself as it is of Pushkin's Cleopatra. In Dostoevsky's evocation of Cleopatra there is both repulsion and the fascination with attractive evil.
52. In its broadest sense the term *bezobrazie* is used by Dostoevsky to define any kind of ugliness (moral, spiritual, aesthetic); very frequently, however, it appears in the context of sexual passion or outrage. Rogozhin in *The Idiot* is referred to as a *bezobraznik*—one who enjoys *bezobrazie;* his sensuality is described as a *bezobraznaja strast'*—a monstrous or disfiguring passion. "It was impossible to imagine anything more monstrous [bezobraznee]," Stavrogin remarks apropos of his rape of a young girl. We learn that in Fyodor Karamazov's *bezobraznyj dom*—his monstrous or shameless house—his first wife was surrounded by *bezobrazie.* Fyodor himself *ljubil bezobraznichat' s zhenskim polom* —liked to debauch with the feminine sex. The pleasure man experiences in moral *bezobrazie* (whether in pure sexual experience or in the vicarious sexual pleasures of violence) is characterized in Dostoevsky's novelistic world by delight in the exceptional, inharmonic, disfigured. Only the "monstrous, abnormal, malignant" can stimulate the bored soul of Cleopatra, according to Dostoevsky. "She has already learned all the secrets of love and pleasures, and before her the Marquis de Sade might seem like a child." "Otvet russkomu vestniku," ibid., p. 217.
53. F. M. Dostoevskij, *Ispoved' Stavrogina* (Munich, 1922), p. 40. L. P. Grossman has noted that the style of Stavrogin's confession is organically linked with its problem content. "The confession of the terrible sinner is expressed in a continual disintegration of word and image, as it were reflecting the chaotic and confused

consciousness of the criminal. The painfulness of the theme insistently demanded some kind of new devices of distorted and wracked language. The ingenious stylist [Dostoevsky] found the key to the resolution of this most difficult problem, discovered the verbal correspondence to the decadent and criminal consciousness of his hero, and gave the first typical model of the 'decadent' style." Cf. L. P. Grossman, "Dostoevskij-khudozhnik," in *Tvorchestvo Dostoevskogo*, ed. N. L. Stepanov, (Moscow, 1959), p. 384.

54. It is indicative, again, of the tremendous importance of the aesthetic element for Dostoevsky that he has Dmitry Karamazov express a deep loathing for the ugly physical features of his father's face (the objective embodiment, one might say, of his moral *bezobrazie*). Indeed, Dmitry says at one point that he fears it will be precisely these repulsive features that will "at the last moment" induce him to kill his father!

55. "Otvet russkomu vestniku," *Stat'i, 13,* 217.

56. The passage from which this line is taken reads as follows: "The teachings of the materialists—universal inertness [*kostnost'*] and the mechanism of matter—mean death. The teachings of true philosophy—the annihilation of inertness, i.e. the center and synthesis of the universe and of its external form—of matter, i.e. God, i.e. eternal life." Cf. Vysheslavtsev, "Dostoevskij o ljubvi i beszmertie (Novyj fragment)," p. 292.

57. "O ljubvi k narodu," *Dnevnik pisatelja, 11,* 184.

58. "G. —bov," *Stat'i, 13,* 95.

59. Konshina, ed., *Zapisnye tetradi,* p. 222.

60. A. S. Dolinin, ed., *F. M. Dostoevskij, materialy i issledovanija* (Leningrad, 1935), p. 297.

61. I discuss this aspect of Dostoevsky's characterization of Dmitry in my article, "Dmitrij Karamazov and the 'Legend,'" in *Slavic and East European Journal, 9* (1965), 257–67.

62. M. P. Klodt was the son of a well-known sculptor; in 1861 he received a gold medal for his painting "The Last Spring" ("Poslednjaja vesna").

63. "Vystavka v akademii khudozhestv," *Stat'i, 13,* 545–46.

64. Ibid., p. 545.

65. A. G. Dostoevskaja, *Dnevnik A. G. Dostoevskoj, 1867 g.* (Moscow, 1923), p. 366. In some comments on Dostoevsky's *The Idiot,* Madame Dostoevsky recalls that her husband stood watching the Holbein painting "as though transfixed" for about 15 or 20 minutes. "His face had the kind of frightened expression that we had had occasion to note many times before his attacks of epilepsy." Cf. "Primechanie A. G. Dostoevskoj k sochinenijam F. M. Dostoevskogo," in *Seminarij po Dostoevskomu,* ed. L. P. Grossman (Moscow, 1922), p. 70.

66. *"Sobor parizhskoj bogomateri:* Roman V. Gjugo," *Stat'i, 13,* 525.

67. Ibid., p. 526.

68. Ibid.

69. Cf. Vysheslavtsev, "Dostoevskij o ljubvi i bezsmertie (Novyj fragment)," p. 297.

6: Reality and Its Representation in Art

1. Belinskij, "Gore ot uma," *Sobranie sochinenij, 1,* 469.

2. The syncretic character of Dostoevsky's realism has been noted by L. P. Grossman and others. Grossman writes: "Close in many respects to the current of

critical representation of reality and frequently offering fine examples of it, the style of the novelist is unique and is qualitatively different. A profound truthfulness of experience gives to his painting the sharp features of a realistic reflection of life. But this is . . . realism of a special type—psychological or grotesque or, in the words of Dostoevsky himself, 'prophetic,' i.e. striving to determine on the basis of the deep currents of contemporary history, the lines of its future development." Grossman, "Dostoevskij-khudozhnik," in *Tvorchestvo Dostoevskogo*, p. 368. J. van der Eng in *Dostoevskij Romancier* ('s-Gravenhage, 1957), pp. 44–45, notes the range of definitions of Dostoevsky's realism in critical literature: "mystical realism," "symbolic realism," "symbolic or transcendental realism," the "realism of an epileptic," "demoniac realism," "fantastic realism," *"réalisme du dernier degré,"* "allegorical realism," "psychological realism."

3. "Dva samoubijstva," *Dnevnik pisatelja, 11,* 423.

4. "G. —bov," *Stat'i, 13,* 82.

5. "Dva samoubijstva," *Dnevnik pisatelja, 11,* 423.

6. V. I. Jacoby received a gold medal for his painting, "Convicts at a Halting Point" ("Prival arestantov") at the Academy of Arts Exhibition.

7. "Vystavka v akademii khudozhestv," *Stat'i, 13,* 531–32. Dostoevsky obviously did not regard photography as an artistic medium. Versilov in *The Raw Youth* (Pt. III, Ch. 7, Sec. i) surely gives expression to Dostoevsky's critical view of photography.

8. Belinsky argues in 1840 that one must distinguish between the *man* and the *artist.* Art has its own laws, he insists, on the basis of which one must examine its works. "The thought, expressed by a poet in a creation, may contradict the personal conviction of the critic, without ceasing to be true and universal, provided the creation is really an artistic one, because man, as a limited individual, may err and nourish false convictions, but the poet, as the organ of the general and universal, as the direct manifestation of the spirit, cannot err and speak a lie. . . . Therefore, to find out whether a thought expressed by a poet in his work is correct, one must first find out whether his creation is really artistic." Belinskij, "Mentsel', kak kritik Gete," *Sobranie sochinenij, 1,* 429–30.

9. See, in particular, the opening section of N. A. Dobrolyubov's extensive essay, "Realm of Darkness." Dobrolyubov distinguishes between the artist as artist and the artist as thinker. "Frequently even in abstract discussions [the artist] expresses concepts strikingly in contradiction with what is expressed in his artistic work." Truth, according to Dobrolyubov, lies in the images created by the artist, in the *types* created by him. Cf. N. A. Dobroljubov "Temnoe tsarstvo," *Izbrannye sochinenija* (Moscow-Leningrad, 1948), p. 104.

10. "Rasskazy N. V. Uspenskogo," *Stat'i, 13,* 548–49.

11. "Vystavka v akademii khudozhestv," *ibid.*, p. 532.

12. Ibid., pp. 530, 532.

13. "Po povodu novoj dramy," *Dnevnik pisatelja, 11,* 100.

14. "Vystavka v akademii khudozhestv," *Stat'i, 13,* 532.

15. Ibid., p. 533.

16. "Po povodu vystavki," *Dnevnik pisatelja, 11,* 42.

17. "Rasskazy N. V. Uspenskogo," *Stat'i, 13,* 549–50.

18. "Vystavka v akademii khudozhestv," *ibid.*, p. 533.

19. "Rasskazy N. V. Uspenskogo," *ibid.*, p. 550.

20. "Detskie sekrety," *Dnevnik pisatelja, 11,* 375.

21. Quoted by G. M. Fridlender, *Realizm Dostoevskogo* (Moscow-Leningrad, 1964), p. 350.

22. *Pis'ma, 3* (No. 558), 225.

23. "Edinichnyj sluchaj," *Dnevnik pisatelja, 12,* 93.

24. The central artistic problem which confronted Dostoevsky when he wrote *Notes from the House of the Dead* unquestionably was that of transcending a naturalistic representation of prison reality, a naked eyewitness account of the "repulsive crust" of prison life. The problem was solved in part by projecting the narrator's life in prison in the form of recollections (as opposed to diary form). The narrator, to be sure, gives us a detailed account of his experience in prison from the first day he set foot there; but the spiritually crushing impact of that experience, as it is conveyed to us, is modified in the perspective of time. See my article, "The Narrator in Dostoevsky's *Notes from the House of the Dead,*" in *Studies in Russian and Polish Literature: In Honor of Waclaw Lednicki* ('s-Gravenhage, Mouton & Co., 1962), pp. 192–216.

25. Alexandre Calame (1810–64).

26. "Vystavka v akademii khudozhestv," *Stat'i, 13,* 543.

27. Apropos of Myshkin's subject for a painting, and in response to Adelaida's observation that it would be a "strange" subject, Myshkin says: "I don't know why . . . in Basel I recently saw one such picture. I'd like very much to tell you. . . . Some day I'll tell you . . . it impressed me very much." G. M. Fridlender suggests that Dostoevsky had in mind here a picture by the German artist Hans Fries (1450–1520) which is called "The Beheading of John the Baptist." G. M. Fridlender, notes to *The Idiot, Sobranie sochinenij v desjati tomakh, 6* (Moscow, 1957), 723.

28. François Diday (1802–77).

29. "Vystavka v akademii khudozhestv," *Stat'i, 13,* 543.

30. "Rasskazy N. V. Uspenskogo," ibid., p. 550.

31. Erich Auerbach, characterizing the disintegration of the concept of reality in the second part of the nineteenth century, calls particular attention to the tendency to turn reality into a function of consciousness. "Reality one and individual was replaced by different strata of reality; i.e. by a conscious perspectivism. Some modern authors have shown us, instead of an objective picture of phenomenon A, phenomenon A as it appears to the consciousness of character B at a certain moment; and they are liable to give us a completely different view of A, either in the consciousness of character C or in the consciousness of character B himself at a different moment in his life." Auerbach views Marcel Proust as the first writer "to apply in a methodical and sustained manner, the conception of the world as a function of consciousness." Erich Auerbach, *Introduction to Romance Languages and Literature* (New York, 1961), p. 251. It seems clear, however, that Dostoevsky anticipated Proust in his literary practice and theory. Dostoevsky's so-called polyphonic novel is the fruit precisely of a conscious perspectivism. In this connection see M. M. Bakhtin's *Problemy poètiki Dostoevskogo* (Moscow, 1963)—a study first published in 1929—in which the author develops the theory of Dostoevsky's "polyphonic novel."

32. "Po povodu vystavki," *Dnevnik pisatelja, 11,* 77–78.

33. *Pis'ma, 2* (No. 318), 150–51. As A. S. Dolinin points out in a note on this letter, Dostoevsky had in mind here a murder committed by the student Danilov in 1865. The circumstances of the crime and the motives of Danilov were somewhat similar to those of Raskolnikov. Ibid., p. 438.

34. L. Simonova, "Iz vospominanij o F. M. Dostoevskom," *Tserkovno-obshchestvennyj vestnik, 17* (1881), p. 5. Quoted by V. V. Vinogradov in *Problema avtorstva i teorija stilej* (Moscow, 1961), p. 535.

35. Letter of A. Maikov to Dostoevsky, March 14, 1868. Quoted by A. S. Dolinin in his notes to *Pis'ma, 2,* 419.

36. Letter of A. Maikov to Dostoevsky, September 30, 1868. Quoted by A. S. Dolinin, ibid., p. 426.

37. "Peterburgskie snovidenija v stikhakh i proze," *Stat'i, 13,* 160.

38. Ibid., p. 156.

39. Fridlender, *Realizm Dostoevskogo,* p. 76.

40. *Pis'ma, 2* (No. 323), 169–70.

41. "Rjazhenyj," *Dnevnik pisatelja, 11,* 83. The chronicler in *The Devils* gives expression to this point of view. He observes at one point in his narrative (Pt. 1, Ch. 2, Sec. vi) that it is difficult to know what was in Varvara Petrovna's heart and that he is not going to undertake in advance to unravel the contradictions in her plan. "As the chronicler I limit myself only to presenting events in a precise form, exactly as they occurred, and it is not my fault if they appear improbable." Of course, the chronicler's pose of objectivity cannot be confused with Dostoevsky the artist who stands at one or two removes from the chronicler. The artist Dostoevsky is not engaged in a mechanical and exact reproducing or detailing of events, of course. What may strike us as improbable at any single moment in the novel loses its aura of improbability in the artist's total presentation of "events"—a presentation, it need hardly be said, which is highly selective and controlled.

42. Ibid.

43. Ibid., p. 84.

44. "Protsess Lasenera," *Stat'i, 13,* 524–25.

45. Quoted by A. S. Dolinin in *V tvorcheskoj laboratorii Dostoevskogo,* p. 147.

46. *Pis'ma, 1* (No. 184), 344.

47. Ibid., p. 343.

48. Ibid., p. 344.

49. "Tri rasskaza Edgara Poè," *Stat'i, 13,* 523.

50. Ibid., p. 524.

51. Ibid., p. 523.

52. "Ot avtora" [Preface to "Krotkaja"], *Dnevnik pisatelja, 11,* 443–44.

53. *Pis'ma, 4* (No. 753), 177–78.

54. Dolinin, ed., *F. M. Dostoevskij, materialy i issledovanija,* pp. 85–86.

55. "Iz knigi predskazanij Ioanna Likhtenbergera, 1528 goda," *Dnevnik pisatelja, 12,* 129.

56. "G. —bov," *Stat'i, 13,* 95.

57. Konshina, ed., *Zapisnye tetradi,* p. 179.

58. Notebook to the *Diary of a Writer.* Quoted by S. Borshchevskij in *Shchedrin i Dostoevskij* (Moscow, 1956), p. 300.

59. "Postydno li byt' idealistom?" *Dnevnik pisatelja, 11,* 349.

60. Opochinin, "Besedy s Dostoevskim," p. 472.

7: The Problem of Type

1. From a review in *Grazhdanin* (1873), No. 1, pp. 21–22. Quoted by V. V. Vinogradov in *Problema avtorstva i teorija stilej,* p. 510. "This review," Vinogradov writes, "was written either by F. M. Dostoevsky himself or, in any case, with his direct participation."

2. "Kul'turnye tipiki," *Dnevnik pisatelja, 11,* 250.

3. "Zuboskal," *Stat'i, 13, 5.*

4. Belinskij, "Pedant," *Sobranie sochinenij, 2,* 216.

5. "Rasskazy bez nachala i bez kontsa," *Literaturnaja gazeta* (1844), No. 1. Quoted by V. V. Vinogradov in "Sjuzhet i arkhitektonika romana Dostoevskogo 'Bednye ljudi' v svjazi s voprosom o poètike natural'noj shkoly," in *Tvorcheskij put' Dostoevskogo,* ed. N. L. Brodskij (Leningrad, 1924), p. 5.

6. *Pis'ma, 1* (No. 123), 257.

7. The term *tip iz korennika* might also be translated as "indigenous type" or type from the heart of the people. The reference to this type appears in the draft-sketches for Dostoevsky's projected novel, "The Life of a Great Sinner." Dostoevsky contrasts this type with the "completely opposite type"—the degenerating scion of a noble family "whom Tolstoy depicted in *Childhood and Boyhood.*" These "types from the stalk" are constantly seeking; their strength is a burden to them; they want "peace from storms." They finally find Christ, "but their whole life is storm and disorder." Konshina, ed., *Zapisnye tetradi,* pp. 107–08. Danila Filippovich was a seventeenth-century peasant, the semilegendary founder of the sect of flagellants.

8. From a review in *Grazhdanin* (1873), No. 4, pp. 125–26. V. V. Vinogradov, who attributes this review to Dostoevsky, republishes the text of the review in Vinogradov, *Problema avtorstva i teorija stilej,* pp. 515–17.

9. See René Wellek's essay "Realism in Literary Scholarship" in his *Concepts of Criticism* (New Haven and London, 1963), p. 226.

10. "Nechto o vran'e," *Dnevnik pisatelja, 11,* 123. "In Russia," Dostoevsky adds, "truth always has a completely fantastic character."

11. See Grossman's "Dostoevskij-khudozhnik," in *Tvorchestvo Dostoevskogo,* p. 336.

12. *Pis'ma, 2* (No. 321), 161.

13. From a review in *Grazhdanin* (1873), No. 4, pp. 125–26. See Vinogradov, *Problema avtorstva i teorija stilej,* p. 516.

14. For a general discussion of Dostoevsky's literary polemics with Chernyshevsky, Dobrolyubov, and the radical camp in the 1860s, see U. A. Gural'nik's "F. M. Dostoevskij v literaturno-èsteticheskoj bor'be 60-x godov," in *Tvorchestvo Dostoevskogo,* pp. 293–329.

15. N. G. Chernyshevskij, "Ne nachalo li peremeny? Rasskazy N. V. Uspenskogo," in *N. G. Chernyshevskij, Èstetika i literaturnaja kritika, Izbrannye stat'i* (Moscow-Leningrad, 1951), pp. 491, 492.

16. Dostoevsky's demand for an ideal in the artistic representation of reality is, of course, not a demand for a glossy idealization of life. He specifically rejects this kind of "idealization" in his essay on N. V. Uspensky. Cf. "Rasskazy N. V. Uspenskogo," *Stat'i, 13,* 551. Dostoevsky insisted upon a forceful, truthful representation of reality. Arkady Dolgoruky in *The Raw Youth* expresses Dostoevsky's viewpoint when he remarks, apropos of the elements of the cynical and even ridiculous in Versilov's "confession": "I was too broad not to understand and to allow realism—which did not, however, mar the ideal" (Pt. III, Ch. 9, Sec. i). What Dostoevsky demands, then, in the depiction of reality, is fullness of perspective, consciousness of the norm, the ideal, above all, the preservation of that ideal. "Realism which is limited by the end of one's nose," Arkady Dolgoruky declares elsewhere in *The Raw Youth,* "is more dangerous than the maddest fantasy, because it is blind" (Pt. 1, Ch. 8, Sec. ii).

17. "Rasskazy N. V. Uspenskogo," ibid., p. 548. It should be noted that Dostoevsky is *not* quoting from Chernyshevsky's article but is offering the reader his summary of Chernyshevsky's views in the form of a quotation. This device makes it

easier for Dostoevsky to set forth his own ideas, but it makes it difficult to get an accurate idea of his opponent's views.

18. Ibid.

19. Ibid., pp. 550–51.

20. "Reality strives toward fragmentation" ("Dejstvitel'nost' stremitsja k razdro-bleniju")—this notion is central to Dostoevsky's whole vision of reality. The force of reality and the force of art are completely antithetical to each other in their strivings. To the centrifugal, disfiguring, fragmenting force of reality, Dostoevsky opposes the aesthetic striving for unity, form, and moral figuration.

21. "Rjazhenyj," *Dnevnik pisatelja, 11,* 91.

22. Ibid., p. 90. Dostoevsky himself, it should be noted, took a great interest in the gathering of lexical material during his imprisonment in Siberia. His Siberian notebook is made up almost exclusively of expressions, sayings, turns of speech, bits of popular ballads, etc. Cf. L. P. Grossman, ed., "F. M. Dostoevskij, Pervaja zapisnaja knizhka," in *Zven'ja, 6* (1936), 413–38.

23. "Rasskazy N. V. Uspenskogo," *Stat'i, 13,* 552.

24. "Rjazhenyj," *Dnevnik pisatelja, 11,* 90.

25. Belinskij, "Gore ot uma," *Sobranie sochinenij, 1,* 468–69.

26. "Po povodu vystavki," *Dnevnik pisatelja, 11,* 77–78.

27. The observation is from an article intended by Dostoevsky for his *Diary of a Writer* in 1876; it is cited by W. Komarowitsch [V. Komarovich] in *Die Urgestalt der Brüder Karamasoff* (Munich, 1928), p. 505. Dostoevsky's original text, of course, is in Russian; Komarovich's translation of Dostoevsky's observation in German reads as follows: "Man spricht über den Realismus in der Kunst. Javert ist kein Realismus, sondern im höchsten Ausmasse ein Idealtypus, aber es gibt nichts Realistischeres als diese Idealgestalt." I translate the word *Idealtypus* in the hyphenated form of ideal-type in order to distinguish it from the notion of "ideal type," that is, the positive, good, or beautiful type of man.

28. "Po povodu vystavki," *Dnevnik pisatelja, 11,* 76, 78.

29. *Pis'ma, 1* (No. 154), 306. Dostoevsky's first opinion of Ostrovsky's work, based only on an acquaintance with excerpts from Ostrovsky's plays, was a negative one. He wrote to his friend Maikov from Siberia in 1856: "Perhaps he knows a certain class of Rus' well, but it seems to me that he is not an artist. Moreover, it seems to me that he is a *poet without an ideal.* Disabuse me of this, send me, for God's sake, the best of his works." *Pis'ma, 1* (No. 75), 167.

30. Ibid., *2* (No. 356), 288–89.

31. A. I. Gertsen, "Zapiski molodogo cheloveka," in *Povesti i rasskazy* (Moscow, 1962), p. 4.

32. "Our contemporary authors for some reason do not understand that for the creation of type it is not necessary that the circumstances of life of their heroes and heroines be unusual ones," we read in an 1873 review attributed to Dostoevsky by V. V. Vinogradov; "[they do not understand] that the more ordinary the life, the more graphic and real will be the emergent types." Quoted by Vinogradov, *Problema avtorstva i teorija stilej,* p. 511.

33. "Malen'kie kartinki," *Dnevnik pisatelja, 11,* 109. The view of Petersburg architecture as characterless was not a new one with Dostoevsky. In a book renowned throughout Europe, Dostoevsky writes in a feuilleton in 1847, it is said that "there is nothing more characterless than Petersburg architecture." Dostoevsky does not deny this, but he notes that all this "diversity of character" attests to the "unity of thought and unity of movement" of St. Petersburg—the different periods in its development. "Peterburgskaja letopis'," *Stat'i, 13,* 21, 23. In his later years Dostoev-

sky simply took a pessimistic view of St. Petersburg's "diversity of character"; he finds in St. Petersburg architecture, particularly the palaces, "all the negativeness of the essence of the Petersburg period, from its very beginning to its end." "Malen'kie kartinki," *Dnevnik pisatelja, 11*, 109. This negative *ideological* view of Petersburg architecture, however, would not seem to exclude a positive aesthetic appreciation of St. Petersburg.

34. "Po povodu vystavki," *Dnevnik pisatelja, 11*, 72.

35. "Knizhnost' i gramotnost': Stat'ja pervaja," *Stat'i, 13*, 101, 103.

36. "Kul'turnye tipiki," *Dnevnik pisatelja, 11*, 250.

37. *Pis'ma, 2* (No. 356), 288.

38. "Odna iz sovremennykh fal'shej," *Dnevnik pisatelja, 11*, 129–30.

39. Konshina, ed., *Zapisnye tetradi*, p. 276.

40. "Ob anonimnykh rugatel'nykh pis'makh," *Dnevnik pisatelja, 12*, 130–31.

41. "Plan oblichitel'noj povesti iz sovremennoj zhizni," *Dnevnik pisatelja, 12*, 135.

42. "Vystavka v akademii khudozhestv," *Stat'i, 13*, 540.

43. Cited by L. P. Grossman in *Biblioteka Dostoevskogo* (Odessa, 1919), pp. 78–79. Variants of the Pushkin speech were published later in Dolinin, ed., *F. M. Dostoevskij, stat'i i materialy, 2*, 537–45.

44. Grossman, *Biblioteka Dostoevskogo*, p. 73.

45. F. M. Dostoevskij, "Rech' o Pushkine," in *F. M. Dostoevskij, stat'i i materialy, 2*, 529.

46. Grossman, *Biblioteka Dostoevskogo*, pp. 71, 72.

47. The priest does not appear in the final version.

48. I. Goncharov, *Sobranie sochinenij v 8 tomakh, 8* (Moscow, 1955), p. 457.

49. Ibid., p. 459.

50. "Imeninnik," *Dnevnik pisatelja, 12*, 35.

51. Ibid., p. 36.

52. Goncharov, "Namerenija, zadachi i idei romana 'Obryv,'" *Sobranie sochinenij v 8 tomakh, 8*, 212–13.

53. Quoted by A. S. Dolinin in *V tvorcheskoj laboratorii Dostoevskogo*, p. 147.

54. Ibid., p. 148.

55. Cf. Grossman, ed., *Seminarij po Dostoevskomu*, p. 30.

56. I discuss this aspect of *Dr. Zhivago* in two articles: "The Symbol of the Wild Duck in *Dr. Zhivago*," *Comparative Literature, 15* (1963), 39–45, and "Doktor Živago and the Living Tradition," *Slavic and East European Journal*, New Series, *4* (1960), 103–17.

57. A parody of Goncharov's theory of the type is evident in certain parts of the letter of Arkady Dolgoruky's mentor. But the total image of the mentor—as a bearer of ideas—is a complex and, chiefly, independent one. He gives expression to some of Goncharov's ideas, but he also transcends them in his understanding. As a personality, Arkady Dolgoruky's mentor has a certain priggish or fastidious quality which Dostoevsky may have identified with Goncharov. Certainly Goncharov (at least in Dostoevsky's view) does not appear to have shared Dostoevsky's passionate literary and ideological concern with current Russian reality in the 1870s. "The other day I met Goncharov," Dostoevsky writes in a letter to Kh. D. Alchevskaja in 1876, "and to my sincere question: does he understand everything in current reality, or has he already ceased to understand something? he directly answered me that 'he had ceased to understand' a great deal. Of course," Dostoevsky continues ironically, "I myself know that this *great mind* not only understands, but even teaches others. . . . 'Precious to me are my ideals and what I have grown so fond of

in life, and I want to spend with them these few years which remain to me, while to study them (he pointed out to me the passing crowd in the Nevsky Prospect) is a burden to me, because my precious time will be spent on them.' " *Pis'ma, 3* (No. 544), 206. Dostoevsky's irritation with Goncharov's personality is plainly evident in one of his letters at the end of his life. "If Goncharov hiccups, they immediately shout in all the newspapers: 'our venerable belletrist has hiccuped,' but me, as though the word had been passed around, they ignore." *Pis'ma, 4* (No. 762), 192.

58. "Rjazhenyj," *Dnevnik pisatelja, 11,* 90.

59. "Po povodu novoj dramy," ibid., p. 99.

60. *Pis'ma, 2* (No. 294), 71.

61. Ibid. (No. 346), p. 264.

62. "Knizhnost' i gramotnost': Stat'ja pervaja," *Stat'i, 13,* 100.

63. "Ob'jasnitel'noe slovo po povodu pechataemoj nizhe Rechi o Pushkine," *Dnevnik pisatelja, 12,* 370.

64. "Odin iz oblagodetel'stvovannykh sovremennoj zhenshchinoj," *Dnevnik pisatelja, 11,* 369.

65. "Knizhnost' i gramotnost'," *Stat'i, 13,* 105.

66. *Pis'ma, 4* (No. 685), 91–92.

67. Ibid. (No. 664), p. 59.

68. Ibid. (No. 694), p. 109.

69. Ibid. (No. 649), pp. 109–10.

70. Ibid., 2 (No. 294), 71.

71. "Starye ljudi," *Dnevnik pisatelja, 11,* 9.

72. "Po povodu vystavki," ibid., pp. 78–79.

73. Ibid., 79.

74. *Pis'ma, 3* (No. 544), 206. In another letter Dostoevsky is critical of the contemporary writer, "from among the new people," for not wanting to know anything of the past. "He does not know either European literature or his own; he has read nothing and he is not going to read anything." "Obosoblenie," *Dnevnik pisatelja, 11,* 222.

8: Art and Aesthetic Education

1. Théophile Gautier, "Préface," *Mademoiselle de Maupin* (Paris, Garnier, 1955), pp. 22, 23, 24.

2. "G.—bov," *Stat'i, 13,* 93. There is another absolutely independent force, apart from art, that serves mankind, Dostoevsky wrote in "Stories of N. V. Uspensky" less than a year after his critique of Dobrolyubov. "This is science, a terrible force, which was born with man and which will never leave him until man ceases to exist on earth." Dostoevsky goes on to say that "we acknowledged all this and still acknowledge it, and it is in vain that we are accused of placing all our hopes for progress and social consciousness upon art alone." "Rasskazy N. V. Uspenskogo," *Stat'i, 13,* 551. But although Dostoevsky equates art and science in their role of serving mankind, it is quite probable that Stepan Verkhovensky fully expresses Dostoevsky's view when he exclaims at the literary quadrille (in *The Devils*) that "science itself would not survive a moment without beauty." There is no indication that Dostoevsky ever linked science, as he does art and beauty, with what for him was the primal force in life: religion. Or is this in the back of his mind when he writes that science and art were "born with man"?

3. " 'Svistok' i 'Russkij vestnik'," *Stat'i, 13,* 190. Dostoevsky never ceases to em-

phasize the moral understructure of all social life; this emphasis upon the moral element he identified with Belinsky. Belinsky knew, Dostoevsky wrote in 1873, that "the moral element is the basis of everything." *Dnevnik pisatelja, 11*, 8. All "social civic ideals," Dostoevsky wrote at the end of his life, are "organically connected with moral ideals." Ibid., *12*, 408.

4. N. A. Dobroljubov, "O stepeni uchastija narodnosti v razvitii russkoj literatury, in *Izbrannye sochinenija* (Moscow, 1948), p. 25.

5. "G. —bov," *Stat'i, 13*, 88, 94.

6. Ibid., *12*, 88. Dostoevsky shared the cult of Hellenism with his generation; it had been nourished on the ideas and ethos of J. J. Winckelmann, Schiller, and others who projected ancient Greece as the lofty ideal to be emulated. Belinsky, twenty years earlier, in his article "Menzel, Critic of Goethe," emphasized that *The Iliad* and the art of Greece in general were part of Russia's inheritance. "Is it possible," he asked, "that the life of the Greeks has not entered into us as an element?" Belinskij, "Mentsel', kritik Gete," *Sobranie sochinenij, 1*, 427. One of Alexander Herzen's heroes of the 1840s (*Notes of a Young Man—Zapiski molodogo cheloveka*) writes in his notebook: "Let these supremely refined [Greek] statues greet a young man at his first step into the realm of consciousness: from the heights of their magnificence these first lessons of civic virtues will fix their gaze upon him."

7. "G. —bov," *Stat'i, 13*, 92.

8. "Ob'javlenija o podpiske na zhurnal 'Vremja,' " ibid., p. 506.

9. "Dva lagerja teoretikov," ibid., p. 240.

10. "Rasskazy N. V. Uspenskogo," ibid., p. 548.

11. "O ljubvi k narodu," *Dnevnik pisatelja, 11*, 185.

12. *Pis'ma, 2* (No. 385), 357.

13. Ibid. (No. 319), p. 155.

14. Cf. "Po povodu vystavki," *Dnevnik pisatelja, 11*, 71.

15. "Sobor parizhskoj bogomateri," *Stat'i, 13*, 526.

16. "Knizhnost' i gramotnost': Stat'ja pervaja," ibid., pp. 106–07.

17. Ibid., p. 106. The people will understand Pushkin "later on." A few months earlier, however, in his critique of Dobrolyubov, Dostoevsky had written: "Pushkin is a banner, a point for uniting all those who thirst for education and development; because he is the most artistic, more than all our poets, hence the most simple, the most captivating, the most comprehensible. He is a national poet precisely because everybody understands him." "G. —bov," ibid., p. 95. The identification of artistry with simplicity and comprehensibilty anticipates Tolstoy's similar emphasis later on in his "What Is Art?"

18. "Knizhnost' i gramotnost': Stat'ja pervaja," ibid., p. 106.

19. "Nechto o vran'e," *Dnevnik pisatelja, 11*, 128–29.

20. Ibid., p. 128.

21. *Zimnie zametki o letnikh vpechatlenijakh, 4*, 62–63.

22. "Po povodu novoj dramy," *Dnevnik pisatelja, 11*, 104.

23. Dostoevsky poses the problem of the Russian nature (or the Russian nature of its educated classes) in its moral and cultural shapelessness and lack of self-respect in *The Gambler*, in particular in the figure of Aleksey Ivanovich. "I want to express everything, everything, everything. I lose all form. I even agree that I not only have not got form but also have not got dignity." "For the most part we Russians are so richly gifted that we need genius in order to obtain decency of form." Aleksey has no use for the empty bourgeois formalities and banalities of the de Grieux and the German barons (whom he disconcerts with his typically "underground" behavior), but he himself is the embodiment for Dosto-

evsky of moral instability among the educated classes, of its inability to concentrate its working energies and to find a firm foundation for creative work. He is the epitomy of Russian shapelessness, or *bezobrazie,* in his uncontrolled, frenetic gambling mania and in his sensual passion which expresses itself in his desire to "beat, disfigure, and strangle" Polina.

24. "Na kakom jazyke govorit' budushchemu stopu svoej rodiny?" *Dnevnik pisatelja, 11,* 362. In this same essay, Dostoevsky defines language as "unquestionably, form, body, the membrane of thought (the explanation of the nature of thought aside), so to speak, the last and final word of organic development." The wealthier the forms of thought, the happier man is in life. We think in a language, Dostoevsky observes further on. We may not think in words, that is, pronouncing the words in thought, as it were, "but still, so to speak, we think 'by the elemental basic force of that language' in which we have proposed to think, if it is possible to so express it." Ibid., p. 360.

25. "Sem'ja i nashi svjatyni," ibid., p. 215.

26. "Neskol'ko slov o Zhorzh-Zande," ibid., p. 315.

27. "Rossijskoe obshchestvo," ibid., p. 173. Dostoevsky wrote to Strakhov in 1870: "Man, on the surface of the earth, has no right to avert his face and to ignore what is taking place on earth, and there are lofty *moral* reasons for this. *Homo sum et nihil humanum.*"

28. "Verna li mysl'," ibid., p. 217.

29. "Zhelanie," *Stat'i, 13,* 527–28.

30. Quoted by Vinogradov, *Problema avtorstva i teorija stilej,* pp. 515–16.

31. "Knizhnost' i gramotnost': Stat'ja vtoraja," *Stat'i, 13,* 133, 134.

32. "Kolonija maloletnikh prestupnikov," *Dnevnik pisatelja, 11,* 165. See also pp. 167, 168.

33. *Pis'ma, 4* (No. 789), 222.

34. Ibid. (No. 766), p. 196.

35. Ibid.

9: Critique of Utilitarian Aesthetic

1. N. G. Chernyshevskij, *Èsteticheskie otnoshenija iskusstva k dejstvitel'nosti,* in N. G. Chernyshevskij, *Èstetika i literaturnaja kritika,* p. 8.

2. Ibid., p. 43.

3. Ibid., pp. 43, 44.

4. From a review of *Èsteticheskie otnoshenija* written by Chernyshevsky himself. Ibid., pp. 54–55.

5. Ibid., pp. 49, 50, 51.

6. "Dva samoubijstva," *Dnevnik pisatelja, 11,* 423.

7. "Otryvok iz romana 'Shchedrodarov,' " *Stat'i, 13,* 328.

8. Ibid., p. 335.

9. Ibid., p. 330.

10. "Ob'javlenija o podpiske na zhurnal 'Vremja,' " ibid., p. 512.

11. "Rasskazy N. V. Uspenskogo," ibid., p. 551.

12. "G. —bov," ibid., 69.

13. *Pis'ma, 1* (No. 61), 143.

14. A. Grigor'ev, *Sochinenija Apollona Grigor'eva,* ed. N. N. Strakhov, *1* (St. Petersburg, 1876), p. 615.

15. Dobroljubov, "Temnoe tsarstvo," in *Izbrannye sochinenija,* pp. 103–04.

16. Dobroljubov, "O stepeni uchastija narodnosti," ibid., p. 26.

17. Dobroljubov, "Kogda zhe pridet nastojashchij den'," ibid., p. 242.

18. N. A. Dobroljubov, "Blagonamerennost' i dejatel'nost'," in *Sochinenija N. A. Dobroljubova, 3* (St. Petersburg, 1908), 272.

19. Ibid., p. 276.

20. Dobroljubov, "Stikhotvorenija Ivana Nikitina," *Izbrannye sochinenija,* p. 422.

21. Ibid., p. 420.

22. "G. —bov," *Stat'i, 13, 95.*

23. Dobroljubov, "Stikhotvorenija Ivana Nikitina," *Izbrannye sochinenija,* p. 426.

24. Dobroljubov, "O stepeni uchastija narodnosti," ibid., p. 25.

25. Ibid., p. 24.

26. Dobroljubov, "Stikhotvorenija Ivana Nikitina," ibid., p. 426.

27. "G. —bov," *Stat'i, 13, 94.*

28. Dumas is not an artist, Dostoevsky writes in this review, because "he cannot restrain himself in his unbridled fantasy from exaggerated effects. Let's allow that the Count of Monte-Cristo is rich; but why the emerald flask for poison? . . . One must have a sense of measure, one must be able to restrain oneself in time." "Vystavka v akademii khudozhestv," ibid., 541.

29. "Paradoksalist," *Dnevnik pisatelja, 11,* 268–69. Dostoevsky writes to S. A. Ivanova in 1870: "Without war man grows numb in comfort, in wealth, and completely loses the capacity for magnanimous thoughts and feelings and imperceptibly becomes hardened and falls into barbarism. I speak about peoples as a whole. Without suffering you will not find happiness. The ideal passes through suffering as gold through fire." *Pis'ma, 2* (No. 353), 284.

30. "Spasaet li prolitaja krov'?" *Dnevnik pisatelja, 12,* 104. "*True* art develops precisely in times of prolonged peace." Yet Dostoevsky's "paradoxicalist" maintains that art and science develop "always in the first period after a war." "Paradoksalist," ibid., *11,* 269.

31. Ibid., p. 269.

32. "G. —bov," ibid., *13,* 90.

33. Ibid., pp. 90–91.

34. Dobroljubov, "Cherty dlja kharakteristiki russkogo prostonarod'ja," *Izbrannye sochinenija,* p. 244.

35. "G. —bov," *Stat'i, 13,* 72.

36. "Po povodu vystavki," *Dnevnik pisatelja, 11,* 74–75.

37. Ibid.

38. Ibid., p. 78.

39. "G. —bov," *Stat'i, 13,* 73.

40. "Primechanie," ibid., p. 352.

41. Ibid., p. 353. It doesn't occur to the "contemporary scribbler (a free translation of the word *feuilletonist*)," Dostoevsky wrote in "Petersburg Visions in Verse and Prose" in 1861, that "without a burning ardor, without meaning, without an idea, without desire all will be routine and repetition, repetition and routine. It does not occur to him that the feuilleton in our century is almost the main thing. All his life Voltaire wrote nothing but feuilletons." "Peterburgskie snovidenija," ibid., p. 155.

42. "Rasskazy N. V. Uspenskogo," ibid., p. 548.

43. "G. —bov," ibid., p. 84.

44. *Pis'ma, 3* (No. 541), 203.

45. " 'Svistok' i 'Russkij vestnik,' " *Stat'i, 13,* 190.

46. Quoted by Borshchevskij in *Shchedrin i Dostoevskij,* p. 300.

47. *Pis'ma, 2* (No. 318), 150.

48. Ibid. (No. 343), p. 252.

49. Ibid. (No. 346), p. 262.

50. Ibid. (No. 345), p. 257.

51. Ibid. (No. 357), p. 291.

52. "Odin iz glavnejshikh sovremennykh voprosov," *Dnevnik pisatelja, 12,* 54.

53. "G. —bov," *Stat'i, 13,* 66.

54. Ibid., pp. 66–67.

55. Ibid., pp. 67–68.

56. Ibid., p. 68.

57. Ibid.

58. "Svidetel' v pol'zu Nekrasova," *Dnevnik pisatelja, 12,* 361.

59. Strictly speaking the opinions that follow here are those of "one camp—the camp of defenders of the freedom and complete independence of art." "G. —bov," *Stat'i, 13,* 66. Dostoevsky, it will be remembered, opens his essay with an imaginary debate between two camps: the art for art's sake camp and the utilitarian camp. He insists that "we do not adhere to any one of the existing opinions." An analysis of Dostoevsky's own views in his critique certainly demonstrates that he achieves a unique synthesis of conflicting positions on the question of the purpose and function of art. But he is nonetheless very close to the "defenders of the freedom and complete independence of art," particularly in his advocacy of the "organic" theory of art; this theory he expounds later on in his critique of Dobrolyubov. Thus, he defends "freedom of inspiration" as the main essence of art. Art has its own norms, laws, its own "integral organic life and, consequently, fundamental and unchangeable laws for this life. Art is as much a need for man as eating and drinking." Ibid., p. 86.

60. Ibid., pp. 65–66. In an essay on Dostoevsky's relations with N. N. Strakhov, A. S. Dolinin called attention to a series of articles by Strakhov in *Svetoch* in 1860 entitled "Pis'ma o zhizni," wherein the author discusses the attributes of the organic world. Here Strakhov stresses that creative development depends not so much on external circumstances as upon the organism itself. In a review of a book by P. L. Lavrov, Strakhov writes: "In an essential, necessary way, will is subordinated only to one thing—namely, *the idea of its freedom,* the idea of *insubordination* [nepodchinenie], of independent and conscious self-determination." Quoted by A. S. Dolinin in, "F. M. Dostoevskij i N. N. Strakhov," in *Shestidesjatye gody,* ed. N. K. Piksanov and O. V. Tsekhnovitser, (Moscow-Leningrad, 1940), p. 240. The idea of "independent and conscious self-determination," of course, is central to Dostoevsky's (and Apollon Grigoriev's) "organic" theory of art.

61. Strakhov, *Biografija, pis'ma i zametki,* p. 275.

62. "G. —bov," *Stat'i, 13,* 94.

63. Ibid., p. 90.

10: The Creative Process

1. *Pis'ma, 2* (No. 1), 551.

2. Arkady Dolgoruky expresses a somewhat analogous thought at the beginning of his memoirs when he asks: "Why does it always turn out that what a wise man says is always far more foolish than what remains within him?"

3. *Pis'ma, 4* (No. 774), 206.

4. Ibid. (No. 726), 136.

5. "Peterburgskaja letopis'," *Stat'i, 13,* 30–31.

6. Ibid., p. 29.

7. Ibid., pp. 10–11.

8. *Pis'ma, 1* (No. 27), 75.

9. Ibid. (No. 28), p. 77.

10. Ibid. (No. 109), pp. 236–37. "They say that there were no corrections in Shakespeare's manuscripts," Dostoevsky writes somewhat in the manner of French neoclassical criticism of Shakespeare. "That's why we find so many [stylistic] enormities and [so much] bad taste in him, but if he had worked, things would have come out better." Ibid., p. 236.

11. Ibid. (No. 75), p. 167. "Tell me," Dostoevsky asks in this same letter, "why the woman-writer is almost never a strict artist? Even such an unquestioned and colossal artist as George Sand more than once did herself injury by her feminine attributes." Ibid.

12. Ibid., 2 (No. 292), 59–60.

13. Ibid. (No. 328), pp. 192, 193.

14. Ibid. (No. 328), p. 190.

15. Ibid. (No. 328), pp. 190, 193.

16. "Budushchij roman," *Dnevnik pisatelja, 11,* 147.

17. Quoted by Dolinin in *V tvorcheskoj laboratorii Dostoevskogo,* p. 134.

18. *Pis'ma, 1* (No. 109), 236–37.

19. Ibid., 2 (No. 353), 283. In this letter to S. A. Ivanova in 1870, Dostoevsky insists that he needs two or three years to work on his projected novel (*The Devils*). He fears he will make a hash of it in eight or nine months; he could work out details, sketch out characters, but there would be "much unevenness and unnecessary prolixity," and a "vast multitude of beautiful elements" would not get into the novel. Ibid.

20. Ibid. (No. 358), p. 294.

21. Ibid. (No. 305), p. 111. Dostoevsky continues: "Would you believe what it means, my angel, to be abroad for a long time and to lose touch with Russia: one doesn't have the thoughts, the ecstasy, or the energy that one has in Russia. Strange as it may seem, it is so." Dostoevsky repeatedly complains (during his stay abroad in 1867–71) of the deleterious effect upon him as a writer of being outside of Russia. See, for example, his letters to S. A. Ivanova, February 6, 1869; to A. Maikov, August 28, 1867; to N. N. Strakhov, March 18, 1871. Yet this period was one of the most intensively creative ones in his life.

22. Ibid. (No. 324), p. 175.

23. Ibid. (No. 323), p. 170.

24. Ibid. (No. 359), p. 297.

25. Cf. "Pis'ma N. N. Strakhova F. M. Dostoevskomu," in *Shestidesjatye gody,* p. 271. After the lines cited, Strakhov continues: "For example, *The Gambler, The Eternal Husband* produced a most clear impression, but all that you put into *The Idiot* went for nought. This shortcoming, of course, is linked with your merits. The nimble Frenchman or German, if he had a tenth of your content, would be extolled in both hemispheres and would enter as a star of the first magnitude into the History of World Literature. And the whole secret, it seems to me, consists in weakening the creative work, lessening the subtlety of analysis, dwelling on one image and a dozen scenes instead of two images and hundreds of scenes. Forgive me, F. M., but it seems to me that until now you have not been coping with your talent, not adapting it to the greatest impact upon the public. I

feel that I am touching upon a great mystery, that I am proposing absurd advice to you—to cease being yourself, to cease being Dostoevsky. But I think that in this form you will still understand my thought."

26. *Pis'ma, 2* (No. 385), 358. Dostoevsky, as is well known, held Strakhov in very high esteem. "He is the only real critic in our time," Dostoevsky wrote Maikov in 1871. Ibid. (No. 372), p. 333.

27. Quoted by V. V. Timofeeva (O. Pochinkovskaja), "God raboty s znamenitym pisatelem," *F. M. Dostoevskij v vospominanijakh sovremennikov* ed. N. K. Grigorenko, et al., 2 (Moscow, 1964), 176.

28. Belinskij, "Gore ot uma," *Sobranie sochinenij, 1,* 461.

29. I. I. Lapshin, *Èstetika Dostoevskogo* (Berlin, 1923), pp. 9–10.

30. *Pis'ma, 1* (No. 238), 427–28.

31. Ibid. (No. 29), p. 80.

32. Ibid. (No. 117), p. 246.

33. Ibid., *4* (No. 772), 201.

34. "It very often happened in my literary life," he wrote in 1864, "that the beginning of a chapter of a novel or story was already in type, while the conclusion still remained in my mind, but *without fail* had to be written for the morrow." "Primechanie," *Stat'i, 13,* 350.

35. *Pis'ma, 4* (No. 769), 198.

36. Ibid., *2* (No. 279), 33.

37. Ibid., *1* (No. 56), 126.

38. Opochinin, "Besedy s Dostoevskim," pp. 471–72.

39. Strakhov, *Biografija, pis'ma i zametki,* pp. 215–16.

40. *Pis'ma, 1* (No. 245), 438.

41. Dostoevskij, *Ispoved' Stavrogina,* pp. 18, 35.

42. "Svidetel' v pol'zu Nekrasova," *Dnevnik pisatelja, 12,* 362.

43. *Pis'ma, 4* (No. 726), 137.

44. Ibid., p. 136.

45. Letter of M. A. Polivanova to Dostoevsky, July 22, 1880. Quoted by A. S. Dolinin in the notes to *Pis'ma, 4,* 432.

46. Ibid. (No. 764), pp. 193–94.

47. Ibid., *2* (No. 1), 550.

48. Ibid., *4* (No. 816), 253.

49. See also Dostoevsky's piece, "Little Pictures," in his *Diary of a Writer* in 1873 where he discusses his walks through St. Petersburg and his impressions of life there. "Malen'kie kartinki," *Dnevnik pisatelja, 11,* 114.

50. "Peterburgskie snovidenija v stikhakh i proze," *Stat'i, 13,* 160–61.

51. "Sreda," *Dnevnik pisatelja, 11,* 19, 20, 21.

52. "Nechto ob advokatakh voobshche," ibid., 196.

53. *Pis'ma, 1* (No. 44), 106.

54. Ibid., p. 108.

55. Ibid. (No. 32), p. 87.

56. Ibid. (No. 44), p. 108.

57. Dostoevsky's almost abnormal shyness, hypersensitivity, and vanity made him the butt of a good deal of wit in the 1840s. See K. Chukovsky's introductory essay, "Dostoevskij i kruzhok Belinskogo," in *N. A. Nekrasov: Kamennoe serdtse (Povest' iz zhizni Dostoevskogo),* ed. K. I. Chukovskij (St. Petersburg, 1922), pp. 3–38. Dostoevsky emerges almost as a hero of one of his own early stories in Nekrasov's extraordinary parody, "The Stone Heart" ("Kamennoe serdtse").

58. *Pis'ma, 1* (No. 146), 293.

11: Correspondences

1. *Pis'ma, 2* (No. 349), 271.

2. Strakhov, *Biografija, pis'ma i zametki*, p. 195.

3. "Our conversations were endless," Strakhov recalls, "and these were the best conversations that ever fell to my lot in life. . . . The chief thing that fascinated me and even was striking in him was his extraordinary mind, the rapidity with which he grasped any thought from merely a word and a hint. In this nimbleness of understanding lies the great charm of conversation, when one can freely give oneself up to a train of thoughts, when there is no need to insist and explain, when a question immediately receives an answer, an objection is made directly against the central thought, agreement is reached when needed, and there are no misunderstandings and obscurities. That is how I conceived those endless conversations which were for me both a great joy and a great pride." Ibid., pp. 224–25. Strakhov, whom Dostoevsky called the leading Russian critic, was, it may easily be seen from his reminiscences of Dostoevsky alone, a fine thinker in his own right; he was no Eckermann (a fact which explains, in part at least, why we have no detailed accounts of his talks with Dostoevsky), but his observations about Dostoevsky are extraordinarily lucid and perceptive. "The shape of my thoughts, and my whole self," Dostoevsky declared in his "Affidavit" filed with the trial commission in 1849, "are known only to a very few of my friends." Strakhov, a friend of later years, was one of these few intimates. Yet as Strakhov himself remarked in the candor of true perceptiveness: "He is too close to me and incomprehensible." Strakhov recalls the "indefatigable mobility" of Dostoevsky's mind and "inexhaustible fruitfulness" of his spirit and adds: "It was as though there was nothing formed in him, so abundantly did thought and feeling crop up, so much unknown and unexpressed was concealed behind what he succeeded in saying." Strakhov speaks of Dostoevsky's "special kind of ambivalence," a quality that Dostoevsky himself dubbed his "reflexion," a capacity to "give oneself up very animatedly to certain thoughts and feelings, yet preserve in one's soul an unyielding and unshakable point from which one looks at oneself, one's thoughts and feelings." Thus, a person always preserves the possibility of judging his thoughts; his feelings and moods can never master him. "Fyodor Mikhailovich always impressed me with the breadth of his sympathies, his ability to understand different and contradictory views." Ibid., pp. 173–74.

4. Ibid., p. 225.

5. Ibid., pp. 204–05.

6. Cf. *Pis'ma, 2* (No. 3), 554.

7. Cf. *Pis'ma, 1* (No. 12), 51.

8. Ibid. (No. 60), p. 139.

9. Strakhov, *Biografija, pis'ma i zametki*, p. 172.

10. Cf. Chizhevskij, *Gegel' v Rossii*, p. 115.

11. Edgar De Bruyne, *L'esthétique du Moyen Age* (Louvain, 1947), p. 86. See also, pp. 86–93.

12. Ibid., p. 92.

13. René Wellek, "Aesthetics and Criticism," in *The Philosophy of Kant and Our Modern World*, ed. Charles W. Hendel (New York, 1957), p. 80.

14. *Pis'ma, 3* (No. 541), 203.

15. Israel Knox, *The Aesthetic Theories of Kant, Hegel, and Schopenhauer* (New York, 1936), p. 39.

16. Kant, *Critique of Judgement,* pp. 79–80.

17. Ibid., p. 42.

18. "Vystavka v akademii khudozhestv," *Stat'i, 13,* 543.

19. "Molodoe pero," ibid., p. 306.

20. "Knizhnost' i gramotnost': Stat'ja vtoraja," ibid., pp. 142, 143.

21. "Rasskazy N. V. Uspenskogo," ibid., p. 553.

22. *Pis'ma, 2* (No. 359), 296–97.

23. Immanuel Kant, *Observations on the Feeling of the Beautiful and Sublime,* trans. John T. Goldthwait (Berkeley and Los Angeles, 1960), p. 60.

24. Bruyne, *L'esthétique du Moyen Age,* p. 158.

25. Kant, *Critique of Judgement,* Part I, p. 157.

26. K. Mochul'skij, *Dostoevskij: zhizn' i tvorchestvo* (Paris, 1947), p. 206.

27. See Strakhov's observations on Dostoevsky's "reflexion," cited in footnote 3 to this chapter.

28. "Vystavka v akademii khudozhestv," *Stat'i, 13, 545.*

29. Kant, *Critique of Judgement,* Part I, p. 172.

30. Ibid., p. 173.

31. Ibid., pp. 173–74.

32. Friedrich Schiller, *Gedanken über den Gebrauch des Gemeinen und Niedrigen in der Kunst,* in Schillers Werke, *8,* 436, 437.

33. Ibid., p. 442.

34. "Vystavka v akademii khudozhestv," *Stat'i, 13,* 546.

35. "Po povodu vystavki," *Dnevnik pisatelja, 11,* 76.

36. *Pis'ma, 3* (No. 396), 20. Apropos of the problem of staging Dostoevsky's novel: Maxim Gorky violently objected, in 1913, to the staging by the Moscow Art Theatre of *The Devils.* He considered the enterprise "aesthetically question-able and, socially, unconditionally harmful." M. Gor'kij, "O 'karamazovshchine,' " in *M. Gor'kij, Sobranie sochinenij v tridtsati tomakh, 24* (Moscow, 1953), 149. "Reading the books of Dostoevsky the reader can correct the thoughts of his heroes; as a consequence they significantly gain in beauty, depth, and humanity." But the stage presentation of the images of Dostoevsky "transfers the spectator from the realm of thought, which permits free debate, into a realm of sugges-tions, hypnosis, into a dark realm of emotions and feelings, even more—of the special "karamazov" kind—maliciously emphasized and intensified; on the stage the spectator sees man created by Dostoevsky in the image and likeness of a 'wild and evil animal.' " Gor'kij, "Eshche o 'karamazovshchine,' " ibid., p. 154. Gorky, like Schiller, sees in the visual image or representation of the ugly a po-tentially dangerous force, an uncontrollable negativity which endangers the reconciling poetry of reality (*das Innere*—as Schiller expressed it); a force which threatens to transform an artistic vision of reality (which Gorky acknowledges in Dostoevsky) into naturalistic distortion. The "socially harmful" consequences of a staging of a Dostoevsky novel, of course, stem directly from this naturalism. As Dostoevsky himself observed: "What goes in a story will not go on the stage. The stage is not a book." Cf. *Pis'ma, 3* (No. 451), 85–86. Aside from whether a stage production of *The Devils* can overcome naturalistic distortion, Gorky un-questionably has raised an aesthetic problem of central importance not only to the stage but, even more, to cinematic representation of reality.

37. "Vystavka v akademii khudozhestv," *Stat'i, 13,* 538. See also *Pis'ma, 3* (No. 451), 85–86, where Dostoevsky advises M. P. Fedorov not to stage "Uncle's Dream."

38. Kant, *Critique of Judgement,* Part II, p. 3.

39. Ibid., p. 21.

40. Grigor'ev, "Paradoksy organicheskoj kritiki (Pis'ma k F. M. Dostoev-skomu)," in *Sochinenija*, p. 631.

41. "O pravde i iskrennosti v iskusstve," ibid., p. 144.

42. The passage is quoted and commented on by John T. Goldthwait in his introduction to Kant, *Observations on the Feeling of the Beautiful and Sublime*, p. 8.

43. A most interesting discussion of Dostoevsky's critical attitude toward Kant's rationalistic ethics may be found in Ja. E. Golosovker's hundred-page essay in Russian, *Dostoevsky and Kant: Reflections of a Reader of the Novel*, The Brothers Karamazov *and of Kant's treatise*, Critique of Pure Reason. In this study of *The Brothers Karamazov*, Golosovker projects Ivan Karamazov as the "dialectical hero of the Kantian antinomies." In the hidden context of the novel, the author argues, Kant represents "European theoretical philosophy in general, especially critical philosophy, and Dostoevsky enters into conscious strug-gle with it on the pages of the novel, while simultaneously conducting an uncon-scious struggle with himself." Cf. Ja. E. Golosovker, *Dostoevskij i Kant* (Moscow, 1963), p. 96.

44. "Knizhnost' i gramotnost': Stat'ja pervaja," *Stat'i, 13,* 110.

45. Schiller, *Über die ästhetische Erziehung des Menschen, 8,* 261 (Twenty-Fourth Letter).

46. Ibid., p. 174 (Third Letter).

47. Ibid., pp. 176, 177 (Third Letter).

48. Ibid., p. 173 (Third Letter).

49. Ibid., p. 198 (Ninth Letter).

50. Ibid., pp. 196–97 (Ninth Letter), p. 200 (Tenth Letter).

51. "Nechto ob advokatakh voobshche," *Dnevnik pisatelja, 11,* 195–96.

52. Schiller, *Über die ästhetische Erziehung des Menschen, 8,* 221–22 (Fifteenth Letter).

53. Ibid., p. 232 (Eighteenth Letter).

54. Ibid., p. 280 (Twenty-Seventh Letter).

55. Ibid., p. 253 (Twenty-Third Letter).

56. Ibid., p. 204 (Tenth Letter).

57. D. I. Chizhevskij, "Shiller v Rossii," *Novyj zhurnal 45* (1956), 128.

58. *Pis'ma, 1* (No. 16), 58.

59. The question of the impact of *Le Génie du Christianisme* upon Dostoev-sky's aesthetics was raised by A. S. Dolinin in his notes to Volume 1 of Dostoev-sky's letters. Cf. *Pis'ma, 1,* 469. I discuss the possible impact of Chateaubriand's aesthetic-religious thought upon *The Brothers Karamazov* in my article, "Cha-teaubriand and Dostoevsky: A Posing of the Problem," in *Scando-Slavica, 12* (1966).

60. Chateaubriand, François René de, *Oeuvres Complètes de M. le Vicompte de Chateaubriand, 14* (Paris, 1826–28), 284–85.

61. Cited by Alice Poirier in *Les Idées artistiques de Chateaubriand* (Paris, 1930), p. 25.

62. Chateaubriand, *Oeuvres Complètes, 11,* 7.

63. Ibid., p. 288.

64. Cited by Poirier, *Les Idées artistiques*, pp. 20–21.

65. Chateaubriand, *Oeuvres Complètes, 11,* 289.

66. Victor Giraud, *Le Christianisme de Chateaubriand 2* (Paris, 1928), 68.

67. Chateaubriand, *Oeuvres Complètes, 2,* 393.

68. See Jean Gibelin, *L'Esthétique de Schelling* (Clermont-Ferrand, 1934), p. xxviii.

69. G. W. F. Hegel, *The Philosophy of Fine Art,* trans. F. P. B. Osmaston *1,* (London, 1920), 86.

70. F. W. J. v. Schelling, *System des transzendentalen Idealismus,* in Werke, *2,* (Leipzig, 1907), 304.

71. Cited by René Wellek in *A History of Modern Criticism: 1750–1950* (4 vols. New Haven, 1955, 1965), *2,* 74. The observations cited here appear in Hölderlin's works, but the particular manuscript involved has been attributed to Schelling. See Wellek's note on this matter. Ibid., p. 367.

72. Schelling, *System des transzendentalen Idealismus,* p. 294.

73. Ibid., p. 302.

74. Ibid., *3,* 16.

75. Bernard Bosanquet, *A History of Aesthetic* (New York, 1957), p. 334.

76. Hegel, *The Philosophy of Fine Art, 1,* 12.

77. Ibid., p. 13.

78. Ibid., p. 42.

79. Ibid., p. 100.

80. Ibid., p. 147.

81. Ibid., p. 212.

82. Ibid., p. 213.

83. Ibid., pp. 233–34.

84. Ibid., p. 219.

85. Ibid., p. 223.

86. Ibid.

87. L. P. Grossman, *Poètika Dostoevskogo* (Moscow, 1925), p. 178.

88. Grossman, "Dostoevskij-khudozhnik," in *Tvorchestvo Dostoevskogo,* pp. 383–84.

89. Ibid., p. 384.

90. V. Zelinskij, ed., *Istoriko-kriticheskij kommentarij k sochinenijam F. M. Dostoevskago* (Moscow, 1885), Part I, p. 91.

91. Strakhov, *Biografija, pis'ma i zametki,* p. 227.

92. Schiller, *Über naïve und sentimentalische Dichtung,* in Schillers Werke, *8,* 369, 370.

Appendix: Dostoevsky and the Fine Arts

1. "Istorija glagola 'stushevat'sja,' " *Dnevnik pisatelja, 12,* 299.

2. V. S. Nechaeva, "Illjustratory Dostoevskogo," in *Tvorchestvo Dostoevskogo,* p. 483.

3. I. I. Lapshin, *Èstetika Dostoevskogo,* p. 11.

4. Dostoevskaja, *Dnevnik A. G. Dostoevskoj,* pp. 118–19.

5. Ibid., p. 167.

6. Pis'ma, *2* (No. 318), 153–54.

7. A. G. Dostoevskaja, "Iz 'Vospominanij,' " in *F. M. Dostoevskij v vospominanijakh sovremennikov, 2,* 45, 46.

8. Dostoevskaja, *Dnevnik A. G. Dostoevskoj,* p. 15.

9. Dostoevskaja, "Iz 'Vospominanij,' " p. 70.

10. *Pis'ma,* (No. 27), 75.

11. Konshina, ed., *Zapisnye tetradi,* p. 197.

12. Dostoevskaja, "Iz 'Vospominanij,' " p. 46.

13. Dostoevskaja, *Dnevnik A. G. Dostoevskoj*, p. 19.

14. Dostoevskaja, "Iz 'Vospominanij,' " p. 46.

15. Dostoevskaja, *Dnevnik A. G. Dostoevskoj*, p. 366. Dostoevsky in a discussion about German art is reported to have said: "Among the Greeks the whole force of their representation of divinity in a beautiful person was expressed in the Venus of Milo; the Italians presented the true Mother of God—the Sistine Madonna; but the Madonna of the best German artist, Holbein? Do you call that a Madonna? A baker's wife! A petit bourgeois! Nothing more!" See B. Brjullov, "Vstrecha s F. M. Dostoevskim," *Nachalo* (1922), No. 2, p. 264. Quoted by P. N. Sakulin in "Rabota Dostoevskogo nad 'Idiotom,' " in *Iz arkhiva F. M. Dostoevskogo, Idiot*, p. 178.

16. Ibid., p. 364.

17. *Pis'ma, 3* (No. 475), 102.

18. Cf. notes to Grigorenko, et al., ed., *F. M. Dostoevskij v vospominanijakh sovremennikov, 2,* 261.

19. Dostoevskaja, *Dnevnik A. G. Dostoevskoj*, p. 19.

20. Lionello Venturi, *History of Art Criticism*, trans. Charles Marriott (New York, 1964), p. 330.

21. Dostoevskaja, "Iz 'Vospominanij,' " p. 70.

22. "G. —bov," *Stat'i, 13,* 70.

23. "Vystavka v akademii khudozhestv," ibid., p. 535.

24. "Obraztsy chistoserdechija," ibid., p. 184.

25. "Vystavka v akademii khudozhestv," ibid., p. 534.

26. Ibid., pp. 535–36.

27. Ibid., pp. 540, 541.

28. "Po povodu vystavki," *Dnevnik pisatelja, 11,* 70.

29. Ibid., p. 71.

30. Ibid., p. 72. "Landscape is flourishing among us and has far outstripped historical painting. Russia with pride may name several respected names." Dostoevsky attributes Russia's success in landscape painting to two factors: first, Russia is a country which leans toward the village; secondly, it is more difficult for academism to take a hold in landscape painting. Cf. "Vystavka v akademii khudozhestv," *Stat'i, 13,* 543.

31. "Po povodu vystavki," *Dnevnik pisatelja, 11,* 73.

32. Ibid., p. 76.

33. "Vystavka v akademii khudozhestv," *Stat'i, 13,* 536.

34. Ibid., p. 542.

35. "Edinichnyj sluchaj," *Dnevnik pisatelja, 12,* 93–94.

36. Grossman, *Poètika Dostoevskogo*, p. 119. For a discussion of Dostoevsky's "verbal painting," see in particular, pp. 116–43.

37. Ibid. Dostoevsky, in Grossman's view, essentially is an artist of light and shadow. In this connection, see also N. M. Chirkov's interesting discussion of the motifs of light and darkness in Dostoevsky's novels (in particular in *The Idiot*) in his study *O stile Dostoevskogo* (Moscow, 1964), pp. 102–23.

38. *Pis'ma, 1* (No. 184), 343.

39. S. D. Janovskij, "Vospominanija o Dostoevskom," *Russkij vestnik, 176* (1885), 814.

40. *Pis'ma, 1* (No. 198), 365.

41. Grossman, ed., *Seminarij po Dostoevskomu*, p. 61.

42. Cf. N. Fon-Fokht, "K biografii F. M. Dostoevskogo," in *F. M. Dostoevskij v vospominanijakh sovremennikov, 1,* 378.

43. Dostoevskaja, "Iz 'Vospominanij,' " p. 47.

44. Fon-Fokht, p. 378.

45. Dostoevskaja, *Dnevnik A. G. Dostoevskoj,* p. 126.

46. S. V. Kovalevskaja, "Iz 'Vospominanij detstva,' " in *F. M. Dostoevskij v vospominanijakh sovremennikov, 1,* 358.

47. *Pis'ma, 3* (No. 560), 231.

48. Dostoevskaja, "Iz 'Vospominanij,' " p. 47.

49. Fon-Fokht, p. 378.

50. Dostoevskaja, "Iz 'Vospominanij,' " p. 47.

51. *Pis'ma, 4* (No. 682), 90.

52. See notes to *Pis'ma, 4,* 394. Dostoevsky, as A. S. Dolinin points out here, was a close friend of A. N. Serov's; the latter wrote a number of articles about Wagner in which he detailed Wagner's aesthetic and philosophical theories.

53. *Pis'ma, 3* (No. 523), 177.

54. Note to *Pis'ma, 3,* 326.

55. Janovskij, "Vospominanija o Dostoevskom," p. 807.

56. "Peterburgskaja letopis,' " *Stat'i, 13,* 21–22.

57. "Malen'kie kartinki," *Dnevnik pisatelja, 11,* 109.

58. *Pis'ma, 1* (No. 172), 321.

59. *Zimnie zametki o letnikh vpechatlenijakh, 4,* 53.

60. *Pis'ma, 2* (No. 315), 139.

61. Ibid. (No. 381), p. 206.

Selected Bibliography

SOURCES

Bel'chikov, N. F., *Dostoevskij v protsesse petrashevtsev,* Moscow-Leningrad, 1936.

Cheshikhin-Vetrinskij, V. E., ed., *F. M. Dostoevskij v vospominanijakh sovremennikov, pis'makh i zametkakh,* Moscow, 1912.

Dolinin, A. S., ed., *F. M. Dostoevskij, materialy i issledovanija,* Leningrad, 1935.

Dostoevskaja, A. G., *Dnevnik A. G. Dostoevskoj, 1867 g.,* Moscow, 1923.

—— *Vospominanija,* ed. L. P. Grossman, Moscow, 1925.

Dostoevskij, F. M., *Ispoved' Stavrogina,* Munich, 1922.

——, *Pis'ma,* ed. A. S. Dolinin, 4 vols. Moscow-Leningrad, 1928-59.

——, *Polnoe sobranie khudozhestvennykh proizvedenij,* ed. V. Tomashevsky and K. Khalabaev, 13 vols. Moscow-Leningrad, 1926–30.

Glivenko, I. I., ed., *Iz arkhiva F. M. Dostoevskogo, Prestuplenie i nakazanie,* Moscow-Leningrad, 1931.

Grigorenko, N. K., et al., ed., *F. M. Dostoevskij v vospominanijakh sovremennikov,* 2 vols. Moscow, 1964.

Grossman, L. P., ed., "Pervaja zapisnaja knizhka," *Zven'ja,* 6 (1936), 413–38.

Komarowitsch, W. L., ed., *Die Urgestalt der Brüder Karamasoff: Dostojewskis Quellen, Entwürfe und Fragmente,* Munich, 1928.

Konshina, E. N., ed., *Zapisnye tetradi F. M. Dostoevskogo,* Moscow-Leningrad, 1935.

Sakulin, P. N., and Bel'chikov, N. F., ed., *Iz arkhiva F. M. Dostoevskogo, Idiot,* Moscow-Leningrad, 1931.

Strakhov, N. N., *Biografija, pis'ma i zametki iz zapisnoj knizhki F. M. Dostoevskogo,* St. Petersburg, 1883.

BACKGROUND AND CRITICAL

Alekseev, M. P., *Rannij drug F. M. Dostoevskogo,* Odessa, 1921.

Annenkov, P. V., *Literaturnye vospominanija,* Leningrad, 1928.

Auerbach, Erich, *Introduction to Romance Languages & Literature,* trans. Guy Daniels, New York, Capricorn Books, 1961.

————, *Mimesis,* trans. Willard Trask, Princeton, Princeton University Press, 1953.

Bakhtin, M. M., *Problemy poètiki Dostoevskogo,* Moscow, 1963. First published in 1929.

Belinskij, V. G., *Sobranie sochinenij v trekh tomakh,* Moscow, 1948.

Bem, A. L. "Khudozhestvennaja polemika s Tolstym: k ponimaniju 'Podrostka,' " in *U istokov tvorchestva Dostoevskogo,* ed. A. L. Bem (Prague, 1936), pp. 192-214.

————, "Pervye shagi Dostoevskogo (genesis romana Bednye ljudi)," *Slavia, 12* (1933), 134–61.

————, "Tolstoj v otsenke Dostoevskogo," in *U istokov tvorchestva Dostoevskogo,* ed. A. L. Bem (Prague, 1936), pp. 167–91.

Berdjaev, N. A., *Mirosozertsanie Dostoevskogo,* Prague, 1923.

Borshchevskij, S., *Shchedrin i Dostoevskij,* Moscow, 1956.

Bosanquet, Bernard, *A History of Aesthetic,* New York, Meridian Books, 1957.

Bowman, H. E., *Vissarion Belinski,* Cambridge, Harvard University Press, 1954.

Brodskij, N. L., ed., *Tvorcheskij put' Dostoevskogo,* Leningrad, 1924.

Bruyne, Edgar De, *L'esthétique du Moyen Age,* Louvain, 1947.

Chateaubriand, François René de, *Le Génie du Christianisme,* in *Oeuvres Complètes de M. le Vicompte de Chateaubriand, 14, Paris,* 1826–28.

Chernyshevskij, N. G., *Èsteticheskie otnoshenija iskusstva k dejstvitel'nosti,* in N. G. Chernyshevskij, *Èstetika i literaturnaja kritika,* Izbrannye stat'i, Moscow-Leningrad, 1951, pp. 3–51.

————, "Ne nachalo li peremeny? Rasskazy N. V. Uspenskogo," ibid., pp. 491–502.

Chirkov, N. M., *O stile Dostoevskogo,* Moscow, 1964.

Chizhevskij, D. I., *Gegel' v Rossii,* Paris, 1939.

————, "Schiller und die 'Brüder Karamazov,' " *Zeitschrift für slavische Philologie, 6* (1929), 1–42.

————, "Shiller v Rossii," *Novyj zhurnal, 45* (1956), 109–35.

Chukovskij, Kornej, "Dostoevskij i kruzhok Belinskogo," in *N. A. Nekrasov: Kamennoe serdtse (Povest' iz zhizni Dostoevskogo),* ed. K. I. Chukovskij (St. Petersburg, 1922), pp. 3–38.

Chulkov, Georgij, *Kak rabotal Dostoevskij,* Moscow, 1939.

Dolinin, A. S., ed., *F. M. Dostoevskij, stat'i i materialy,* 2 vols. St. Petersburg, 1922; Leningrad, 1925.

————, *V tvorcheskoj laboratorii Dostoevskogo,* Moscow, 1947.

Dobroljubov, N. A., *Izbrannye sochinenija,* Moscow, 1948.

————, *Sochinenija N. A. Dobroljubova,* 4 vols. St. Petersburg, 1908.

Eng, Johannes van der, *Dostoevskij Romancier,* 's-Gravenhage, 1957.

Engel'gardt, B., "Ideologicheskij roman Dostoevskogo," in *Dostoevskij, stat'i i materialy,* ed. A. S. Dolinin, *2* (Leningrad, 1925), 71–108.

Evnin, F. I., "Zhivopis' Dostoevskogo," *Izvestija Akademii nauk SSSR (Otdelenie literatury i jazyka), 18* (1958), 131–48.

Fet, A. A., *Polnoe sobranie stikhotvorenij,* ed. B. Ja. Bukhshtab, Leningrad, 1959.

Fridlender, G. M., "Dostoevskij-kritik," in *Istorija russkoj kritiki,* ed. B. P. Gorodetskij, A. Lavretskij, and B. S. Mejlakh, *2* (Moscow-Leningrad, 1958), 269–88.

———, *Realizm Dostoevskogo,* Moscow-Leningrad, 1964.

Gerhardt, Dietrich, *Gogol' und Dostojewskij in ihrem künstlerischen Verhältnis, Slavisch-Baltische Quellen und Forschungen, 10,* Leipzig, 1941.

Gibelin, Jean, *L'esthétique de Schelling,* Clermont-Ferrand, 1934.

Giraud, Victor, *Le Christianisme de Chateaubriand,* 2 vols. Paris, 1928.

Golosovker, Ja. E., *Dostoevskij i Kant,* Moscow, 1963.

Gor'kij, M. "Eshche o 'karamazovshchine,' " in *M. Gor'kij, Sobranie sochinenij v tridtsati tomakh, 24* (Moscow, 1953), 151–57.

———, "O 'karamazovshchine,' " ibid., pp. 146–50.

Gorodetskij, B. P., *Istorija russkoj kritiki,* 2 vols. Moscow-Leningrad, 1958.

Grigor'ev, A. *Sochinenija Apollona Grigor'eva,* ed., N. N. Strakhov, *1,* St. Petersburg, 1876.

Grossman, Leonid P., *Biblioteka Dostoevskogo,* Odessa, 1919.

———, "Dostoevskij i Evropa," *Russkaja mysl',* No. 11 (1915), pp. 54–93.

———, "Dostoevskij-khudozhnik," in *Tvorchestvo Dostoevskogo,* ed. N. L. Stepanov (Moscow, 1959), pp. 330–416.

———, *Poètika Dostoevskogo,* Moscow, 1925.

———, "Problema realizma u Dostoevskogo," *Vestnik Evropy,* No. 2 (1917), pp. 65–100.

———, "Stilistika Stavrogina," in *F. M. Dostoevskij, stat'i i materialy,* ed. A. S. Dolinin, *2* (Leningrad, 1925), 139–48.

———, ed., *Seminarij po Dostoevskomu,* Moscow, 1922.

———, ed., *Tvorchestvo Dostoevskogo,* Odessa, 1921.

Gural'nik, U. A., "F. M. Dostoevskij v literaturno-èsteticheskoj bor'be 60-x godov," in *Tvorchestvo Dostoevskogo,* ed. N. L. Stepanov (Moscow, 1959), pp. 293–329.

Hegel, G. W. F., *The Philosophy of Fine Art,* trans. F. P. B. Osmaston, 4 vols. London, G. Bell and Sons, Ltd., 1920.

Hendel, Charles W., ed., *The Philosophy of Kant and Our Modern World,* New York, Liberal Arts Press, 1957.

Ivanov, I. I., *Istorija russkoj kritiki,* St. Petersburg, 1900.

Ivanov, Vyacheslav, *Freedom and the Tragic Life: A Study in Dosto-evsky,* trans. Norman Cameron, New York, 1957.

Kant, Immanuel, *Observations on the Feeling of the Beautiful and Sub-lime,* trans. John T. Goldthwait, Berkeley and Los Angeles, University of California Press, 1960.

Katkov, M. N., "Vstuplenie k razboru Pushkina," *Russkij vestnik, 1* (1856), 155–73, 306–25.

Kirpotin, V. Ja., *Dostoevskij i Belinskij,* Moscow, 1960.

——, *F. M. Dostoevskij: tvorcheskij put'* 1821–1859, Moscow, 1960.

Knox, Israel, *The Aesthetic Theories of Kant, Hegel, and Schopenhauer,* New York, Columbia University Press, 1936.

Krestovsky, Lydie, *La laideur dans l'art à travers les âges,* Paris, Editions du Seuil, 1947.

Lapshin, I. I., *Èstetika Dostoevskogo,* Berlin, 1923.

Lauth, R., *Die Philosophie Dostojewskis,* Munich, 1950.

Lavretskij, A., *Èstetika Belinskogo,* Moscow, 1959.

Lo Gatto, Ettore, ed., *L'èstetica e la poetica in Russia,* Florence, 1947.

Losskij, N., *Dostoevskij i ego khristianskoe miroponimanie,* New York, Chekhov Publishing House, 1953.

Mochul'skij, K., *Dostoevskij: zhizn' i tvorchestvo,* Paris, 1947.

Nechaeva, V. S., "Illjustratory Dostoevskogo," in *Tvorchestvo Dosto-evskogo,* ed. N. L. Stepanov (Moscow, 1959), pp. 472–509.

Opochinin, E. N., "Besedy s Dostoevskim," in *Zven'ja,* ed. L. P. Gross-man, *6* (1936), 454–95.

Piksanov, N. K., and Tsekhnovitser, O. V., ed., *Shestidesjatye gody,* Moscow-Leningrad, 1940.

Poirier, Alice, *Les Idées artistiques de Chateaubriand,* Paris, Les Presses Universitaires de France, 1930.

Pypin, A. N., *Belinskij, ego zhizn' i perepiska,* St. Petersburg, 1908.

Schelling, F. W. J., *Werke,* ed. Otto Weiss, 3 vols. Leipzig, Fritz Eckardt Verlag, 1907.

Schiller, Friedrich, *Schillers Werke,* ed. L. Bellermann, Leipzig und Wien, Bibliographisches Institut, 1895–97.

Setschkareff, Wsewolod, *Schellings Einfluss in der russischen Literatur der 20er und 30er Jahre des XIX. Jahrhunderts,* Berlin, 1939.

Stammler, Heinrich, "Dostoevsky's Aesthetics and Schelling's Philos-ophy of Art," *Comparative Literature, 7* (1955), 313–23.

Stepanov, N. L., ed., *Tvorchestvo Dostoevskogo,* Moscow, 1959.

Venturi, Lionello, *History of Art Criticism,* trans. Charles Marriott, New York, E. P. Dutton & Co., 1964.

Vinogradov, V. V., *Evoljutsija russkogo naturalizma: Gogol' i Dosto-evskij,* Leningrad, 1929.

———, *Problema avtorstva i teorija stilej,* Moscow, 1961.

———, "Sjuzhet i arkhitektonika romana Dostoevskogo 'Bednye ljudi' v svjazi s voprosom o poètike natural'noj shkoly," in *Tvorcheskij put' Dostoevskogo,* ed. N. L. Brodskij, Leningrad, 1924.

Vysheslavtsev, V., "Dostoevskij o ljubvi i bezsmertie (Novyj fragment)," *Sovremennyja zapiski, 50* (Paris, 1932), 293.

Wellek, René, *Concepts of Criticism,* New Haven and London, Yale University Press, 1963.

———, *A History of Modern Criticism: 1750–1950,* 4 vols. New Haven, Yale University Press, 1955, 1965.

Zamotin, I. I., *Sorokovye—Shestidesjatye gody,* Petrograd-Moscow, 1915.

Zander, L. A., *Tajna dobra,* Frankfurt am Main, Possev-Verlag, 1960.

Zelinskij, V., ed., *Istoriko-kriticheskij kommentarij k sochinenijam F. M. Dostoevskogo,* Moscow, 1885.

Zenkovsky, V. V. [Zen'kovskij, V.], *Aus der Geschichte der ästhetischen Ideen in Russland im 19. und 20. Jahrhundert,* 's-Gravenhage, 1958.

———, *A History of Russian Philosophy,* trans. George L. Kline, 2 vols. New York, Columbia University Press, 1953.

———, "Problema krasoty v mirosozertsanii Dostoevskogo," *Put',* No. 37 (1933), pp. 36–60.

Index